BECOMING GOLD

S̲ʜ̲ᴀɴɴᴏɴ Gʀɪᴍᴇs

BECOMING GOLD

ZOSIMOS OF PANOPOLIS AND THE
ALCHEMICAL ARTS IN ROMAN EGYPT

Shannon Grimes, PhD

PANOPOLIS SERIES
VOLUME ONE

RUBEDO

2018

THE PANOPOLIS SERIES
CRITICAL FORAYS INTO THE
GRÆCO-EGYPTIAN ALCHEMICAL CORPUS
SERIES EDITOR: AARON CHEAK, PHD

Volume One

—

Becoming Gold:
Zosimos of Panopolis and the
Alchemical Arts in Roman Egypt

By Shannon Grimes, PhD

—

First published in 2018 by
RUBEDO PRESS
AUCKLAND, NEW ZEALAND
WWW.RUBEDO.PRESS

ISBN: 978-0-473-40775-9 (softcover)
ISBN: 978-0-473-40776-6 (hardback)

© Rubedo Press 2018
Shannon Grimes asserts the moral right
to be identified as the author of this work.
All rights reserved. No part of this work may be reproduced
without express permission from the publisher.
Brief passages may be cited by way of criticism,
scholarship, or review, as long as full
acknowledgement is given.

Design and Typography
by Aaron Cheak

Cover illustrations by David Roberts (1796–1864):
Central Avenue of the Hall of Columns at Karnak (1838)
Excavated Temple of Gyrshe, Nubia (1838)

SCRIBE SANGUINE QUIA SANGUIS SPIRITUS

FOR JASON

Solve et coagula

Contents

List of Illustrations	9
Abbreviations	11
A Note on Conventions	12
Acknowledgements	13
INTRODUCTION	**15**
HISTORIOGRAPHICAL ISSUES	19
CHAPTER SUMMARIES	25
PRIMARY SOURCES	27

1. **ZOSIMOS AND GRECO-EGYPTIAN ALCHEMY, REVISITED** — 29

    ZOSIMOS AND STATUE MAKING — 34
    COLOR TRANSMUTATION — 41
    PHILOSOPHIES OF NATURE — 53

2. **ALCHEMY IN PANOPOLIS** — 69
    Temples and Trade Guilds

    PRIESTS OF THE HOUSE OF LIFE — 70
    TEMPLE CULTURE IN THE PANOPOLIS REGION — 76
    TRADE GUILDS AND WORKSHOPS — 87
    CRAFT KNOWLEDGE — 94
    ZOSIMOS'S ASSOCIATES AND RIVALS — 101
    CONCLUSION — 111

3. **ALCHEMY AS A SPIRITUAL EXERCISE** — 115

    VIRTUE AND THE PURIFICATION OF THE SOUL — 117
    CONTEMPLATING NATURE AS A SPIRITUAL EXERCISE — 120

	ALCHEMY AND SACRIFICE IN 'ON EXCELLENCE'	127
	'ON EXCELLENCE': LESSON ONE	131
	'ON EXCELLENCE': LESSONS TWO AND THREE	146
	CONCLUSION	151
4.	**ON GNOSIS AND NATURAL METHODS** *Jewish and Christian Influences in Zosimos's Work*	155
	HEBREW METALLURGY AND ALCHEMY	156
	KING SOLOMON THE EXORCIST	167
	THE BOOK OF ENOCH AND THE ORIGINS OF ALCHEMY	173
	THE ANTHROPOS, OR PRIMAL HUMAN	181
	JEWISH/CHRISTIAN COLLEAGUES	192
5.	**SPIRITS IN THE MATERIAL WORLD** *Alchemy, Theurgy, and the Divine Cosmos*	194
	WHAT IS THEURGY	197
	COSMIC KNOWLEDGE VS. THEURGICAL KNOWLEDGE	200
	THE DIVINE HIERARCHY	210
	LINKING SPIRIT & MATTER THROUGH THEURGIC RITES	216
	GOD-MAKING	225
	CONCLUSION	241
6.	**CODA**	243
	Bibliography	249
	Index	275
	About the Author	281

LIST OF ILLUSTRATIONS

1. Polychromic statuary, 1. *Bes-image of the god Hor-asha-khet.* Bronze inlaid with gold, electrum, auriferous silver, copper and copper-alloy. Ptolemaic Egypt (4th–2nd century BCE). The Metropolitan Museum of Art, New York. Public domain · 37

2. Polychromic statuary, 2. *The divine adoratrice, Karomama.* Bronze inlaid with gold, silver, and electrum. Pharaonic Egypt, 22nd Dynasty (943–716 BCE). Photo copyright Musée du Louvre, Paris, Dist. RMN-Grand Palais / Georges Poncet. Used with permission · 39

3. Polychromic statuary, 3. *The divine adoratrice, Karomama: detail of metallic inlay (necklace, reverse view).* Bronze inlaid with gold, silver, and electrum. Pharaonic Egypt, 22nd Dynasty (943–716 BCE). Photo copyright Musée du Louvre, Paris, Dist. RMN-Grand Palais / Georges Poncet. Used with permission · 40

4. Black bronze statuary, 1. *Sphinx of King Siamon.* Black bronze inlaid with gold. Pharaonic Egypt, 21st Dynasty (978–959 BCE). Photo copyright Musée du Louvre, Paris, Dist. RMN-Grand Palais / Christian Decamps. Used with permission · 40

5. Black bronze statuary, 2. *Ritual statuette of Thuthmose III.* Black bronze inlaid with gold. Pharaonic Egypt, 18th Dynasty (ca. 1479–1425 BCE). The Metropolitan Museum of Art, New York. Public domain · 43

6. *Zosimos and Theosebeia conversing next to a furnace.* From the *Tome of Images (Mushaf as-ṣuwar).* Arabic manuscript, thirteenth century. Public domain · 104

7. *Zosimos and Theosebeia depicted bearing the discs of the sun and moon on their heads.* From the *Tome of Images (Mushaf as-ṣuwar)*. Arabic manuscript, thirteenth century. Public domain · 105

8. *The Phialē.* An alchemical apparatus from the *Chrysopoeia of Cleopatra* (Codex Marcianus 299). Greek Manuscript, tenth–eleventh century. Public domain. · 133

9. *The Greek Letter Theta*, which "contains the whole key to the visible art" · 190

Abbreviations

Auth.Mem   *Zosime de Panopolis: Mémoires authentiques*
            MERTENS, Michele, trans., ed.
            Les alchimistes grecs, vol. IV, part I. 2nd ed.
            Paris: Les Belles Lettres, 2002
CAAG   *Collection des Anciens Alchimistes Grecs.* 3 vols.
            BERTHELOT, Marcellin, and Ch.-Ém. RUELLE, trans., ed.
            1888. Osnabrück: Otto Zeller, 1967
CH   *Corpus Hermeticum*
            COPENHAVER, Brian P., trans., ed.
            Cambridge: Cambridge University Press, 1992
CMA   *La Chimie au Moyen Age.* 3 vols.
            BERTHELOT, Marcellin, and R. DUVAL
            1893. Osnabrück: Otto Zeller, 1967
DM   IAMBLICHUS, *De Mysteriis Ægyptiorum*
            E. CLARKE, J. DILLON, and J. HERSHBELL, trans., ed.
            Writings from the Greco-Roman World Series, no. 4.
            Atlanta: Society of Biblical Literature, 2003
P.Leid   *Papyrus de Leyde, Papyrus de Stockholm Recettes*
            HALLEUX, Robert, trans. & ed.
            Les alchimistes grecs, vol. I.
            Paris: Les Belles Lettres, 1981

A Note on Conventions

ALL GREEK TECHNICAL TERMS have been Romanised following the conventions of the ALA/LC system of transliteration, with the exception of proper names and other terms that have already been assimilated into English scholarly usage (e.g., for Ζώσιμος, we retain Zosimos, rather than Zōsimos; for Δημόκριτος we retain Democritus rather than Dēmokritos). Exceptions to these usages are made when citing bibliographic works that employ different conventions.

Unless noted otherwise, when quoting from primary or secondary texts, square brackets are used to indicate editorial interpolations made by the author of the present work. By extension, ellipses within square brackets, [...], indicate an editorial omission rather than an original omission. Lacunæ in source texts (e.g. due to damage or deterioration) as well as their reconstructions, are indicated by angled brackets: ‹...›. Ellipses alone indicate ellipses as used in the original text.

Acknowledgements

ALTHOUGH SCHOLARSHIP can feel very solitary at times, it is actually a collaborative effort involving networks of colleagues, mentors, students, family, and friends who have directly contributed or offered support along the way. I'd like to express my gratitude to some of the key players.

I'll start with some of my colleagues at Meredith College, beginning with Dr. Carmen Christopher. It is challenging for faculty at teaching-focused college like ours to make time for scholarship, which led Carmen to the brilliant idea of starting a faculty writing group, which has been a vital source of motivation, inspiration, and support for many of us. My former dean, Dr. Garry Walton, also helped me carve out time to work on this project and allowed me hire one of our brightest French majors, Berekia Divanga, to help me read and translate French sources more quickly and eloquently than I could have done on my own. Also crucial were Shanna Alley, the library goddess who procured my interlibrary loan requests, which were legion, and Dr. Michael Novak, who carefully read and commented on drafts of my first chapters.

Special thanks go to my gifted editor and publisher, Dr. Aaron Cheak, who approached me about the Panopolis Series at a most serendipitous time; it has been a pleasure to work with him, and an honor to have *Becoming Gold* as the inaugural volume in this series. Thanks also to Daniel Burnham, who prompted me a few years ago to look deeper into Zosimos's Egyptian roots (I haven't looked back), and to peer-reviewer Dr. Kyle Fraser, whose feedback on earlier drafts helped me strengthen my arguments.

Last, but not least, I'd like to thank my sons, Jackson and Hunter, and especially my husband, Jason, for giving me the time and mental space to write, and doing so with love and minimal complaint. Jason, this one's for you.

Introduction

Zosimos of Panopolis, who flourished in Roman Egypt around the turn of the fourth century CE, is a seminal figure in the history of western alchemy, reverently lauded by later alchemists as "the divine Zosimos", "crown of philosophers", and "friend of truth".[1] He is often regarded as the first person to frame alchemy as a spiritual practice due to championing the idea that the purification of metals corresponds to the purification of the soul.[2] While his writings are the most religiously significant works in the Greco-Egyptian alchemical corpus, which dates from the first through eighth centuries CE, it is a bit misleading to think of Zosimos as a founding father of religious alchemy, because there is ample evidence for religious elements in the ancient Near Eastern crafts of metalworking, glassmaking, and dye-making in which "alchemy" has its roots.[3] This book will demonstrate some of the ways

[1] On honorific titles given to Zosimos, see MERTENS, *Zosime de Panopolis: Mémoires authentiques,* Les Alchimistes Grecs, Tome IV, 1re partie (Paris: Les Belles Lettres, 1995), xi. See also the portrayal of Zosimos and his female colleague, Theosebeia, as mystical sages in an Arab alchemical manuscript, *Mushaf as-suwar* in Theodor ABT, ed., *The Book of Pictures: Mushaf as-suwar by Zosimos of Panopolis* (Zurich: Living Human Heritage Publications, 2007). Abt argues that Zosimos is the author of this text, but I do not believe that this is the case. The text incorporates some authentic Zosimean material, but elaborates on it and turns it into a dialogue between Zosimos and Theosebeia. See HALLUM's discussion in *The Tome of Images: An Arabic Compilation of Texts by Zosimos of Panopolis and a Source of the* Turba Philosophorum", *Ambix* 56.1 (March 2009): 79–81.

[2] A.-J. FESTUGIÈRE calls him the "father of religious alchemy" in *La Révélation d'Hermès Trismégiste,* vol. I, 2nd ed. (Paris: Gabalda, 1950), 260-262.

[3] See, for example, Mircea ELIADE, *The Forge and the Crucible,* 2nd ed., trans.

that Zosimos carries on these ancient traditions. Zosimos believes that piety, meditation, and divine revelation contribute to the efficacy of his work with metals, and that close observation of the properties of matter can bring one closer to the divine mind. His religious ideas are steeped in a heady blend of traditional Egyptian religion, Greek philosophy, Hermetism, and Jewish/Christian Gnostic thought.[4] Little is known about adherents of Hermetism and Gnosticism in the first few centuries CE; we have collections of their sacred texts, but hardly any first-hand accounts from the people who embraced these teachings and practiced them in their daily lives. Zosimos's writings, therefore, give us a rare glimpse of a practitioner's perspective, which is invaluable for scholars of late ancient Mediterranean religions. Unfortunately, Zosimos is not widely known outside of scholarship on the history of alchemy.

This study of Zosimos began as a doctoral dissertation, and while some of the core material remains intact, much has been changed and expanded as my research has taken new directions over the years.[5] This current work, *Becoming Gold*, has benefitted from a wave of scholarship on Greco-Egyptian alchemy in the

    Stephen CORBIN (Chicago: University of Chicago Press, 1978 [1962]); and Claude TRAUNECKER, « Le Château de l'Or de Thoutmosis III et les magasins nord du temple d'Amon », *Cahiers de Recherches de l'Institut de Papyrologie et d'Égyptologie de Lille* 11 (1989): 89-111.

4   Gnosticism is a contested category among scholars of early Christianity. However, I find it useful as a descriptor of the type of metaphysics exemplified in the Nag Hammadi manuscripts. I capitalize "Gnostic" and related terms when referring to the Christian and Jewish varieties that flourished during the Roman period, particularly in Egypt. Gnostic texts are predominantly Christian, though there is evidence that some Gnostic texts originated in Jewish circles. For overviews of debates over the category "Gnosticism", see David BRAKKE, *The Gnostics: Myth, Ritual, and Diversity in Early Christianity* (Cambridge: Harvard University Press, 2010); and April D. DECONICK, "Gnostic Spirituality at the Crossroads of Christianity: Transgressing Boundaries and Creating Orthodoxy", in *Beyond the Gnostic Gospels: Studies Building on the Work of Elaine Pagels*, ed. E. IRICINSCHI, L. JENOTT, N. DENZEY LEWIS, and P. TOWNSEND (Tübingen: Mohr Siebeck, 2013).

5   See Shannon GRIMES, "Zosimos of Panopolis: Alchemy, Nature, and Religion in Late Antiquity", PHD diss., Syracuse University, 2006.

past decade, as well as an influx of studies on Roman Egypt from many different disciplines, including socio-economics, politics, religion, art history, and archæology.⁶ I have become increasingly interested in the Egyptian roots of Zosimos's life and work and have concluded that ancient temple traditions of statue-making are absolutely critical for understanding Zosimos and the origins of alchemy.⁷ Scholars have tended to gloss over the Egyptian contexts, largely because the literature is written in the language of Hellenistic natural philosophy, which obscures its Egyptian roots, and when Egyptian themes are explicit, they seem closer to the realm of legend—temple columns spontaneously cracking open to reveal alchemical secrets hidden inside, for example, or romanticized descriptions of the priesthood as keepers of secret and powerful knowledge, all of which were common tropes in Greco-Roman literature.⁸ But in Zosimos's case, there is enough evidence to realistically conclude that he was indeed an Egyptian priest, and that his work was in line with ancient temple traditions.

I am certainly not the first to speculate that alchemy originated in Egyptian temples, but to date there have not been many sustained efforts to demonstrate this. Jack Lindsay's *The Origins of Alchemy in Græco-Roman Egypt* (1970) is sometimes cited as one of the first books to argue for Egyptian origins, but despite his title, his intent is not to demonstrate Egyptian origins as much as to argue that alchemists were the first scientists. He claims that alchemy arose from a crisis in thought, when Egyptian craftsmen were plagued by questions that their tradition could not answer and began to look to Greek philosophy, thereby breaking through "into

---

6 For an overview of recent work in this field, see Christina RIGGS, ed., *The Oxford Handbook of Roman Egypt* (Oxford: Oxford University Press, 2012).
7 Special thanks go to Daniel Burnham for an email exchange back in 2013 that nudged me farther down the Egyptian path.
8 See Matteo MARTELLI's discussion of this in *The Four Books of Pseudo-Democritus. Sources of Alchemy and Chemistry: Sir Robert Mond Studies in the History of Early Chemistry*. Leeds: Maney Publishing; *Ambix* 60, supplement 1 (2013), S64-S65.

the world of scientific contemplation and model making".⁹ Lindsay's book contains a wealth of information, but his discussions of Egyptian origins are scattershot with Greco-Roman, Persian, and Christian ideas from a wide historical range. Better arguments for the Egyptian origins of alchemy have come from Egyptologists. François Daumas, for example, has analyzed Egyptian names and attributes in alchemical literature, as well as allusions to alchemy in Egyptian texts, and shown that there are numerous *rapprochements* between them.¹⁰ Philippe Derchain has examined the House of Gold and ritual inscriptions at the ruins of the Temple of Dendara and argued that alchemy originates from the sacred metallurgy practiced by temple statue makers.¹¹ Also important is Sydney Aufrère's work, *L'Univers minéral dans la pensée Égyptienne* (1991), which is invaluable for understanding the theologies of metals and precious stones that informed the work of temple artisans; he, too, argues that Greco-Egyptian alchemy is rooted in ancient temple traditions, though his discussion of alchemy is brief (four pages out of a two volume work).¹² There have been other significant articles and book chapters investigating the ancient Egyptian roots of alchemy, and scholars are getting bolder about making such claims.¹³ *Becoming Gold* contributes to these efforts, and hopefully pushes them further.

9   Jack LINDSAY, *The Origins of Alchemy in Græco-Roman Egypt* (London: Frederick Muller, 1970), 391. On page 390, he makes the claim that alchemists are the first scientists.

10 See François DAUMAS, "L'alchimie a-t- elle une origine égyptienne?", in *Das römisch–byzantinische Ägypten* (Mainz am Rhein: P. von Zabern, 1983), 109–118.

11 Phillipe DERCHAIN, "L'Atelier des Orfevres à Dendara et les origins de l'Alchimie", *Chronique d'Egypte* LXV (1990), 219-242. See also Claude TRAUNECKER, « Le Château de l'Or de Thoutmosis III et les magasins nord du temple d'Amon », op.cit.

12 See Sydney AUFRÈRE, *L'Univers Minéral Dans La Pensée Égyptienne*, vol. II (Paris: Le Caire, 1991), 801–804.

13 See, for example, Terence DUQUESNE, "Egypt's Image in the European Enlightenment", *Seshat* 3 (1999): 32–51; Erik HORNUNG, *The Secret Lore of Egypt: Its Impact on the West*, trans. D. LORTON (Ithaca: Cornell University Press, 2001), ch. 4; and Aaron CHEAK, "The Perfect Black: Egypt and Alchemy", in *Alchemical Traditions: From Antiquity to the Avant-Garde*, ed. A. CHEAK (Auckland: Rubedo Press, 2019 [2013]).

This book on Zosimos is not a biography, *per se*, because we know so little about his life, but more of a cultural biography, a study of how Zosimos's writings are shaped by his various social, cultural, and intellectual milieux. I carefully situate his writings in specific socio-cultural contexts of Roman Egypt (particularly the Thebaid region) at the turn of the fourth century, beginning with Egyptian priestly culture and temple and trade guild economies, moving into Zosimos's blending of Egyptian, Greco-Roman, Jewish, and Christian ideas. I hope to illuminate some of the fascinating cultural and intellectual exchanges that were occurring in Upper Egypt in the last century of "paganism", as Christianity was gaining currency, and many Egyptian temples were declining under Roman administration. This cultural biography of Zosimos is aligned with recent historiographical trends in alchemy that focus on case studies, or "microhistories", rather than broad surveys as a means of arriving at more nuanced understandings of the varieties of alchemy being practiced in particular times, cultures, and places.[14] I aim to use Zosimos as a lens that will bring broader issues pertaining to the origins of alchemy and the religious dynamics of Roman Egypt into sharper focus.

Historiographical issues

One of my historiographical concerns has been whether to use the term "alchemy" in describing Zosimos's work, since the term is anachronistic for this time period. Zosimos and other Greco-Egyptian alchemists more commonly refer to their work as the "sacred art" (*hiera technē*); they also use the terms *chrysopoeia* and *argyropoeia* (gold-making and silver-making), and, more rarely, they call it *chēmia* (also *chēmeia* or *chymia*).[15] Zosimos's use of

---

14 For an overview of these trends see Marcos MARTINÓN-TORRES, "Some Recent Developments in the Historiography of Alchemy", *Ambix* 58.3 (Nov 2011): 215–237.
15 On the etymology of the word "alchemy", See William NEWMAN and

the term *chēmia* is one of the earliest known appearances of the word; another early instance allegedly comes from the emperor Diocletian in an edict from around 300 CE, issued against "the old writings of the Egyptians, which treat of the *chēmia* of gold and silver".[16] There is much speculation about where this term comes from: many think it derives from the ancient Egyptian word *km* ("black") or *kmt*, "the black earth"; Greco-Roman writers also used *"Chēmia"* as a sobriquet for Egypt, referring to the black, fertile land along the Nile.[17] Interestingly, Zosimos's town, Panopolis, was known to Herodotus and other Greek writers as Chemmis, or Chemmo, which is probably also related to *kmt*/Chēmia.[18] Therefore, I retain the use of the term "alchemy" because this Arabic word (from *al-kīmiyā*) is thought to derive from the *chēmia* of the Greco-Egyptian alchemists, and it has a lexical resonance with the land of Egypt and names for Panopolis, in particular. Another reason I retain this term is that in modern usage, alchemy denotes a form of chemistry that has religious, even mystical dimensions, which aptly describes Zosimos's work with metals. The modern use of this term, however, needs a little more unpacking.

Alchemy has often been labeled as a "pseudo-science" and

Lawrence PRINCIPE, "Alchemy vs. Chemistry: The Etymological Origins of a Historiographical Mistake", *Early Science and Medicine* 3 (1998), 38; Robert HALLEUX, *Les Textes Alchimiques* (Turnhout, Belgium: Brepols, 1979), 45–47; and Jack LINDSAY, *The Origins of Alchemy in Graeco-Roman Egypt*, ch. 4.

16 See M. MARTELLI and M. RUMOR, "Near Eastern Origins of Græco-Egyptian Alchemy", in K. GEUS and M. GELLER, eds., *Esoteric Knowledge in Antiquity* (Berlin: Max Planck Institute for the History of Science, Preprint 454, 2014), 38; and "Alchemy", in *Oxford English Dictionary*, online version (March 2016).

17 OED, ibid.

18 On the different names for Panopolis throughout history, see Karolien GEENS, "Panopolis, a Nome Capital in Egypt in the Roman and Byzantine Period", PHD diss., Katholieke Universiteit Leuven (2007), 1, 110. Geens thinks that "Chemmis" is a Greek variant of the ancient Egyptian name for the town, Khent-Min ("sanctuary of Min"), which seems likely. Islamicate rulers named the town Akhmim (its present name), which etymologically derives from the names of Chemmis, Khent-Min, and *km*.

associated with magic and occultism. Lawrence Principe and William Newman have famously claimed that these characterizations are related to two basic approaches to the historiography of alchemy, which have their roots in Enlightenment scientific debates and in Romantic critiques of Newtonian science. The first approach, which could be called the Enlightenment approach, dates from the beginning of the eighteenth century when etymological distinctions between "alchemy" and "chemistry" began appearing in force as an attempt to distinguish alchemy from the burgeoning science of chemistry.[19] Prior to this time, the terms alchemy and chemistry had been used interchangeably in reference to all types of chemical experiments, pharmacology, and to gold-making, but in the eighteenth century "alchemy" came to be used almost exclusively to designate gold-making practices, which by now had become widely associated with charlatanism and fraud.[20] Enlightenment writers often describe chemistry as a light of reason triumphantly shining forth from the deluded darkness of the alchemical past, and these Enlightenment metaphors and attitudes continue to appear in contemporary histories of alchemy.[21]

According to Principe and Newman, the initial consequence of this separation of alchemy and chemistry is that the religious and esoteric aspects of alchemy became more pronounced, and by the nineteenth century, alchemy was popularly associated

19 Lawrence M. PRINCIPE and William R. NEWMAN, "Some Problems with the Historiography of Alchemy", in W. NEWMAN and A. GRAFTON, eds., *Secrets of Nature: Astrology and Alchemy in Early Modern Europe* (Cambridge: MIT Press, 2001), 386.
20 A fuller treatment of this etymological shift can be found in another article by the same authors. See W. NEWMAN and L. PRINCIPE, "Alchemy vs. Chemistry: The Etymological Origins of a Historiographical Mistake", *Early Science and Medicine* 3 (1998): 32–65.
21 Ibid. Many scholarly works on early Greco-Egyptian alchemy, especially those written by historians of science, convey these "Enlightenment" attitudes. See, for example, F. Sherwood TAYLOR, *The Alchemists* (St. Albans: Paladin, 1976 [1952]); A. J. HOPKINS, *Alchemy: Child of Greek Philosophy* (New York: AMS Press, 1967 [1933]); and a more recent article by P. T. KEYSER, "Alchemy in the Ancient World: From Science to Magic", *Illinois Classical Studies* 15 (1990): 353–378.

with natural magic, theurgy, astrology, and other so-called occult sciences.[22] The association of alchemy and the occult has often been used to discredit alchemy, to reinforce a distinction between "rational" chemistry and "irrational" alchemy. However, nineteenth-century "occultists" (as they were then called) celebrated and popularized the notion of alchemy as an esoteric mystical practice. They claimed that the chemical operations were actually codes for spiritual realities, used as a foil to conceal the mystical wisdom of alchemy from the uninitiated. This esoteric interpretation of alchemy, which Principe and Newman call the "spiritual" interpretation, has been influential in twentieth-century studies of alchemy, both popular and academic. They cite works on alchemy by C. G. Jung and Mircea Eliade as examples of a predominantly "spiritual" approach because of their claims that alchemy is essentially a psychological and spiritual pursuit in which chemistry plays only a secondary role, if it is even practiced at all.[23] Principe and Newman do not discuss the notion promoted by Antoine Faivre and other scholars of Western esotericism that alchemy is part of a pervasive esoteric religious current in Western culture, but this approach to the study of alchemy would no doubt fall under their rubric of "spiritual" interpretations, as well.[24]

Given that alchemy has been associated with religion, mysticism, magic, theurgy, and astrology throughout its history, which will become abundantly clear in this present work on Zosimos, I take some issue with the historical narratives presented by Principe and Newman because they tend to minimize and even disparage the religious and "occultish" aspects of alchemy, even though they acknowledge that prior to the eighteenth century, the religious

---

22 PRINCIPE and NEWMAN, "Some Problems with the Historiography of Alchemy", 387.
23 Jung's psychological theories of alchemy have been enormously influential on twentieth-century alchemical scholarship, including Eliade's treatment of the subject.
24 For examples of an esoteric approach to alchemy, see FAIVRE, *Access to Western Esotericism* (Albany: SUNY Press, 1994), esp. Part One, 13, 52.

and chemical aspects of alchemy were closely intertwined.²⁵ But they do have a point in that relegating alchemy to the categories of *either* science *or* religion skews our understanding of alchemy. I will give two extreme examples of this that I've seen in studies of Zosimos. Arguing from the scientific/technological side, Jean Letrouit challenges the idea that Zosimean alchemy is religious at all and argues that Zosimos uses religion polemically to ridicule his competitors. He insists that Zosimos is a craftsman and that it is wrong to see him as a religious thinker.²⁶ On the other hand, religion scholar Naomi Janowitz makes the opposite argument, that alchemy is primarily religious. She claims that Zosimos and other religious thinkers co-opted aspects of the metallurgical arts for religious purposes, and that late antique alchemy is best understood as a ritual practice.²⁷ In my estimation, both views are inaccurate and not well-supported by the literature. Greco-Egyptian alchemy, particularly Zosimean alchemy, is best understood as an amalgamation of religion, science, and magic. Although scholars from various fields have made significant contributions to the historiography of Greco-Egyptian alchemy, the field has long been dominated by scientists and historians of science, and by scientific ways of thinking that privilege empirical data and rationalism. Given that alchemy is such an interdisciplinary phenomenon—incorporating religion, natural philosophy, art, languages, history, and literature, as well as science and technology—alchemical studies can only benefit from more interdisciplinary perspectives, and indeed,

---

25 For a similar critique, and for debates surrounding this "new historiography" of alchemy, see Brian VICKERS, "The 'New Historiography' and the Limits of Alchemy", *Annals of Science* 65 (2008): 127–156; and the rebuttal by William NEWMAN, "Brian Vickers on Alchemy and the Occult: A Response", *Perspectives on Science* 17.4 (2009): 482–506.
26 Jean LETROUIT, "Hermetism and Alchemy: Contribution to the Study of Marcianus Græcus 299 (=M)", in ed. C. GILLY and C. van HEERTUM, eds., *Magia, Alchimia, Scienza dal '400 al '700: L'iflusso di Ermete Trismegisto* (Florence: Centro Di, 2002), vol. 1, 88.
27 Naomi JANOWITZ, *Icons of Power: Ritual Practices in Late Antiquity* (University Park, PA: Pennsylvania State University Press, 2002), 111–114.

this is a growing trend.[28] As a religion scholar, I focus mainly on the religious and cultural dimensions of Zosimos's work, but this is not to reduce alchemy to a religious practice. I feel strongly that the spiritual and material aspects of alchemy need to be viewed in tandem, and I approach this by looking at the ways in which Zosimos's religiosity permeates his work with metals and his views of the natural world.

Indeed, the relationship between spirit and matter forms the theoretical underpinning of Zosimos's work: how the One (the divine source) becomes the All (the manifest world), and how the All returns to the One. The relationship between the One and the All is *the* central metaphysical concern in Egyptian Hermetism, Neoplatonism, and Gnosticism. How did the world come into being? Is spirit present in matter, and to what degree? How do spirit and matter co-mingle, and how do they separate? The answers to these questions resulted in various theologies about the process and purpose of creation, the nature of good and evil, and how the human soul/spirit could fulfill its destiny by returning to the divine source. The relationship between the One and the All is also a prominent feature of early alchemical texts, which make use of both Egyptian and Greek philosophical concepts to speculate on the qualities and interactions of the four elements (earth, water, air, and fire) and the underlying unity of the universe that binds everything together. Zosimos intermingles various religious and philosophical approaches in his writings, and the paths he travels between the One and the All reveal his habits of thought and his approach to the alchemical art of divinizing matter, or becoming gold.

---

28   See MARTINÓN-TORRES, "Some Recent Developments in the Historiography of Alchemy", 236. Martinón-Torres mentions that if the history of alchemy is to become a discipline in its own right, training is needed in several of the fields I've just mentioned, but interestingly, he leaves out religion.

Chapter summaries

This book opens with an introduction to Greco-Egyptian alchemy, which is typically defined as (1) the application of Hellenistic natural philosophy to ancient craft traditions, and (2) as efforts to transmute base metals into gold. I challenge these definitions and attempt to provide a more nuanced view by examining Greco-Egyptian alchemical recipes in light of what is known about Egyptian metal statuary, which is distinctively polychromatic. Temple artisans had developed advanced techniques for coloring metals, and I argue that Egyptian alchemy is rooted in this tradition. I also discuss some Egyptian ontological concepts that are evident in alchemical theory, and show how Zosimos and other alchemists were harmonizing Egyptian theories with Greek philosophy as well as other religious and philosophical ideas.

The second chapter fleshes out what the alchemical profession might have been like in Panopolis and the Thebaid region around the time that Zosimos was active. I focus particularly on temple culture and discuss the roles of scribal priests, metallurgists and craft traditions, and the economies in which alchemists made their living. I make the case that Zosimos was a scribal priest who was responsible for preserving and translating ancient Egyptian metallurgical recipes, and that he was a high-ranking craftsman—a goldsmith—who supervised other temple metallurgists. His relationships with other alchemists, namely his colleagues Theosebeia and Neilos, are discussed here, as well as the economic relationships between temples and trade guilds in Roman Egypt. This chapter also addresses the syncretism that was so commonplace in the Greco-Roman era, and some of the socio-economic aspects of this cultural and religious exchange as it pertains to alchemy and the Egyptian priesthood. Traditions of craft secrecy that may have limited the exchange of ideas and techniques are also discussed.

Having situated Zosimos in his broader professional and cultural contexts, I begin in the third chapter to examine his writings in more depth, particularly his religious approach to alchemy. In a number of his writings, Zosimos outlines various spiritual exercises for contemplating the deeper meaning of alchemical work, which involves purifying the soul and transforming the self. I examine several of these exercises, which appear in different texts, but the bulk of this chapter involves a close reading of Zosimos's allegory of the alchemical opus, *On Excellence*, in which he portrays alchemy as a sacrificial ritual. I show how he draws upon Egyptian mortuary traditions and statue-making rituals in this allegory to convey alchemy as the sacred art of "god-making", which involves both the creation of divine statues and the divinization of the embodied soul.

The last two chapters continue to flesh out Zosimos's religious approach to alchemy, though from different angles. Zosimos discusses Hebrew alchemy more than any author in the Greco-Egyptian corpus, and in Chapter Four I examine these references and show how he uses Jewish and Christian thought to differentiate between "natural" and "unnatural" methods of alchemy; I argue that competing concepts of Fate, divine power, and the natural order are at the heart of these alchemical debates. Zosimos is clearly inspired by so-called Gnostic texts as well as some Jewish pseudepigraphical works, and I examine the way he harmonizes ideas from these texts with Egyptian teachings in order to present a universal theory of alchemy.

The final chapter looks at alchemy as a form of theurgy, or "god-work". I compare Zosimean alchemy with the theurgical writings of the Neoplatonic philosopher, Iamblichus, who was a contemporary of Zosimos, and argue that they share similar foundations, especially their critiques of human reason and insistence that higher knowledge comes through divine revelation; their ritual use of material objects to sympathetically link the natural and divine realms and thereby facilitate the soul's ascent; as well as their shared goal of divinizing the embodied soul. Neoplatonism was arguably the most influential philosophical school in late ancient Mediterranean culture, and with theurgy, Neoplatonism began to take a more religious and ritualistic turn, borrowing heavily from ancient Near Eastern cultures in the process. Iamblichus wrote his tome on theurgy in the persona of an Egyptian Hermetic priest; since Zosimos was an actual Hermetic priest, this makes for an interesting comparison, showing how Hellenistic and Egyptian philosophers were borrowing ideas from each other. This comparison allows for a deeper examination of Zosimos's work in light of this prevailing philosophical movement in late antiquity.

Primary sources

The surviving remains of Zosimos's writings come from Byzantine and Syriac anthologies of early Greco-Egyptian alchemical works, preserved in Greek, Syriac, Arabic, and Latin. The Greek manuscripts, dating from the tenth to fifteenth centuries, contain 109 pages of Zosimos's writings and are the largest collection of his works.[29] A French translation of these manuscripts, entitled *Collection des Anciens Alchimistes Grecs*, was published in 1888 by M. Berthelot and C.-E. Ruelle, but it is difficult to sort out Zosimos's writings in this collection since many are folded into or lumped together with ancient commentaries on Zosimos's works. More recently, in the late 1980s, philologist Michèle Mertens undertook the project of sorting out Zosimos's writings in these Greek manuscripts. She has catalogued them and organized them into four groups: *Authentic Memoirs*, *Chapters to Eusebia*, *Chapters to Theodorus*, and the *Book of Sophe* and the *Final Account*, which together constitute the last group. In 1995 she published an excellent French translation of the *Authentic Memoirs* as part of the Budé series, *Les Alchimistes Grecs*, edited by H. D. Saffrey. Her cataloguing of

---

29   The Greek manuscripts are *Marcianus græcus* 299 (tenth or eleventh century), *Parisini græcus* 2325 (thirteenth century) and 2327 (fifteenth century), and *Laurentianus græcus* 86, 16 (fifteenth century). For complete information on these manuscripts and a catalogue of Zosimos's writings in the Greek, Syriac, Arabic, and Latin alchemical manuscripts, see Michèle Mertens's introduction in *Zosime de Panopolis: Mémoires authentiques*, Les Alchimistes Grecs, Tome IV, 1re partie (Paris: Les Belles Lettres, 1995), xii–cxii.

the Greek material by Zosimos is of immense value to scholars of early alchemy.

About sixty-four pages of Zosimos's writings appear in three Syriac alchemical manuscripts from the fifteenth and sixteenth centuries, housed at Cambridge University and at the British Museum.[30] These were collected by Berthelot, translated into French by R. Duval, and published in 1893 in a three volume series entitled *La Chimie au Moyen Age*. The Syriac collection contains different material than the Greek, including a substantial amount of Zosimos's religious writings and letters to his colleague, Theosebeia.

A few pages of Zosimos's authentic works can also be found in Arabic and Latin manuscripts that date from the thirteenth to fifteenth centuries, the majority of which are also found in the Greek manuscripts.[31] Benjamin Hallum recently discovered a few additional authentic writings of Zosimos in a twelfth century Arabic manuscript housed at the Egyptian National Library in Cairo, including some fragments which are not found in any of the Greek or Syriac manuscripts.[32]

---

30 The Cambridge manuscript is numbered Mm 6.29 (fifteenth century); the two at the British Museum are Egerton 709 (fifteenth century) and Oriental 1593 (fifteenth or sixteenth century). See MERTENS, *ibid*, lxxiv and lxxvii.

31 For a list of names and contents of the Arabic and Latin manuscripts, see MERTENS, ibid., lxxviii-lxxxvi. See also MERTENS, "Project for a New Edition of Zosimus of Panopolis", in *Alchemy Revisited: Proceedings of the International Conference on the History of Alchemy at the University of Groningen, 17–19 April 1989*, ed. Z. R. W. M. von MARTELS (Leiden: Brill, 1990), 122 n. 7.

32 The manuscript is Cairo, Dar al-Kutub MS 23 kimiyä' M. See Benjamin HALLUM, *Zosimus Arabus: The Reception of Zosimos of Panopolis in the Arabic/Islamic World* (PHD diss., Warburg Institute, 2008), Ch. 5.

Zosimos and Greco-Egyptian Alchemy, Revisited

THE WRITINGS OF ZOSIMOS OF PANOPOLIS (late third–early fourth century CE) afford us more of a glimpse into the Egyptian roots of alchemy than any other early alchemical texts, yet the Egyptian elements have rarely been examined because scholars have focused instead on its Greek influences. Greco-Egyptian alchemy is said to have originated in the first century CE, when craftsmen began to apply Greek natural philosophy to their crafts and develop theories of transmutation, or how one substance can transform into another. But our operating assumptions need to be re-evaluated from time to time, and so by way of introducing Zosimos of Panopolis, I will also be probing the defining features of Greco-Egyptian alchemy—whether the transmutation of base metals into gold was in fact their primary aim, and whether Hellenistic philosophy should continue to be privileged as a defining feature of early alchemical literature.

The works of Zosimos are found in Byzantine and Syriac anthologies dating from the tenth or eleventh century through the sixteenth century; these collections contain copies of original alchemical works dating from the first through eighth centuries CE. The anthologies are missing pages and organized rather haphazardly; for example, recipes attributed to Zosimos and other alchemists are inserted into the middle of an allegory by Zosimos, thereby disrupting the unity and flow of that work.[1] The Syriac

---

1   For a discussion of the manuscripts and dating of the Byzantine collection, see Lawrence M. PRINCIPE, *The Secrets of Alchemy* (Chicago: University of Chicago Press, 2013), 11–12. For insertions interrupting the flow of Zosim-

manuscripts have additional challenges: in addition to lacunæ and interpolations from later time periods (which are also found in the Greek texts), one of them, Cam. Mm.6.29, suffers from moisture damage, making it difficult to translate. To date, the Syriac manuscripts have been the least studied by scholars of Greco-Egyptian alchemy, though they contain several important Zosimean texts, many of which I will be using here.[2]

As Lawrence Principe points out, it is important to keep in mind the "corrupt" nature of these anthologies:

> [the] compilers chose to copy what they thought was important—which could be neither representative of the original texts nor what the original authors themselves would have considered crucial. Hence, the overall picture of what Greco-Egyptian alchemists thought and did is skewed by the way their writings were excerpted centuries later.[3]

The Egyptian contexts of Zosimos's writings are detectable, but not always explicit, and one must excavate through layers of translation of languages and ideologies in order to recover them. Zosimos was writing for a Hellenized audience, translating Egyptian concepts and harmonizing them with Greek philosophy and Jewish and Christian religious thought. It is likely that some of the Egyptian polytheistic elements were excised or reframed by later Christian and Muslim scribes who copied these recipes. One must also be attentive to the ways these texts have been viewed through

---

os's writings, see, for example, CAAG III.1–5.

2   Not all of the Zosimean texts in Cam. Mm.6.29 appear to be authentic, but I concur with DUVAL (the nineteenth-century translator of these texts), who thinks that many of them might be. They need to be used with caution. See overviews of the Syriac texts in MERTENS, *Zosime de Panopolis*, lxxiv-lxxviii; and Erica C. D. HUNTER, "Beautiful Black Bronzes: Zosimos's treatises in Cam. Mm.6.29", in Alessandra GIUMLIA-MAIR, ed., *I bronzi antichi: Produzione e tecnologia* (Montagnac: Éditions Monique Mergoil, 2002), 655–656.

3   PRINCIPE, *The Secrets of Alchemy*, 12.

modern lenses that bifurcate science and religion; this split is inadequate for understanding ancient worldviews where concepts like science and religion can only be approximated, and their counterparts, natural philosophy and piety, were most often intertwined.

The earliest extant copies of "alchemical" documents are the Leiden and Stockholm Papyri, which were allegedly found in a tomb near Thebes in Upper Egypt and date to the late third or early fourth century CE—the same time frame and vicinity as Zosimos—though they show evidence of being copies of earlier texts.[4] These papyri feature recipes dealing with metallurgy, dyeing, and the manufacture of *faux* precious stones; some of the recipes are also found in earlier Greek alchemical texts dating to the first century, which indicates that alchemy has its origins in decorative arts that involved color fabrication.[5] Many of the techniques in these early alchemical texts had been practiced by Near Eastern craftsmen for millennia, though our texts from the Roman period reveal some new advances in these arts—namely, distillation and the discovery of the chemical properties of sulfur, arsenic, and mercury vapors.[6]

4   See Robert HALLEUX, *Papyrus de Leyde, Papyrus de Stockholm Recettes, Les Alchimistes Grecs, Tome I* (Paris: Les Belles Lettres, 1981), 5–14. The recipes are technical in nature, devoid of the Hellenistic philosophical or religious speculations that accompany other alchemical texts, and because of this there is debate about whether they should be considered alchemical texts. However, some of these recipes are similar to those found in earlier alchemical works, such as the *Physika kai Mystika* ("Natural and Secret Things", first or second century CE, attributed to DEMOCRITUS), which do contain philosophical reflection. See Earl R. CALEY, trans., and Wm. B. JENSEN, ed., *The Leyden and Stockholm Papyri: Greco-Egyptian Chemical Documents from the 4th Century AD* (Cincinnati: University of Cincinnati, 2008), 3–4; and HALLEUX, 24–30.
5   The recipes in the Leiden Papyrus (*P. Leid.* X) are metallurgical, whereas the Stockholm Papyrus deals mostly with dyeing. On the antiquity of arts of coloration, see R. J. FORBES, *Studies in Ancient Technology* I (Leiden: Brill, 1955), 125–128. See also A. J. HOPKINS, "Earliest Alchemy", *The Scientific Monthly* 6.6 (1918): 531–533; and Philip BALL, *Bright Earth: Art and the Invention of Color* (New York: Farrar, Straus, and Giroux, 2002), ch. 4.
6   Some scholars have claimed that alchemy is based on the discovery of distillation, but there are indications that distillation was known, in some

32　CHAPTER ONE

Alchemical authors often (though not always) include philosophical speculation on color changes and chemical reactions, which are described in terms of the transmutation of the four elements, the unity of nature ("One is All" is a popular alchemical slogan),[7] and the death and resurrection of the "spirits" of metals. For example, in a second-century text known as *The Dialogue of Cleopatra and the Philosophers*, Ostanes asks Cleopatra, a teacher of alchemy, to "Enlighten us, casting your light upon the elements. Tell us how the highest descends to the lowest and how the lowest rises to the highest, and how that which is in the midst approaches the highest and is united to it, and what is the element which accomplishes these things".[8] Cleopatra responds:

> The waters, when they come, awaken the bodies and spirits, which are imprisoned and weak. For they again undergo oppression and are enclosed in Hades, and yet in a little while they grow and rise up and put on diverse glorious colors like the flowers in springtime, and the spring itself rejoices and is glad at the beauty they wear. [...] When they are clothed in the glory

---

form, to Sumerians, Babylonians, and to ancient Greeks. However, the distillatory techniques and apparatuses of Greco-Egyptian metallurgists are "revolutionary" compared with earlier descriptions. See Robert MULTHAUF, *The Origins of Chemistry* (London: Oldbourne, 1966), 109. For a description of an ancient Sumerian still, see P. T. KEYSER, "Alchemy in the Ancient World: From Science to Magic", 362–363. For a discussion of the development of Greek and Greco-Egyptian distillation techniques, see F. S. Taylor, *The Alchemists* (St. Albans: Paladin, 1976 [1952]), 39–50.

7　See the *Chrysopoeia of Cleopatra* (second c. CE) in CAAG I, Fig. 11, 132, which consists of various diagrams of chemical symbols and apparatus, along with drawings of the serpent Ouroboros inscribed with statements such as: "One is All", and "One is All and through it is All and by it is All and if you have not All, All is nothing". F. S. TAYLOR's translation, "Origins of Greek Alchemy", *Ambix* 1 (1937–38): 43.

8　TAYLOR's translation, *The Alchemists*, 55–56. The full text is found in CAAG IV.20, under the (probably late) title of *Book of Comarius, Philosopher and High Priest. Teachings of Cleopatra on the Divine and Sacred Art of the Philosopher's Stone*.

from the fire and the shining color thereof, then will appear their hidden glory, their sought-for beauty, being transformed to the divine state of fusion.[9] [...] For the womb of fire has given them birth and they have clothed themselves in glory. It has brought them to a single unity; their likeness has been perfected in body, soul and spirit and they have become one. For fire has been subjected to water, and earth to air, in the same way as air with fire, and earth with water, and fire and water with earth, and water with air, and they have become one.[10]

Though religious concepts such as rebirth and the unity of body, mind, and spirit are found in this text and in others from the same period, Zosimos of Panopolis is usually hailed as the founder of religious alchemy. This book makes the case that Zosimos was an Egyptian artisan-priest and that alchemy originated in the art of making divine statues, which had been a sacred art for thousands of years; religious approaches to metals and metallurgy had long been present in other forms of Egyptian ritual, as well.[11] Instead of thinking of Zosimos as the first religious alchemist, it is more accurate to say that his works are the earliest examples in the Greco-Egyptian alchemical corpus of someone who *theologizes* alchemy; he is probably not the first Egyptian priest to do so, but he is one of the last of his kind. In 392 CE, the Roman emperor Theodosius officially closed most of the Egyptian temples; the empire had be-

---

9   Ibid. Compare with CAAG IV.20.8-10.
10 Adapted from a translation by C. A. BROWNE, in "Rhetorical and Religious Aspects of Greek Alchemy, Part II", *Ambix* 3 (1948): 24. About three-fourths of the entire CLEOPATRA dialogue is reprinted in a commentary on an alchemical poem by ARCHELAOS (seventh–eighth century), which is where this portion of the translation comes from. The text is the same as that of the Cleopatra dialogue in the *Book of Comarius*, CAAG IV.20.16.
11 For an excellent study of Egyptian "theologies" of metals and their use in religious rites and art forms, see Sydney AUFRÈRE, *L'Univers Minéral dans la Pensée Égyptienne*, 2 vols. (1991).

come Christianized and iconoclasm was rampant, which put an end to the professional role of the Egyptian temple artisans.[12] The alchemical corpus needs to be studied in light of the intellectual networking and shifting socio-political circumstances in Roman Egypt. In my view, Zosimos was not trying to create anything new as much as preserve a time-honored tradition and express it in ways that would have universal appeal in an increasingly multicultural and multi-religious Egyptian society.

ZOSIMOS AND STATUE MAKING

Zosimos gives more insight into his profession than other authors in the Greco-Egyptian corpus, who rarely describe the professional contexts in which they are working, or what the end products of their technical recipes will be. Evidence that Zosimos was involved with statue-making comes from one of the Syriac texts, *On the Work of Copper (Letter Waw)*, where he gives instructions for making and coloring anthropomorphic statues, techniques he claims can also be used on figurines of animals, fish, birds, trees, and various other objects.[13] For the male statue, he says to make "a Phrygian [or radiant?] figure, which is not inferior, so that those viewing it believe that they are seeing a living body".[14] He gives

---

12 See Ragnhild FINNESTAD, "Temples of the Ptolemaic and Roman Periods: Ancient Traditions in New Contexts", in Byron SHAFER, ed. *Temples of Ancient Egypt* (Ithaca, NY: Cornell University Press, 1997), 237. On iconoclasm in Roman Egypt at the turn of the fourth century, see David FRANKFURTER, *Religion in Roman Egypt: Assimilation and Resistance* (Princeton: Princeton University Press, 1998), 277–284.

13 CMA, Syr. II.6.2.

14 CMA, Syr. II.6.8. I am here using Erica HUNTER's partial English translation of the Syriac text, in "Beautiful Black Bronzes: Zosimos's treatises in Cam. Mm.6.29", in *I bronzi antichi: Produzione e tecnologia*, Atti del XV Congresso Internazionale sui Bronzi Antichi, Università di Udine, 22–26 Maggio, 2001, ed. A. GIUMLIA-MAIR (Montagnac: Éditions Monique Mergoil, 2002), 656–658. Hunter says that Phrygian is probably the original meaning, but could be a derivative of the Syriac PGR, which means "radiant". HUNTER, 659.

further instructions for making it the color of "castor oil". The castor oil plant is mentioned in Leiden Papyrus x as an ingredient that can whiten metal alloys, and the resulting color is beautiful and of high quality.[15] Achieving beautiful color and sheen is important to this work: the female figurine he describes is made from four parts silver and one part gold. "This mixture", he says, "resembles female flesh; it glows whilst it shines".[16] Zosimos also mentions crafting statues of Agathodaimon (the "good spirit") and the deities of Fortune, Earth, and the Nile, which were all popular deities in the Roman period.[17] In another text, *On Electrum*, he refers to manuals for making amulets.[18] These statues and amulets were undoubtedly used for religious purposes. The small cast statues that Zosimos describes would have been installed in the temples themselves, used as funerary offerings in private tombs, and sold to wealthier clients for religious and/or decorative purposes. Figurines made from debased or less precious metals would have been sold at festivals or at the markets near the temple entrances, along with terracotta figurines manufactured by local craftspeople; these religious objects for household or funerary use were made in consultation with the temple priests who ensured that proper religious iconography was used in their design.[19]

The beautifully-colored statues that Zosimos describes are in line with other evidence from the Greco-Egyptian alchemical corpus, where most of the metallurgical recipes are for coloring metals. Ancient Egyptian statues are distinctive for their polychromatic qualities, and the techniques that temple artisans developed

---

15   *P. Leid.* x, 21.
16   CMA, Syr. II.6.9. HUNTER's translation.
17   CMA, Syr. II.6.31. Images of Mother Earth and the Nile are commonly found in funerary sculpture from late ancient Egypt. See Thelma THOMAS, *Late Antique Egyptian Funerary Sculpture: Images for this World and the Next* (Princeton: Princeton University Press, 1999), 63–64.
18   CMA, Syr. II.12.5.
19   See FRANKFURTER, *Religion in Roman Egypt*, 132, 140, 215; and FRANKFURTER, "Religious Practice and Piety", in C. RIGGS, ed., *The Oxford Handbook of Roman Egypt* (Oxford: Oxford University Press, 2012), 322.

for coloring metals reached new heights in the Third Intermediate Period (1070–664 BCE). Élisabeth Delange notes that the polychromy has been difficult to detect, because metals transform over time, but newer methods of chemical analysis have been able to identify the subtle, intentional uses of color by the artist.[20] The production of polychromic statuary persisted into the Ptolemaic and Roman periods, and artifacts from this time period show that a single statue might be made of several different metals and contain a variety of hues, achieved through bronzing and surface treatments, gilding, or inlays.[21] In *On the Work of Copper*, Zosimos boasts about these polychromic statues, stating that people were "seized with fear at the sight of the images; they thought that they were animated and that they had the colors of living nature".[22] Being "seized with fear" at the sight of a divine image is a standard Egyptian response to the majesty of the god it represents.[23] The life-like form and vivid colors of the divine image facilitate an encounter with the holy, the *mysterium tremendum et fascinans* of the living god.

---

20 Élisabeth DELANGE, "The Complexity of Alloys: New Discoveries About Certain 'Bronzes' in the Louvre", in M. HILL with D. SCHORSCH, eds., *Gifts for the Gods: Images from Egyptian Temples*, Catalog of exhibition held at the Metropolitan Museum of Art, New York Oct. 16, 2007–Feb. 18, 2008 (New Haven: Yale University Press, 2007), 39. This remarkable color artistry is also attested by Marsha HILL in "Heights of Artistry: The Third Intermediate Period (ca. 1070–664 BC)", in the same volume, 52.

21 See, for example, Deborah SCHORSCH's technical analysis of a statue of Bes from the fourth–second century BCE in SCHORSCH, "The Manufacture of Metal Statuary: 'Seeing the Workshops of the Temple'", in M. HILL and D. SCHORSCH, eds., *Gifts for the Gods*, 196.

22 CMA Syr. II.6.31. My translation of DUVAL's French: « Les hommes étaient saisis de crainte à la vue des images; ils pensaient qu'elles étaient animées et qu'elles tenaient leurs couleurs de la nature vivante ; à tel point qu'ils n'osaient pas les regarder en face, par crainte de la nature vivante des membres et de la figure de l'objet façonné ».

23 See Erik HORNUNG, *Conceptions of God in Ancient Egypt: The One and the Many*, trans. J. BAINES (Ithaca: Cornell University Press, 1982), 197; and Robert RITNER, *The Mechanics of Ancient Egyptian Magical Practice* (Chicago: Oriental Institute of the University of Chicago, 1993), 24.

FIGURE 1. POLYCHROMIC STATUARY, I
BES-IMAGE OF THE GOD HOR-ASHA-KHET

*Bronze inlaid with gold, electrum, auriferous silver, copper, & copper-alloy.
Ptolemaic Egypt (4th–2nd century BCE). The Metropolitan Museum of Art, New York.*

Egyptian statues are also noteworthy for their interesting textural designs (achieved through scoring), and for their lustration effects. Some figures are elaborately "tattooed" with hieroglyphs and divine symbols. One of the unattributed books in the Syriac alchemical manuscripts, *Letter Beta*, attests to this practice and gives several recipes for "writing" with precious metals, many in the form of encaustic inlays using liquid adhesives, gum arabic, or fish glue: "With this, you can write letters of gold on vases ‹...›, on statues, and on all that you wish, so as to make it look like golden letters".[24] This manuscript also contains recipes for silver letters and for black, as well as for writing with silver on copper, or black on gold.[25] Recipes for writing with gold and silver are also found in Leiden Papyrus x.[26] Artifacts that display this kind of writing or tattooing include blackened cult statues known as black bronzes; the elaborate gold and silver inlays create a brilliant, scintillating effect against the black background. In *On the Work of Copper*, Zosimos gives some recipes for blackening copper and silver. According to Pliny the Elder (first c. CE), the Egyptians customarily colored their silver statues black "so as to see portraits of their god Anubis in their vessels".[27] Pliny quips that the use of blackened silver "passed over even to our [Roman] triumphal statues, and, wonderful to relate, its price rises with the dimming of its brilliance".[28] Zosimos says that the recipes for blackening silver were closely guarded: "This essential recipe was most important for the ancients, and it was kept hidden. Not only was the secret mandatory, but it was also prescribed by all the oaths that sanctioned its mystery".[29] The high market value of these blackened cult statues

---

24 CMA Syr. 1.2.1 (Letter Beta). My translation of Duval's French: « Avec ceci, écris des lettres d'or sur des vases ‹...›, sur des statues et sur tout ce que tu voudras, de façon à faire paraître les lettres dorées ».
25 Ibid.
26 On writing with gold, see *P.Leid.*x 33, 38, 44, 49, 51, 56, 61, 68, 69, 76; on writing with silver, 77.
27 Pliny, *Natural History*, 33.46. Translated by H. Rackham.
28 Ibid.
29 CMA, Syr. 11.6.4. My translation of Duval's French: « Il faut savoir

FIGURE 2. POLYCHROMIC STATUARY, II
THE DIVINE ADORATIRCE, KAROMAMA

Bronze inlaid with gold, silver, & electrum;
Pharaonic Egypt, 22nd Dynasty (943–716 BCE). Musée du Louvre, Paris.

FIGURE 3. POLYCHROMIC STATUARY, III
KAROMAMA: DETAIL OF METALLIC INLAY (REVERSE)

*Bronze inlaid with gold, silver, & electrum;
Pharaonic Egypt, 22nd Dynasty (943–716 BCE). Musée du Louvre, Paris.*

FIGURE 4. BLACK BRONZE STATUARY, I
SPHINX OF KING SIAMON

*Black bronze inlaid with gold; Pharaonic Egypt, 21st Dynasty (978–959 BCE).
Musée du Louvre, Paris.*

is attested as far back as the Bronze Age, where in ranked lists of religious offerings, black bronze alloys are listed behind gold and silver in value, but before bronze and copper.[30]

The emphasis on coloring metals that we see in the alchemical corpus lines up in many ways with what we now know about the polychromy and design of Egyptian metal statuary. Zosimos and other early Egyptian alchemists were most likely working in this ancient artisanal tradition.

Color transmutation

Although alchemy is commonly thought of (and sometimes ridiculed) as the attempt to change lead into gold, there is a lack of evidence that Zosimos and other early alchemists believed they were literally transforming base metals into precious ones. They seem to be well-aware that they were either coloring metals to give them the appearance of pure gold or silver (or other hues), or purifying gold and silver from natural contaminants, as the case may be.

One of the earliest known references in Greco-Roman literature to metallic transmutation, meaning that one substance can completely transform into another, comes from the first century CE in Pliny's discussion of orpiment, a mineral that is golden-yellow or golden-orange in color. He reports that Caligula, who was "extremely covetous for gold", once ordered great quantities of orpiment to be smelted.[31] Pliny says that orpiment did, in fact, "produce excellent gold", but in such small quantities that Caligula abandoned the project and "no one afterwards has repeated the

---

comment se faisait le traitement des enduits et de l'incération, d'après le premier livre sur les modifications de l'argent, son amollissement, ou son noircissement. Cette recette capitale était la principale pour les anciens, et elle était tenue cachée. Non seulement le secret était obligatoire, mais il était aussi prescrit par tous les serments qui en sanctionnaient le mystère ».

30   DELANGE, "The Complexity of Alloys", 41.
31   PLINY, *Natural History*, 30.22. Translated by H. RACKHAM.

experiment".³² Regardless of whether the story is historically accurate, it does appear that Pliny thinks it possible for orpiment to be transmuted into gold. F. S. Taylor explains that definitions of gold in antiquity were more malleable than they are today:

> The men of those times had no conception that there existed one and only one exactly defined chemical individual called *gold*. There were all sorts of golds, some very good, others not so good. They were, however, all "gold" to the ancients, not mixtures of one pure gold with varying proportions of base metal. Gold was something shining, heavy, yellow, untarnishable, and resistant to fire.³³

On the other hand, specialists in metallurgy, especially the artisan-priests discussed earlier in this chapter, exhibit a more sophisticated understanding of the different qualities and kinds of gold, and would certainly be able to distinguish gold from smelted orpiment. Various assay tests were used in antiquity to detect pure gold from adulterated gold. These include weight tests and the touchstone test, which involves rubbing gold on a black stone and examining the color of the streak it left behind.³⁴ A fire test known as cupellation was also used. Cupellation, which is still used today, is a method of refining gold by heating it with lead, which causes base metals and other impurities to oxidize and separate from the gold; when used as an assay test, cupellation can reveal the presence of base metals and other impurities by the oxides that appear.³⁵ These assaying techniques were certainly known to me-

---

32   Ibid.
33   TAYLOR, *The Alchemists*, 34.
34   Ibid. Also, see J. F. HEALY, *Mining and Metallurgy in the Greek and Roman World* (London: Thames and Hudson, 1978), 203–209.
35   Cupellation was known to ancient Egyptians and Babylonians, and even today it is considered the most accurate assaying method. See Joseph NEEDHAM, *Science and Civilisation in China*, vol. 5, part II (Cambridge: Cambridge University Press, 1974), 36–41.

FIGURE 5. BLACK BRONZE STATUARY, II
RITUAL STATUETTE OF THUTHMOSE III

*Black bronze inlaid with gold. Pharaonic Egypt, 18th Dynasty (ca. 1479–1425 BCE).
The Metropolitan Museum of Art, New York.*

tallurgists, but the average person may not have been able to tell the difference between gold and orpiment, and may have indeed believed that anything closely resembling gold in weight and color *is* gold; this is probably also true of the average person today.

Most of the recipes in the Greco-Egyptian corpus are for the manufacture and coloring of metal alloys, the debasing of gold (i.e., making gold of different carat weights), and the superficial coloring of metals with tinctures.[36] There are also recipes for making dyes, mordants, and inks, as well as for making artificial gemstones and pearls. Some of the comments in the Leiden Papyrus indicate that the recipes could be used for counterfeiting:

> *P. Leid.* x, 39: [The metal] will be like the finest quality *asem* (i.e., electrum, a natural alloy of silver and gold), to the point that it will deceive even the artisans.[37]

> *P. Leid.* x, 37 (on making imitation gold rings): [T]he objects of copper appear as gold and can neither be detected by fire nor by rubbing on the stone.[38]

In the 1970s, Joseph Needham introduced the terms "aurifiction" and "aurifaction" to distinguish between gold-faking and gold-making, and the terms are still frequently used today in studies of alchemy. Aurifiction is knowingly making imitation gold, or other precious metals, in some cases with the intent to deceive.[39] Aurifaction, by contrast, is defined by Needham as a "belief that it is possible to make gold (or 'a' gold, or an artificial 'gold') indistinguishable from, and as good as (if not better than),

---

[36] TAYLOR, "A Survey of Greek Alchemy", *The Journal of Hellenic Studies* 50, part 1 (1930), 127-130. For more detail about these techniques, see TAYLOR, *The Alchemists*, 36-50.

[37] NEEDHAM quotes these passages, but with different numbering, in *Science and Civilisation in China*, vol. 5, part 11, 18. The translations here are adapted from Halleux, *Papyrus de Leyde, Papyrus de Stockholm Recettes*.

[38] Ibid., No. 37.

[39] NEEDHAM, 10. The parenthetical remark is a shortened version of Needham's.

natural gold, from other quite different substances, notably the ignoble metals".[40] He claims that this was the belief of Greco-Egyptian alchemists, whom he thinks were probably *not* professional metallurgists, but rather philosophers who erroneously believed that they were making real gold because, like the average person, they considered gold to be anything that had the form or quality of gold.[41]

One of the earliest Greco-Egyptian alchemical texts, *Physika kai Mystika* ("Natural and Secret Things", first century CE, attributed to Ps.-Demokritos) is cited by Needham as an example of aurifaction. This text contains numerous recipes for tinting metals and making alloys, some of which are similar to recipes in Leiden Papyrus X, but Ps.-Democritus often makes claims like, "thus you will obtain gold", which Needham interprets as a belief in the transmutation of base metals.[42] However, he takes these phrases about obtaining gold out of context. Looking at the entire recipe, one can see that these recipes are about gold-coloring, not making real gold: "Add yellow silver (i.e., electrum) and you will have gold; with the resulting gold you will have coral of gold reduced in a metallic body".[43] "Coral of gold" is described in other alchemical recipes as a red-colored substance used to tint gold.[44] Most of the recipes for "gold-making" in this text are for obtaining a golden-colored tincture (or varnish?) called "shell of gold".[45]

40 Ibid, 11.
41 Ibid, 10-11.
42 Ibid, 20. On the similarities to *Leiden Papyrus* X, see BERTHELOT's notes to CAAG II.1.
43 See CAAG II.1.4, which is the same recipe cited by NEEDHAM. J. M. STILLMAN (Needham cites Stillman's translation of this recipe) claims that these recipes clearly intend to "give copper or bronze a superficial silver or gold color by the use of mercury alloys or arsenic alloys". See J. M. STILLMAN, *The Story of Alchemy and Early Chemistry* (New York: Dover, 1960 [1924]), 157.
44 See, for example, CAAG II.2.5, where coral of gold is described as a powerful substance that has the color of cinnabar.
45 See CAAG II.1.6-7. According to BERTHELOT's lexicon, "shell of gold" is also known as "liquor of gold", CAAG II, 16.

Needham's theory that Greco-Egyptian alchemists were primarily philosophers who misunderstood or repurposed the recipes of the artisans has continued to raise questions about divisions between the theoretical and technical aspects of alchemy.[46] Matteo Martelli, for example, has recently noted that Greco-Egyptian alchemists—including Zosimos—seem more focused on the intellectual, text-oriented aspects of ancient alchemy, on interpreting ancient recipes rather than doing experimental work with metals. He proposes that there was likely a separation, yet also a dialectical relationship, between craftsmen and alchemists.[47] Zosimos's writings (and their temple context) help to fill in this seeming gap between theory and practice. Zosimos indicates that alchemical texts were copied and produced by scribal priests, who supervised temple artisans that most likely worked in a variety of mediums.[48] This does not indicate a stark division between scribes and artisans, the former being intellectual dilettantes with only a superficial knowledge of metallurgy, and the latter being skilled craftspeople. These scribal priests were master craftsmen who, according to Zosimos and other alchemical texts, held the rank of "prophet": this high ranking group of priests was responsible for seeing that rituals and temple procedures were performed correctly.[49] As master craftsmen, they would be experienced in the work, but in their supervisory role they would have had more responsibi-

---

[46] Older theorists of alchemy did not make such a divide, though BERTHELOT and others have puzzled over the differences in alchemical texts, some of which (they think) indicate transmutation of base metals, and others that clearly indicate they are making imitation gold. NEEDHAM introduces this theory of two distinct groups, the aurifictors (artisans), and aurifactors (philosophers) as a way of explaining these apparent discrepancies. See NEEDHAM, 46.

[47] MARTELLI, "Greek Alchemists at Work: The 'Alchemical Laboratory' in the Greco-Roman Egypt", *Nuncius* 26 (2011): 310–11.

[48] CMA, Syr. II.6.4, 19. On senior artisans having priestly status, see Joachim Friedrich QUACK, "Religious Personnel: Egypt", in Sarah Iles JOHNSTON, ed., *Religions of the Ancient World: A Guide* (Cambridge: Harvard University Press, 2004), 290.

[49] Ibid; on role of prophet, see QUACK, 289.

lity for interpreting, collecting, and creating recipes and overseeing the work of others. Zosimos appears to be one of these priestly master craftsmen (see chapter 2), which explains his deep engagement with the textual tradition, but he was also a highly skilled metallurgist, not merely a dabbler.[50]

My own view of metallic transmutation in this period is closer to that of Arthur Hopkins, a scholar of Greco-Egyptian alchemy writing in the early twentieth century, who argued that Greco-Egyptian notions of alchemical transmutation are essentially describing changes in *color*, not fundamental transformations from one metal into another.[51] According to Hopkins, the notion of transmuting base metals into gold did not originate with Greco-Egyptian alchemists, but rather came about in the thirteenth century as a result of centuries of European misinterpretations of Arabic translations of Greco-Egyptian ideas. He claims that the concept of transmutation was always debated and never universally shared among alchemists.[52] I do not completely agree with Hopkins (he relies heavily on Greek philosophy to explain these theories, and I look more toward Egyptian religious traditions), but the idea of color transmutation seems to be most consistent with the literature and the evidence of Egyptian polychromic statuary. The Greco-Egyptian texts, as Hopkins says, abound in "color words": "[m]etals are defined by their color or even by the color which they are capable of receiving. Moreover, colors are aggressive, alchemical gold being capable of imparting yellowness to base metal alloys".[53] The equation of "gold" with the golden colors produced on metals is replete throughout the early alchemical corpus.

50   See, for example, STILLMAN's assessment of Zosimos in *The Story of Alchemy and Early Chemistry*, 167.
51   HOPKINS first argued this in "Earliest Alchemy", published in 1918 (op. cit., n. 1), and elaborated on his "color theory", as it came to be known, in "A Modern Theory of Alchemy", *Isis* 7.1 (1925).
52   See HOPKINS, "Earliest Alchemy", 536; and "A Modern Theory of Alchemy", 70–72 (a view that I do not share because it overlooks processes of interpretation and innovation).
53   Ibid, 68.

Hopkins claims that a certain color sequence—black, white, yellow, and red-violet (*iōs*)—represents four stages of color transmutation.⁵⁴ The first step, blackening (*melanōsis*), involves making an alloy out of copper and lead.⁵⁵ Oxidation gives this alloy a black color. The second step is to whiten the metal (*leukōsis*), or impart a silver color to the alloy. Next, the alloy is yellowed (*xanthōsis*), or made "gold". The final step is the reddening (*iōsis*), which is the creation of a reddish or violet colored tincture that is apparently formed within the gold-colored alloy. While these colors and procedures are mentioned in the Greco-Egyptian alchemical texts, they are not discussed as stages of transmutation, as Hopkins describes, but rather as a particular process for making gold-colored alloys using a type of reflux apparatus that was either called the *kērotakis*, or topped by a metal sheet called a *kērotakis* (the Greek word for a hot palette used by artists to keep their wax paints warm); this apparatus was allegedly invented by a female alchemist known as Maria the Jewess (ca. second c. CE).⁵⁶

Modern-day scientists have been able to reproduce the black–white–yellow color stages, but ancient alchemists do not give precise instructions for obtaining the much sought-after *iōs*, or red-violet.⁵⁷ Although *iōs* carries different meanings in the alchemical texts, it often refers to a powerful reddish-gold substance that

54 See HOPKINS, "A Modern Theory of Alchemy", 65–66; and *Alchemy: Child of Greek Philosophy*, 92–103. This color sequence occurs frequently in European alchemical literature, where the colors are also associated with stages of spiritual growth, but this does not appear to be the case for Greco-Egyptian alchemy.
55 There are a few different methods that make use of different base metals. See HOPKINS, "A Study of the Kerotakis Process as Given by Zosimus and Later Alchemical Writers", *Isis* 29.2 (1938). In this article HOPKINS outlines different methods of the four-stage coloration process, and corrects some of his earlier interpretations.
56 See TAYLOR, "A Survey of Greek Alchemy", 131–133. Benjamin HALLUM claims that it is misleading to refer to the entire apparatus as a *kērotakis*, when the *kērotakis* is actually the metal sheet atop the device. See HALLUM, "Zosimus Arabus: The Reception of Zosimos of Panopolis in the Arabic/Islamic World" (PhD diss., Warburg Institute, 2008), 188.
57 See TAYLOR, ibid., and KEYSER, "Alchemy in the Ancient World", 365–366.

is used to impart a golden color to metals.⁵⁸ *Iōs* could also refer to the creation of violet-colored bronzes or surface films.⁵⁹ Jewelry and other objects made of violet and rose-colored gold have been found in Egyptian tombs, including that of Tutankhamun. Analysis has shown that the violet film is not a lacquer or varnish, but an iron oxide produced from within the metal by heating; the violet color does not dissipate when fired, and even intensifies in some cases.⁶⁰ The production of this violet film from within the metals correlates to descriptions in Greco-Egyptian alchemical texts.

Some of Zosimos's instructions for gold and silver-making may actually be recipes for making an alloy known in the Greco-Roman period as "Corinthian bronze".⁶¹ There are different theories as to what Corinthian bronze actually is, since the term fell out of usage by the tenth century CE, and references to it in ancient literature are imprecise.⁶² Despite its Greek name, it was known in antiquity as an Egyptian product, and it was highly prized throughout the Roman Empire because it could be made to look exactly like gold or silver, but it was less expensive; it was also harder and more durable and, like gold, it was resistant to tarnish and rust.⁶³ One of the more well-attested examples of Corinthian bronze in antiquity is the Nicanor Gate in the Jewish Temple,

---

58 Another name for this reddish substance is "coral of gold". See note 28 above. *Iōs* also means "poison" or "rust", and the word is used to describe various surface tarnishes; *iōs* of copper is verdigris, for example. See HOPKINS, *Alchemy: Child of Greek Philosophy*, 97 n. 12; and BALL, *Bright Earth: Art and the Invention of Color*, 64.
59 See HOPKINS, *Alchemy: Child of Greek Philosophy*, 100–102; and KEYSER, "Alchemy in the Ancient World", 366.
60 A. LUCAS, *Ancient Egyptian Materials and Industries* (London: Edward Arnold, 1962), 233–234.
61 See Alessandra GIUMLIA-MAIR and P. T. CRADDOCK, *Corinthium aes: das schwarze Gold der Alchimisten* (Mainz am Rhein: P. von Zabern, 1993); GIUMLIA-MAIR, "Zosimos the Alchemist, Manuscript 629, Cambridge, Metallurgical Interpretation", in GIUMLIA-MAIR, ed., *I bronzi antichi*, op. cit.; and David JACOBSON, "Corinthian Bronze and the Gold of the Alchemists", *Gold Bulletin* 33.2 (2000).
62 See JACOBSON, 64.
63 Ibid.

which was commissioned in Alexandria and brought to Jerusalem in the first century CE.[64] But since Corinthian bronze was expensive, it was more commonly used for smaller items, including figurines like the ones mentioned in Zosimos's *On the Work of Copper*; this work contains recipes for Corinthian bronze (including blackened varieties), as does Leiden Papyrus x.[65] Examining recipes from these and other alchemical texts, David Jacobson argues that this alloy was produced by a method called depletion gilding:

> By scouring the Greek, Latin, and Syriac literature, it is possible to reconstruct the manufacture of Corinthian Bronze. We learn that its production involved further processing after alloying. This included a heat-treatment followed by a quench and burnishing. All these constituent steps are consistent with depletion gilding (or silvering), whereby copper is oxidized and removed from the surface of the bronze item by acid pickling, leaving the surface with a gold (or silver) layer.[66]

Jacobson notes that the process of depletion gilding follows the blackening, whitening, and yellowing sequence described in the Greco-Egyptian alchemical texts.[67] The resulting gold or silver, perfect because of its tarnish-resistant incorruptibility, seems a likely candidate for some of the "gold" of which the alchemists speak.

Olivier Dufault rightly notes that Greco-Egyptian alchemists did not have theories of transmutation, but used the word *ekstrophē* and its cognates to describe various types of transformation, from

---

64 Ibid, 60–61.
65 CRADDOCK and GIUMLIA-MAIR, cited above in footnote 55, think that the blackened patinas described in Zosimos's texts are a blackened form of Corinthian bronze, but JACOBSON disagrees because in ancient literature, Corinthian bronze is most often described as having a lustrous golden or silver appearance. See JACOBSON, 64.
66 JACOBSON, 61.
67 Ibid., 65.

the superficial coloring of metals to the complete transformation of substances; *ekstrophē* could also refer to the "the extraction (the 'turning inside-out') of what was hidden in a substance".[68] The production of a color from within the metal (*iōs*), and the depletion gilding process, whereby copper is extracted from the surface layers so that only gold or silver remains, bring us closer to the meaning of transmutation in the alchemical corpus. For Zosimos, this was also a spiritual process in which impurities are removed from the surface layers of the self so that the soul's divine beauty and precious value can shine forth.

The idea of alchemy as both a chemical and spiritual transformation is embedded in its technical language. There are copious references to metallic "bodies" and "spirits" in Greco-Egyptian alchemical literature. The bodies (*sōmata*) are the physical metals, and the spirits (*pneumata*) of metals refer to their color, to tinctures, and also to volatile substances such as mercury, sulfur, and arsenic, which act upon the metals.[69] The link between color and spirit is also found in ancient Egyptian language, where color is synonymous with essence, or the fundamental character of an object.[70] Distillation technologies may have added new layers of meaning, for metallurgists could readily observe the sublimation of vapors in glass tubes, providing them with images of the "spirits" of metals leaving their bodies.[71] In *The Dialogue of Cleopatra* cited at the beginning of this chapter, the metallic bodies and spirits are imprisoned in the underworld (the apparatus in which the metals are

---

68 Olivier DUFAULT, "Transmutation Theory in the Greek Alchemical Corpus", *Ambix* 62.3 (Aug. 2015): 216.
69 See BERTHELOT's discussion, CAAG I, 247–250.
70 HORNUNG, *Idea into Image*, 27. Hornung also explains that hieroglyphs were always written in different colors, which indicate the essence of the depicted object.
71 In Greek, *pneuma*, or spirit, also means "breath". Aristotle wrote that metals and minerals are formed by inhalations and exhalations of the earth (*Meteor*.III, 378a.20–378b.5). This was probably a common conception even before Aristotle. Miners would have been intimately familiar with vapors and gases in the mines (some of which are poisonous), and may have described them as breaths or spirits.

being fired), and eventually the spirits rise up like flowers in springtime, imparting glorious colors to the metallic bodies. Zosimos is quoted by another alchemist as saying: "The mystery of the gold tincture is to change the bodies into spirits, in order to tint them into the state of spirituality".[72] To color a metal, then, is to bring it to a state of "spirituality", or to "spiritualize" it.[73] The Greek word "incorporeals" (*asōmata*) is used more or less interchangeably with spirits, as can be seen in this passage attributed to Zosimos: "This conversion is called transmutation (ἐκστροφή) after the incorporeals have taken a body, by the effect of the art".[74] Here the incorporeals, the "spirits" or volatile substances, are the agents of transmutation. From these examples, one can see how transmutation centers on coloring, or spiritualizing the metals, and how easily the technical language of alchemy slips into religious concepts.

Given the preponderance of evidence for advanced techniques of metallic polychromy in ancient Egypt, which is reflected in the alchemical texts, can we still claim that Egyptian alchemists were philosophers inexperienced in metallurgy (aurifactors), or that their work centered on transmuting base metals into pure gold? Again, to emphasize Dufault's point, while there are several descriptions of transmutation in the alchemical corpus, there are no explicit *theories* of transmutation.[75] It has been the work of modern scholars, speculating on the origins of the idea of transmutation (transmutation *does* commonly appear in alchemical texts from the medieval period forward),[76] who have proposed different

---

72   ZOSIMOS, quoted by PELAGIUS, CAAG IV.1.9.20. My translation.
73   The phrase "spiritualize" is used several times in this quotation (ibid.) to refer to the coloring of a metal. For example, "Les agents de transformation dissolvent et spiritualisent; les agents coopérateurs sont ceux que l'on projette au moment de la fusion".
74   See CAAG III.28.7. Adapted from HOPKINS' translation in *Alchemy: Child of Greek Philosophy*, 119. This text might not be an authentic writing of Zosimos, as it seems to be quoting Zosimos in section 5.
75   See DUFAULT, "Theories of Transmutation", 217.
76   See Vladimir KARPENKO's discussion of these theories in "The Chemistry and Metallurgy of Transmutation", *Ambix* 39.2 (July 1992): 47–62.

theories supposedly held by the ancient Greco-Egyptian alchemists. These theories are said to derive from Greek philosophy and, to a lesser degree, from magico-religious beliefs that were popular in the Greco-Roman world.[77] It is to this topic of philosophical and religious influence that I shall now turn.

Philosophies of nature

The early alchemical authors often discuss their work with metals in the language of Hellenistic natural philosophy, and as mentioned at the beginning of the chapter, this is often used as a defining characteristic of Greco-Egyptian alchemy. When I first began writing about Zosimos I didn't question this way of framing alchemy, but over the years I've come to resist it because I find that it obscures the antiquity of these metallurgical arts and implies that ancient Near Eastern artisans had no theoretical underpinning to their work until Greek philosophy came along. Egyptian and Mesopotamian civilizations were observing the natural world and forming evidence-based theories of the heavens and earth long before the Greeks.[78] Their explanations of natural phenomena were often steeped in religious language and concepts, whereas Greek philosophers tended to express their investigations of nature in more secular, materialistic terms. A rough equivalent for "scientists" in Greek is *physiologoi*, or natural philosophers; this is what Aristotle called the pre-Socratic philosophers who attempted to

---

[77] DUFAULT has analyzed the prevailing theories and classified them into three major types: the natural sympathy theory, the maturation theory, and the form-transfer theory. He focuses more on the philosophical aspects of these theories, and less on the religious elements proposed by FESTUGIÈRE (natural sympathy) and ELIADE (maturation theory). See DUFAULT, 218–225.

[78] See, for example, FORBES, *Studies in Ancient Technology* 1; and Marshall CLAGETT, *Ancient Egyptian Science*, 3 vols. (Philadelphia: American Philosophical Society, 1989–1999).

explain the causes and structure of the physical world.[79] Ancient Greece had its mathematicians, physicists, astronomers, geographers, physicians, zoologists, and so forth, all of whom were inquirers into nature and exhibited some form of empirical method and reasoning.[80] However, what we call religion and science were often closely intertwined in natural philosophy: nearly all philosophers believed that nature was divine, though they had differing conceptions of nature and the divine. Some science bordered on the mystical, such as the mathematics of Pythagoras, who was revered as a holy man and whose approach to numbers was sometimes symbolic and spiritual. And natural sciences were sometimes associated with magic, especially medicine and astrology, which was considered a branch of astronomy. Pliny, for example, claims that magic originated from medicine combined with astrology.[81]

As Peter Harrison points out, science has typically been defined in opposition to religion, and historians of science usually trace its beginnings to the pre-Socratic philosophers of ancient Greece, who "broke away from the myths of their forebears and sought rational explanations for phenomena".[82] Even though this notion of Greek natural philosophy as being "religion-free" is false, it helps explain why it gets privileged as a valid theoretical

---

79 G. E. R. LLOYD, *Magic, Reason, and Experience: Studies in the Origins and Development of Greek Science* (Indianapolis: Hackett Publishing Company, 1999 [1979]), 32.
80 LLOYD has identified three criteria by which we can claim that the Greeks possessed similar concepts to modern science: (1) the demarcation of natural and divine causes; (2) the development of mathematics and logical argumentation, used to formulate demonstrations and proofs; and (3) increasing use of methods of demonstration and proof, combined with empirical observation and research, to extend the empirical base of knowledge. I am paraphrasing Tambiah's summary of Lloyd's criteria. See Stanley TAMBIAH, *Magic, Science, Religion and the Scope of Rationality* (Cambridge: Cambridge University Press, 1990), 9.
81 See PLINY, *Natural History* 30.1.1.
82 Peter HARRISON, *The Territories of Science and Religion* (Chicago: University of Chicago Press, 2015), 22–23. As Harrison points out, it is a mistake to think of the pre-Socratics as secular philosophers because ideas about the divine play an important role in their works.

framework for alchemy, which is often seen as a precursor of modern chemistry, whereas ancient Near Eastern religious ideas tend to be overlooked or deemed irrelevant.[83] However, it would unfair to explain this solely as a matter of Western biases toward science and rationalism, because part of the problem is textual. The Greco-Egyptian alchemical corpus has many references to Greek natural philosophy, yet explicit references to Egyptian ideas are rare; it understandable, therefore, that scholars have looked primarily to Hellenistic philosophy as a theoretical foundation for alchemy.

Cristina Viano, who has made the most significant investigations into the Greco-Egyptian alchemists' use of Aristotelian and Platonic theories of matter, points out that Zosimos and other alchemists seem to be harmonizing different aspects of Aristotle and Plato, using them selectively in ways that show agreement with their alchemical techniques, but that they were not using Greek philosophy in any systematic way for experimental verification of their work.[84] Olivier Dufault concurs, adding that early alchemists did not adhere to one particular school of thought, but often combined elements from Aristotle, Plato, and Stoicism, whose theories contradict each other. He writes:

> It seems to make little sense to continue assuming that alchemical writers were operating on philosophical grounds, especially if the result is to conclude that they were bad philosophers. Greek philosophy is not the only single interpretive key of the Greek alchemical corpus;

[83] See for example, Paul KEYSER, who claims that "Near Eastern peoples were not inclined to seek explanations for these [chemical] processes", and that it is the Greek pre-Socratic philosophers, who seek to "understand the world not in terms of the actions of anthropomorphic deities alone but also in terms of 'natural' forces" who provide the building blocks for alchemical theory. KEYSER, "Alchemy in the Ancient World", 358.

[84] Cristina VIANO, "Les alchimistes gréco-alexandrins et le Timée de Platon", in C. VIANO, ed., L'alchimie et ses racines philosophiques. La tradition grecque et la tradition arabe (Paris: Vrin, 2005), 93, 107. See also VIANO, "Aristote et l'alchimie grecque: La transmutation et le modèle aristotélicien entre théorie et pratique", Revue d'histoire des sciences 49.2-3 (1996): 189–213.

rather, philosophy was only one of the systems of reference within which alchemical writers described dyeing and metallurgical practices.[85]

Other interpretive frameworks for Greco-Egyptian alchemy need to be looked at more closely, and it should not be presumed that all alchemists had the same frameworks. Zosimos, for example, indicates that there were different schools of thought, and he often complains about the wrongheadedness of his rivals.[86] He uses religious ideas as his primary mode of interpretation, and many of these religious ideas are blended with Platonic philosophy. He also refers to Aristotle and uses language and concepts from pre-Socratic physics. Furthermore, his discussions of religion and philosophy often incorporate different cultural perspectives on alchemical theory and practice. This blending of religious, philosophical, and cultural interpretation begins to make more sense in light of Egyptian ways of knowing.

Erik Hornung explains that Egyptian thought is associative and characterized by a "flexible and pluralistic approach":

> The [Egyptian] idea that there is no single answer, that everything is flow and every answer provisional, is worth investigating today, in an age that has focused attention on fragmentation while continuing to cling to a history of absolutes. Without systematic and logical thought, the great achievements of ancient Egyptian culture are unthinkable. But Egyptian thought steers clear of monocausal simplification, convincing instead through refinement and association, through mastery of both word and image.[87]

---

85   DUFAULT, 225.
86   See, for example, *Auth.Mem.* 1 (On Apparatus and Furnaces) and CAAG III.51 (Final Account).
87   Erik HORNUNG, *Idea into Image: Essays on Ancient Egyptian Thought*, trans. E. BREDECK (New York: Timken, 1992), 14.

The associative nature of Egyptian thought can be seen in their writing and iconography, which features word play and punning, not as a form of humor, but as a way of conveying that words and images contain multiple layers of meaning and resonance.[88] Syncretism, or cultural synthesis, is also a part of this associative thinking, and becomes increasingly more so in the Ptolemaic and Roman periods. Due to increased contact with Greek culture and education, Egyptians began incorporating Greek ideas and traditions and harmonizing them with their own. Cultural synthesis was even more prominent in the Roman period, as were universalizing tendencies.[89] Harmonizing different philosophies, religions, and sciences was often an attempt to articulate a universal theory of everything, especially the workings of the natural world. Many theories of nature in the Greco-Roman era involved a belief in cosmic sympathy and antipathy, whereby all parts of the universe are linked together by invisible forces, and each living thing contains an immanent vital force that is naturally attracted to some forces and repelled by others. Cosmic sympathy, which exhibits a kind of associative thinking, is native to ancient Egyptian thought, though it is not exclusive to Egypt. Garth Fowden points out that in Egyptian religion, cosmic sympathy "manifests itself as the magical power, *heka*, that pervades the universe and in the divine, especially solar, energies that enliven the whole world".[90] *Heka* is what links all phenomena and sympathetic powers into one unified whole. In myth, Heka (in god-form) is described as the first creation of primeval creator god (sometimes identified as the solar god Re), and in the Greco-Roman period Heka was known as the

---

88 On punning as theology, see David LORTON, "The Theology of Cult Statues in Ancient Egypt", in M. B. DICK, ed., *Born in Heaven, Made on Earth: The Creation of the Cult Image in the Ancient Near East* (Winona Lake, IN: Eisenbrauns, 1999), 134–135.

89 See Françoise DUNAND and Christiane ZIVIE-COCHE, *Gods and Men in Egypt: 3000 BCE to 395 CE*, trans. D. LORTON (Ithaca: Cornell University Press, 2004), 234–235.

90 Garth FOWDEN, *The Egyptian Hermes: A Historical Approach to the Late Pagan Mind* (Princeton: Princeton University Press, 1986), 76.

ka of Re and lord of all *kas* (vital spiritual energies); *heka*, then, is the creative power and animating force of the natural world.[91] As a magical power, *heka* is morally neutral and can be harnessed for many purposes, whether benevolent or malevolent.[92]

In the twentieth century, scholars commonly characterized late antiquity as an era when rational science and philosophy were in decline, usurped by the popularity of irrational "occult sciences" based on cosmic sympathy.[93] The astrological belief that the planets influence human behavior, and that certain days and times are more conducive to some activities than others, is an example of cosmic sympathy and antipathy. Alchemy and *materia medica*—a type of pharmacology based on the idea that the vital forces of plants, animal parts, metals, and so forth, have an impact on the health of humans—are frequently listed as examples of occult sciences in this period, because of their emphasis on discovering and manipulating the hidden forces of nature. Zosimean alchemy is very much based in the idea of cosmic sympathy, but this needs to be qualified, because theories of cosmic sympathy range from magical spells and folk remedies to more technical and philosophical works, and Zosimos approves of some of these forms and eschews others.

An Egyptian named Bolus of Mendes (ca. 200 BCE) is usually credited as the first to popularize cosmic sympathy for a Hellenistic audience. He is said to have written a book entitled *On Sympathies and Antipathies*, as well as works on natural remedies, astrology, and the properties of stones, which were popular in the first century BCE.[94] Bolus was known as "the Democritean", and one ancient

---

91 An excellent discussion of *heka* as a principle of creation and as a god can be found in Robert RITNER, *The Mechanics of Ancient Egyptian Magical Practice* (Chicago: Oriental Institute of the University of Chicago, 1993), 17–27.
92 Ibid, 20.
93 On the decline of rationalism and the rise of occult sciences, see, for example, E. R. DODDS, *The Greeks and the Irrational*, 244–248; and FESTUGIÈRE, *La Révélation d'Hermès Trismégiste*, vol. 1 (entire work).
94 A list of some of BOLUS's works are found in the *Suda*, and cited by

source explains that Bolus pretended that his books were authored by Democritus, the famous atomistic philosopher (fifth c. BCE).[95] By the first century CE, Democritus had achieved legendary status as a magician who learned the secrets of the cosmos from the *magoi* of the East.[96] Democritus is an important figure in early alchemical literature, and he is often quoted by Zosimos. Many scholars have speculated that Bolus of Mendes is the principal source of the pseudo-Democritean alchemical texts, since Bolus began the trend of portraying Democritus as a master of the hidden properties of nature.[97] I doubt that they are one and the same, however, because the range of ideas attributed to Democritus is so diverse.[98] The Ps.-Democritean writings on *materia medica*, for example, are very different from the Ps.-Democritean writings on alchemy. Pliny gives an example of the former. In his *Natural History*, he reports that according to Democritus, if one burns the head of a chameleon on logs of oak, it will cause a rainstorm; the chameleon's right

HERSHBELL, in "Democritus and the Beginnings of Greek Alchemy", 5. On the popularity of Bolus's works in the first century BCE, see Robert M. GRANT, *Miracle and Natural Law in Græco-Roman and Early Christian Thought* (Amsterdam: North Holland, 1952), 9.

95 The ancient source is Columella, a first-century CE agricultural writer. See HERSHBELL, "Democritus and the Beginnings of Greek Alchemy", 6. The connection, if any, between the theories of Democritus of Abdera and those of Bolus of Mendes is obscure, since only fragments of Democritus's writings have survived. HERSHBELL argues that the Ps.-Democritean alchemical literature can be given an atomistic interpretation, but he bases this on Democritus's alleged use of the term *"physis"* to refer to atomic particles; since *physis*, or nature, has a broad range of meaning, the connection is rather tenuous. Ibid, 13–14.

96 See Matthew DICKIE, *Magic and Magicians in the Greco-Roman World* (London: Routledge, 2001), 117–124.

97 This connection between Bolus of Mendes and the alchemical writings of Ps.-Democritus is commonplace, and has been made by BERTHELOT and many other well-known scholars of early alchemy. For more information, see HERSHBELL, "Democritus and the Beginnings of Greek Alchemy".

98 Matteo MARTELLI, in his recent work on Ps.-Democritus, also doubts that Bolus of Mendes is the author of the Ps.-Democritean alchemical texts. See MARTELLI, *The Four Books of Pseudo-Democritus*, Sources of Alchemy and Chemistry, Ambix 60, supplement 1 (2013), S36–S44.

60   CHAPTER ONE

eye, when mixed with goat's milk, removes ulcers from human eyes; and its tongue has the power to influence the outcome of court cases.[99] Pliny thinks that the writings of Democritus "smack of sorcery".[100] This is also the opinion of the second-century author Aulus Gellius, who writes, "Many fictions of this kind have been attached to the name of Democritus by ignorant men sheltering under his reputation and authority".[101]

The alchemical literature attributed to Democritus is of a different character. It consists mainly of technical recipes and is based upon practical, empirical observation. The Ps.-Democritean text, *Physika kai Mystika*, consists of numerous procedures for dyeing wool, coloring metals that conclude with some portion of the following slogan: "Nature rejoices in nature, nature triumphs over nature, nature dominates nature".[102] This slogan, which appears frequently in early alchemical literature and appears to be of Egyptian origin, is an expression of cosmic sympathies and antipathies, or *heka*: the powers of one "nature" to attract, repel, or transform.[103] "Nature", here, refers to substances and to the influences that one particular substance has upon another, yet also hints at the unity of nature in which all substances partake. Ps.-Democritus stresses the importance of critical inquiry and experiment in order to properly understand the actions of various substances:

---

99   PLINY, NH 28.29.112–118. Cited by LINDSAY, *The Origins of Alchemy in Græco-Roman Egypt*, 114–115. Most of the works attributed to Democritus have been lost, except for numerous Ps.-Democritean alchemical texts. Much of what is known about Democritean works on *materia medica* comes from Pliny.
100 Ibid.
101 AULUS GELLIUS, *Attic Nights* x.12. Cited by LINDSAY, ibid., 15.
102 See Matteo MARTELLI's recent translation, *The Four Books of Pseudo-Democritus*, which includes the Greek text(s), and Robert STEELE's translation, in *The Alchemy Reader: From Hermes Trismegistus to Isaac Newton*, ed. Stanton LINDEN (Cambridge: Cambridge University Press, 2003), 38–43.
103 This slogan is also found in the surviving fragments of the astrological treatise of Nechepso-Petosiris. See J. BIDEZ and F. CUMONT, *Les Mages Hellénisés*, vol. 1 (New York: Arno Press, 1975), 245–246.

> [T]he young men are much in error, and will not put much faith in what is written, since they are ignorant of the matter, not noticing that physicians, when they wish to prepare a useful drug, do not make it inconsiderately, but first test it, whether it is a warming [substance], and how much cold, or humid or other substance necessary, joined with it will make a medium temperament [...]. As they consider that we speak in fables and not mystically [secretly], they display no diligence in inquiring into the species of things.... If the young men had been skilled in this kind of knowledge, applying their minds judiciously to the actions of substances, they would have suffered less loss; they know not the antipathies of nature, that one species may change ten, as a drop of oil stains much purple, and a little sulfur burns many things.[104]

For Ps.-Democritus and other early alchemical authors, theories of cosmic sympathy and antipathy are conceptualized in terms of the transmutation of the four elements of nature—fire, air, water, and earth—and their corresponding properties, hot, dry, wet, and cold, which is an example of how Greek philosophical concepts were being incorporated into Egyptian alchemy. *The Dialogue of Cleopatra and the Philosophers*, cited at the beginning of this chapter, discusses alchemy as a science of the transmutation of the four elements, but this is not the only avenue for observing the workings of natural world. In the following passage, she asks the philosophers to observe the ways in which different plants are nourished by the elements:

> Look at the nature of plants, whence they come. For some come down from the mountains and grow out of the earth, and some grow up from the valleys and some come from the plains. But look how they develop, for it

---

[104] STEELE's translation, in *The Alchemy Reader*, 41

is at certain seasons and days that you must gather them, and you take them from the islands of the sea, and from the most lofty place. And look at the air which ministers to them and the nourishment circling around them, that they perish not nor die. Look at the divine water which gives them drink and the air that governs them after they have been given body in a single being.[105]

Cleopatra emphasizes natural patterns and rhythms. Some plants are native to the mountains, while others thrive at sea level, just as certain metals and stones are native to particular places. Plants are harvested at certain times of the year and on certain days, according to particular phases of the moon or positions of the stars. Many alchemists believe that metals are also subject to these natural rhythms, and that their work should be performed in accordance with them. For example, Zosimos gives a recipe for a whitening agent made from lime that takes forty-seven days to prepare. First, the lime is corroded in strong vinegar for seven days, and then the resulting substance is exposed to the elements for forty days, where it is repeatedly dried and moistened by the sun and the dew. He believes that the natural rhythms of sun and dew are crucial to the maturation of the whitening agent, just as these rhythms are essential for the growth of plants.[106] Zosimos often speaks of "natural methods" and "timely tinctures", and it appears that he is referring to these types of methods, as well as to performing certain procedures at astrologically opportune moments.

This emphasis on being in harmony with the natural order is at the very core of Egyptian religious practice: it is the principle of *maat*. *Maat*, or divine order, came into being when the cosmos was formed out of primeval chaos: *maat* is evident in the orderly motions of the heavens, the regularity of the changing seasons, and in

---

105 Translated by F. S. TAYLOR, *The Alchemists*, 55.
106 *Auth.Mem.* XIII.1. Compare with CAAG III.2.1. It is possible that the seven days in this recipe, followed by forty days, were chosen for symbolic reasons.

the laws of nature. It is the ideal state of perfection that all of creation should strive for, because it is in harmony with the will of the creator.[107] Maat is also the principle of truth, righteousness, and justice that provides the pattern for social order; as Siegfried Morenz puts it, *"maat is the heart of Egyptian ethics"*.[108] Pharaohs are expected to govern according to *maat*, and individuals are expected to "speak *maat* and do *maat*" in their everyday affairs.[109] One's life should be conducted according to this spirit of righteousness and justice, and at the end of life, according to the Egyptian *Book of the Dead*, one will be judged accordingly: the gods will place the heart of the deceased on one side of a scale, and the feather of Maat (in goddess form) on the other; those who have lived their lives according to *maat* will be deemed "justified".[110] The laws of *maat* are not made explicit, but must be discerned through observation, experience, and wisdom. There can be diverse opinions about what is right or just in the realm of human actions, but opinions become even more varied when it comes to the cosmic order because speculations of this sort venture into mysterious physical and metaphysical terrain.

Different understandings of the cosmic order mean that there are various methods of working with its vital energies. In *On Apparatuses and Furnaces (Letter Omega)*, Zosimos indicates that there is a disagreement over the art of opportune tinctures (καιρικαὶ καταβαφαί, *kairikai katabaphai*).[111] He complains that some of his colleagues are appealing to their personal daimons and relying too

---

107 See Erik HORNUNG, *Conceptions of God in Ancient Egypt: The One and the Many*, trans. J. BAINES (Ithaca: Cornell University Press, 1982), 213.
108 Siegfried MORENZ, *Egyptian Religion*, trans. A. KEEP (Ithaca: Cornell University Press, 1973), 116.
109 *Maat* features prominently in pharaonic texts and in wisdom literature. See MORENZ, ibid, 115–119.
110 Geraldine PINCH, *Egyptian Mythology: A Guide to the Gods, Goddesses, and Traditions of Ancient Egypt* (Oxford: Oxford University Press, 2002), 160.
111 MERTENS reads καταβαφαί as « teintures en profondeur », meaning coloring deep within the mass as opposed to superficial treatments (βαφαί); the latter is the term that Zosimos uses more frequently, though not in this text. See MERTENS, *Zosime de Panopolis: Memoires Authentiques*, 62 n. 9.

heavily upon certain types of astrology for the successful outcome of their experiments, and not enough on time-honored techniques and equipment.[112] When the daimons, under a favorable astral aspect, grant them success, they ridicule the traditional methods, but when they fail, they are forced to admit that those methods have some validity.[113] Zosimos says that due to astrological influences and timing, daimons can be beneficent at one moment, and maleficent at another: this is why it is important to understand the cosmic order, for even the behavior of daimons is subservient to it.[114] "People like this are unacceptable both to God and to men of philosophy", Zosimos says of his rivals:

> They are always following Fate, now to this opinion and then to its opposite. They have no conception of anything other than the material; all they know is Fate.
>
> In his book *On Natures*, Hermes calls such people mindless, only marchers swept along in the procession of Fate, with no conception of anything incorporeal, and with no understanding of Fate herself, who conducts them justly. Instead they insult the instruction she gives through corporeal experience, and imagine nothing beyond the good fortune she grants.[115]

Fate is the force that presides over the cosmos, the realm of nature and change. In the Greco-Roman era, Fate is associated with chance and the ever-changing whims of fortune, but also with di-

---

112   *Auth.Mem.* 1.2-3. Thanks to Kyle FRASER for feedback on an earlier draft of this section. On this point about overreliance on astrology, see Kyle FRASER, "Zosimos of Panopolis and the Book of Enoch: Alchemy as Forbidden Knowledge", *Aries* 4.2 (2004): 138, 140.
113   *Auth.Mem.* 1.3. For a fuller discussion of astral daimons and these differing approaches to timely tinctures, see chapter 4.
114   Ibid. See MERTENS's commentary, *Zosime de Panopolis*, 63 n. 10; and JACKSON's in *Zosimos of Panopolis on the Letter Omega*, 42 n.11.
115   *Auth.Mem.* 1.3-4. JACKSON's translation.

vine providence and natural law.[116] Zosimos associates Fate with the latter, which is also closer to the spirit of *maat*. Alchemists who summon daimons in their work are under the illusion that they are manipulating cosmic energies, but in reality, Fate is controlling them because they fail to comprehend that the daimons are subject to a natural order, governed by a higher divine source. Zosimos associates the unnatural methods of his rivals with magic, which he defines as using "force" upon Fate, rather than letting Fate "work in accordance with her own nature and (divine) decree".[117] "The spiritual man", he exhorts, "need not rectify anything through the use of magic, not even if it is considered a good thing".[118]

Maat is an important concept in Egyptian ontology. As the divine order of things, *maat* conceals and reveals the intricate patterns of creation. Its opposite is chaos, or *isfet*. These opposites are complementary: the threat of disorder and death is always encroaching upon *maat*. In Egyptian myth, the gods sail in their sun boat through the darkness of the underworld each night, where monsters continually threaten them and must be annihilated. Using magic, or *heka*, the gods protect themselves and destroy the haunting demons. The sun god returns to the world, *maat* is restored, and creation begins anew. This pattern recurs in the victorious return of the light each morning, and when darkness falls, chaos threatens to engulf once again.[119] The cycle of death and rebirth, the establishment of order out of chaos, is a recurring

---

116 In Greek thought, the association of Fate with nature and divine providence is largely due to Stoic influences. See A. A. Long, *Hellenistic Philosophy: Stoics, Epicureans, Sceptics* (Berkeley: University of California Press, 1986), 163–165.

117 *Auth.Mem.* 1.7. JACKSON's translation, with the addition of (divine) from MERTENS' translation. The passage is talking about Necessity (ἀνάγκη), which, in antiquity, was synonymous with Fate (εἱμαρμένη). See MERTENS' comments, *Zosime de Panopolis*, 74 n.36.

118 *Auth.Mem.* 1.7. JACKSON's translation.

119 The elements and patterns of Egyptian ontology described in this paragraph can be found in richer detail in DUNAND and ZIVIE-COCHE, *Gods and Men in Egypt*, ch. 2.

image in Egyptian alchemical texts.[120] The "blackening" stage of alchemy is often represented by underworld imagery: metals imprisoned in their underworld tombs, dying so that they may be reborn. Zosimos indicates in several texts that this pattern is essential to working with metals as well as to one's own spiritual journey.[121]

For Zosimos, to become spiritually awake—or a "man of light" (*Phōs*), as he calls it—is to become gold. Gold was known in Egypt as the "flesh of the gods", and it represents divinity. In the Roman period, the wealthy deceased would be buried with gilded skin and gold-plated body parts so that they might have eternal life and light in the darkness of death.[122] There is a resonance between transmuting base metals into gold and transmuting oneself into an illuminated being, and Egyptians would have thought of this not only as an analogical connection, but a vital, energetic one linking gold, sun, light, spirit, and god. But gold was not the only metal used for divine statues, nor was it the only color that alchemists sought to create. Egyptian metallurgy is polychromatic; to render color to a metal, to make it scintillate and glow, is to spiritualize it. Egyptian alchemy is also variegated in an ideological sense: Egyptian ontology and traditions of god-making share a palette with Greek natural philosophy and varieties of Jewish thought and Christian Gnosticism. Zosimos blends these (and more) together so that he might become wiser about the world and the people in it, and ultimately become enlightened.

In sum, looking at the Egyptian contexts of early alchemy brings new perspective to the study of these ancient texts. The recipes for coloring metals that dominate the contents of the Greco-Egyptian alchemical corpus, along with the occasional re-

---

120   See Aaron CHEAK's masterful article on Egyptian religious themes in early alchemy, "The Perfect Black: Egypt and Alchemy", in *Alchemical Traditions: From Antiquity to the Avant-Garde*, ed. A. CHEAK (Auckland: Rubedo Press, 2018 [2013]).

121   See especially Zosimos's allegory, *On Excellence* (*Auth.Mem.* x-xii), discussed in chapter 3 of this volume.

122   See Beatrix GESSLER-LÖHR, "Mummies and Mummification", in *The Oxford Handbook of Roman Egypt*, 675–676.

ferences to Egyptian temple culture, fit well with the evidence of polychromic metal statuary that was a hallmark of Egyptian artistry, used especially for creating divine statues. The term that Zosimos often uses for alchemy, *hiera technē*, or the 'sacred art', is befitting to the art of manufacturing statues of the gods. In this temple context, Egyptian philosophy is the underlying theoretical model for the creation of divine statues. This creative act is performed in accordance with *maat*, the divine cosmic order, which is discerned through observation of the natural world. The metals themselves must undergo a death prior to their creation, and the art of statue-making replicates the creation of the world, with divine beings coming into existence out of a molten, inchoate mass. This ritualistic art form and the theology that informs it long predates Greek philosophy. Zosimos's writings give us the best sense of this *hiera technē* in the Roman period, and how temple traditions were being harmonized with ideas and techniques from other cultures, reflecting the unprecedented levels of cultural and religious synthesis that were occurring in Egypt at the turn of the fourth century.

ALCHEMY IN PANOPOLIS

Temples and Trade Guilds

EGYPT HAS LONG BEEN ROMANTICIZED as a land of mystery and profound wisdom, and idealized views of Egypt (and the Near East) have been consequential for studies of alchemy. Some have embraced alchemy as a font of esoteric wisdom that originated in Egypt, others have dismissed the Egyptian references in alchemical texts as romantic fictions; many have circumvented the Egyptian context altogether. It is true that familiar Egyptian tropes, which are frequently the stuff of legend, can be found in the Greco-Egyptian corpus. *Physika kai Mystika*, for example, a first century Ps.-Democritean text, includes a story about Democritus and his fellow initiates whose master, a famous Persian mage named Ostanes, had died before teaching them a certain alchemical procedure called "harmonizing natures".[1] But one day, when the students were gathered in the temple for a banquet, a column in the sancta sanctorum suddenly split open to reveal the mystery—a text containing the formula: "Nature delights in nature, nature conquers nature, nature masters nature".[2]

By contrast, Zosimos's accounts of the priesthood seem more realistic. He gives pedestrian details that suggest actual work experience in a temple environment, including his instructions for

[1] This story is thought to be either an interpolation, or an epitomization of content from another Ps.-Democritean text by a later compiler. See Jackson HERSHBELL, "Democritus and the Beginnings of Greek Alchemy", 11; and Matteo MARTELLI, *The Four Books of Pseudo-Democritus*, 18–19.

[2] *Physika kai Mystika*, MARTELLI's translation, ibid, 83–85.

making religious statues that were mentioned in the previous chapter. Zosimos, a native Egyptian, is writing for other craft specialists, and many of them were probably artisan-priests, but not all; these professional contexts need to be examined more closely. This chapter fleshes out some of the socio-cultural contexts of Roman Egypt, and Panopolis in particular, in order to gain more insight into the working lives of Zosimos and other Upper Egyptian metalsmiths at the turn of the fourth century.

PRIESTS OF THE HOUSE OF LIFE

Egyptian temples were dwelling places for the divine, designed as microcosmic images of the world. Byron Shafer explains:

> The enclosure wall and sacred lake were Nun [the watery chaos], the sanctuary was the place of the First Creation, the hypostyle hall and the bases of the walls were the liminal swamp, the columns were plants, the ceilings were sky, the floors were earth, the vaults were netherworld, the pylon was the mountains of the eastern horizon, and the axial way was the path of the sun [...]. To be in the temple—whether through priestly service or limited "public" access—was to experience the body of god, to commune with god physically and sacramentally.[3]

The priests performed ritual re-enactments of cosmic creation, along with daily devotions to the gods, as a means of invoking the divine presence in the world and upholding the cosmic order (*maat*).[4] Much of the work of the temple took place in inte-

---

3   See Byron SHAFER, "Temples, Priests, and Rituals: An Overview", in B. SHAFER, ed., *Temples of Ancient Egypt* (Ithaca: Cornell University Press, 1997), 8.
4   Ibid. See also Siegfried MORENZ, *Egyptian Religion*, 88.

rior spaces that could only be entered by initiated priests, but there were courtyard shrines, chapels, and occasionally some interior temple rooms that were open to the public for worship.[5]

Priests of different ranks handled various temple duties, which included things like performing cult rituals, healings, and dream interpretations; singing and playing music; and chiseling hieroglyphs and divine images into temple walls. Other kinds of priestly work extended beyond the temple buildings themselves. Funerary practices, such as embalming and mummification of both humans and animals, were handled by mortuary priests and specialists, and priests were hired by families to perform liturgies at the tombs. Administrators of various kinds were also needed to handle temple finances and oversee its landholdings and its many contract employees, such as farmers, bakers, beekeepers, weavers, construction workers, and artisans; some of these administrators were priests, others were government officials.[6] Both the temple and mortuary cults played a major role in the Egyptian economy. Priests were typically well-paid, and the office was hereditary, passed down from the father's side.[7] Historically, the temples were under royal control, so people could also be appointed to priestly office at the discretion of the king.[8]

Higher ranking priests were literate, and some of the larger temples had an institution called the House of Life, which was devoted to priestly knowledge and craftsmanship and played a role in temple administration.[9] The priests of the House of Life were

---

5 Emily TEETER, *Religion and Ritual in Ancient Egypt* (New York: Cambridge University Press, 2011), 77–84.
6 Serge SAUNERON, *The Priests of Ancient Egypt*, trans. D. LORTON (Ithaca: Cornell University Press, 2000), 56–57.
7 On priests making a good salary, see TEETER, *Religion and Ritual in Ancient Egypt*, 36–38; and Françoise DUNAND, "Book II: Ptolemaic and Roman Egypt", in F. DUNAND and C. ZIVIE-COCHE, *Gods and Men in Egypt: 3000 BCE to 395 CE*, trans. D. LORTON (Ithaca: Cornell University Press, 2004), 212.
8 SAUNERON, 45–47. For information on government/clergy relations in the Ptolemaic and Roman periods, see DUNAND, 206–213.
9 See FINNESTAD, "Temples of the Ptolemaic and Roman Periods", 228. On page 191 of this work, Finnestad indicates that under Ptolemaic and

scholar-scribes who worked in annexes that housed temple libraries and scriptoriums. Ragnhild Bjerre Finnestad outlines the various subjects that they studied:

> In these centers of learning, a variety of disciplines were pursued: mythology, liturgy, iconography, arithmetic, geometry, law, medicine, astronomy, the interpretation of dreams, the study of the Nile and its inundation, and all other sciences pertaining to Egypt: geography, topography, history, and philology (the language of the hieroglyphic texts was dead).[10]

Artisans and craftsmen were under the supervision of the House of Life; some of the artisans who worked for the temple were priests of varying ranks, but others were contract hires, commissioned for specific jobs.[11] Zosimos's writings indicate that he was intimately familiar with the workings of the House of Life. He mentions that priests are the keepers of the ancient books of the sacred art (alchemy), and that access to these books is restricted; copies of these texts can only be read in the sanctuary of the temple.[12] Zosimos refers to several of these books by name, and in some cases there is evidence that he is directly quoting from the works of older alchemists, namely Ps.-Democritus and Maria the Jewess; as Michèle Mertens says, he "had their works under his eyes".[13] He is clearly involved in the interpretation of

> Roman rule, the scholarly activity of the temples took on a special significance because they had become "the chief official repositories of Egyptian learning". On this point, see also Alan H. GARDINER, "The House of Life", *Journal of Egyptian Archaeology* 24.2 (1938): 159; and SAUNERON, 133–134.

10   FINNESTAD, 228.
11   SAUNERON, 134.
12   CMA, Syr. 11.6.19. Compare with similar statements about secret knowledge of the House of Life in Papyrus Salt 825, which dates from the Ptolemaic period.
13   Michèle MERTENS, "Alchemy, Hermetism, and Gnosticism at Panopolis c. 300 A.D.: The Evidence of Zosimus", in A. EGBERTS et al., eds., *Perspectives*

ancient metallurgical recipes, which were apparently difficult to decipher. Hieroglyphs were still in use by priests in the Roman period, though they were not as common as hieratic (priestly) or demotic (popular) cursive scripts. These writing systems are notoriously difficult to translate, and this was the case even for ancient scribes.[14] Also, the Greco-Egyptian alchemical corpus makes use of symbolic notation systems for different substances—metals are designated by planetary symbols, for example—but the symbolic representations show inconsistency and signs of change over time, which further complicates the work of translation.[15] According to Zosimos, those who could interpret and translate the texts achieved some renown: "the diverse symbols of the priests were explicated by the former masters and the different prophets [high-ranking Egyptian priests], whose names became celebrated, and who prevailed with all the power of science".[16] Even though Zosimos is engaged in this work, he claims that he does not seek fame like the others.[17] Jan Assmann explains that in the Greco-Roman period, hieroglyphs were stylized as a form of cryptography, and it was a mark of priestly elitism to be able to read and interpret the signs (only priests could read hieroglyphics and hieratic script).[18]

      on Panopolis: An Egyptian Town from Alexander the Great to the Arab Conquest (Leiden: Brill, 2002), 169. Evidence of his direct quotes can be seen in Auth. Mem., VII, 1, 3–4 (Maria) and Auth. Mem., I, 1.195–197; and CAAG II.53, 1.14–15 (Democritus).

14   On the difficulties of translation of these writings, see Richard JASNOW and Karl-Theodor ZAUZICH, *Conversations in the House of Life: A New Translation of the Ancient Egyptian Book of Thoth* (Wiesbaden: Harrassowitz Verlag, 2014), 3–10; and Leonard LESKO, "Ancient Egyptian Cosmogonies and Cosmology", in Byron SHAFER, ed., *Religion in Ancient Egypt* (Ithaca: Cornell University, 1991), 88–89.

15   F. Sherwood TAYLOR, *The Alchemists*, 51–54.

16   CMA, Syr. II.6.4. My translation of DUVAL's French: « Ainsi que nous l'avons dit, les divers symboles des prêtres ont été expliqués par les anciens maîtres et les différents prophètes, dont le nom est devenu célèbre, et qui ont prévalu avec toute la puissance de la science ».

17   Ibid.

18   Jan ASSMANN, *The Mind of Egypt: History and Meaning in the Time of the Pharaohs*, trans. A. JENKINS (New York: Metropolitan Books, 2002),

74				CHAPTER TWO

He writes: "Cryptographic principles invaded the whole system of hieroglyphic writing [...] Almost every religious center developed its own script system. The difficulty of deciphering script grew proportionately, and there is little doubt that the Egyptians themselves considered it a secret code accessible only to the initiated".[19] Whether or not Zosimos is interpreting hieroglyphs, this mystique surrounding Egyptian priestly writing is not simply a romantic fiction, but firmly embedded in the temple scribal culture of Zosimos's day.

The scribal priests of the House of Life are the keepers of ancient libraries; they research and recopy old, decaying papyrus scrolls, and they also produce new creative works. They are scholars who translate wisdom across the ages and across different modes of language, culture, and expression. Zosimos's work as an alchemical hermeneut suggests that he was a scribal priest. The patron deity of the House of Life is Thoth, the god of writing and magic. In the Greco-Roman period, Thoth was equated with the Greek god, Hermes, and these names are mentioned in the Greco-Egyptian alchemical corpus, both as alchemical authors and as gods.[20] Zosimos is a devotee of Thoth and well-versed in Hermetic literature.[21] Another indication that Zosimos was associated with the House of Life is his emphasis on astrological timing for the preparations of tinctures. Astronomer-priests, the *hōroskopoi* and *hōrologoi*, were important members of the House of Life; they observed and kept records of the movements of the heavenly bodies, and were consulted regarding propitious moments for both religious and non-cultic acts.[22] Zosimos claims that favorable timing

---

      414–415.
19   Ibid, 417–418.
20   See, for example, the Zosimean text *Auth. Mem.* I: *On Apparatus and Furnaces (Letter Omega)*, where the alchemical author, Hermes, and the divine entity, Thoth, are mentioned several times.
21   For example, *Auth. Mem.* I (ibid) and X-XII (his allegory, *On Excellence*) contain numerous allusions to philosophical works in the *Corpus Hermeticum*. I discuss these Hermetic connections more fully in chapters 3, 4, and 5.
22   FINNESTAD, "Temples of the Ptolemaic and Roman Periods", 228. See

is important in metallurgy, and he criticizes others for not adhering to this tradition.[23] According to Clement of Alexandria, who gives a stylized description of Egyptian priests carrying the forty-two essential books of the temple library, the scribal priests come after the astronomers in the procession (and perhaps also in rank), but they, too, will have mastered some knowledge of astronomy:

> [the scribes] must be acquainted with what are called hieroglyphics, and know about cosmography and geography, the position of the sun and moon, and about the five planets; also the description of Egypt, and the chart of the Nile; and the description of the equipment of the priests and of the places consecrated to them, and about the measures and the things in use in the sacred rites.[24]

In order to have priestly rank as an artisan, one had to be a senior artisan, and Zosimos appears to have been a master craftsman, a teacher of teachers.[25] Zosimos describes other master craftsmen as "prophets", a high-ranking class of priests who had administrative roles in the temple, but it isn't clear whether Zosimos had this status. As we have seen, temple administration, including the overseeing of artisans and builders, was one of the functions of priests in the House of Life. Zosimos served as an advisor to his colleague, Theosebeia, who taught the alchemical arts to groups of disciples; his advisory role to her suggests that he was of a higher rank.[26] Some of the frustration Zosimos expresses with

---

also SAUNERON, *The Priests of Ancient Egypt*, 64–65.
23 See, for example, *Auth. Mem.* 1.2–4.
24 CLEMENT OF ALEXANDRIA, *Stromata* VI.4; cf. FRANKFURTER, *Religion in Roman Egypt*, 239; see also ASSMANN, *The Mind of Egypt*, 412–413; and FOWDEN, *The Egyptian Hermes*, 58–59.
25 On senior artisans having priestly status, see J. F. QUACK, "Religious Personnel: Egypt", 290.
26 On THEOSEBEIA and her disciples, see CMA, Syr. II.8.1; Theosebeia may have been a priestess, but evidence is shaky. She is referred to as a priestess

regards to his colleagues—his frequent complaints that they are mistranslating, misinterpreting, or failing to follow the ancient recipes---also implies some administrative and didactic responsibility on his part. Even if he didn't have the rank of prophet, he seems to have been in the role of a supervisor or overseer, and he clearly achieved some distinction in his work, since his writings were admired and found worthy of preservation by later alchemists.

Even though each Egyptian temple was constructed as a cosmos in miniature and had certain features in common, each temple also had unique local and regional features. We don't have specific information about which temple(s) Zosimos was affiliated with, but I will turn now to a discussion of Panopolis and the Thebaid region, where Zosimos allegedly lived and worked, in order to add some local perspective.[27]

Temple culture in the Panopolis region

There were several temples and shrines in Panopolis, but the main temple and largest structure in the city was the Temple of Min.[28]

   in CMA, Syr. VII.19, but this does not appear to be an authentic Zosimean text.
27 Most ancient sources call Zosimos a Panopolite; Photius calls him a Theban from Panopolis, but this probably refers to the Thebaid region and not the city of Thebes. In one source, the *Suda,* he is called an Alexandrian, and many historians of alchemy have gone on to claim that Zosimos was an Alexandrian. I agree with Michele MERTENS that there is no reason to doubt the majority of sources that claim he was from Panopolis and probably spent at least part of his life there. See MERTENS's discussion in "Alchemy, Hermetism, and Gnosticism at Panopolis", 165–166.
28 Robert ALSTON says there were about eight temples in Panopolis in the late Roman period. This figure is based on *P.Berl.Bork*, an early fourth century list of houses and buildings in Panopolis, which is incomplete. Some of the temples/shrines in this list are dedicated to Greek deities, and one appears to be a Christian church. See ALSTON, *The City in Roman and Byzantine Egypt* (London: Routledge, 2002), 156. There is no reference to the largest temple in the city, the Temple of Min. See also Zbigniew BORKOWSKI's critical edition of *P.Berl.Bork, Une description topographique*

Min is an ithyphallic fertility god whom the Greeks associated with Pan. Egyptian cities were often named after their patron deities, which is why the town was known as Panopolis; before the Ptolemaic period, the city was known as Khent-Min.[29] According to ancient descriptions, the Temple of Min was one of the grandest in Egypt, perhaps comparable to the magnificent Thebaid temples of Dendera, Edfu, or Philae, which are still standing today.[30] Unfortunately, the temple was dismantled in the fourteenth century. Early travelers report a famous stone monument in Panopolis with a zodiac on one side, and a Greek inscription commemorating work on the Temple of Min in the twelfth year of Hadrian (108 CE) on the other.[31] Medieval Arab writers describe the temple as being painted blue and beautifully decorated with images of gods, humans, animals, and birds, as well as "dreadful, inhuman forms that terrify the beholder and fill him with wonder and amazement".[32] Symbols of priestly sciences like medicine, alchemy, and astronomy also featured prominently on the walls, and medieval Muslim scholars are reported to have lived for a time in the temple in Panopolis/Akhmim (as well as other Egyptian temples) in order to study these sciences by deciphering the symbols.[33] Akhmim was

---

   des immeubles à Panopolis (Warsaw: Panstwowe Wydawnictwo Naukowe, 1975).

29 Karolien GEENS, "Panopolis, a Nome Capital in Egypt in the Roman and Byzantine Period", PHD diss., Katholieke Universiteit Leuven (2007), 1, 110.

30 Ibid, 134.

31 Mark SMITH, "Aspects of the Preservation and Transmission of Indigenous Religious Traditions in Akhmim and its Environs During the Græco-Roman Period", in *Perspectives on Panopolis: An Egyptian Town from Alexander the Great to the Arab Conquest*, 239.

32 Quotation from IBN JUBAYR, who visited the temple in May, 1183. Cf. Okasha EL-DALY, *Egyptology: The Missing Millennium: Ancient Egypt in Medieval Arabic Writings* (London: UCL Press, 2005), 52. See also GEENS, "Panopolis, a Nome Capital in Egypt", 325. A full treatment of Arabic descriptions can be found in K. KUHLMANN, *Materialien zur Archäologie und Geschichte des Raumes von Achmim* (Mainz am Rhein: Philipp von Zabern, 1983).

33 EL-DALY, 51; GEENS, 325.

known to Arab scholars throughout the medieval period as a center for the study of alchemy.[34]

The Temple of Min had a House of Life that was active well into the Roman period, and its priests were devoted to the god Thoth; an epithet for these scribal priests was "those who know the forms of the ancestors".[35] Given the large number of demotic papyri that have been found in the region, it appears to have been an important production center for demotic translations of wisdom literature and funerary texts, including a unique *Book of the Dead* tradition.[36] Astronomy and astrology, which were virtually inseparable in the Greco-Roman period, also seem to have been an emphasis; more zodiacs have been found and attested to in Panopolis than anywhere else in Egypt.[37] Medieval Arab travelers have described a ceiling zodiac and architraves adorned with celestial images that they saw at the Temple of Min.[38] Several zodiacs have also been found in tombs in the area, as well as ostraca painted with astral iconography.[39] Zosimos indicates that there are debates over different approaches to astronomy/astrology as it pertains to alchemy, particularly the art of propitious timing, which is an ancient craft tradition, yet appears to be in danger of being superseded by newer theories.[40] This shows that astronomy/astrology was being discussed, debated, and theorized, and was a topic of

[34] EL-DALY, 163.
[35] SMITH, 242.
[36] Ibid, 237–238; see also Malcolm MOSHER, Jr., "The Book of the Dead Tradition at Akhmim During the Late Period", in *Perspectives on Panopolis*, op. cit., 201–209.
[37] SMITH, 242–243.
[38] GEENS, 324–325.
[39] SMITH, 242–243.
[40] Some of the earliest records of propitious timing come from Mesopotamian glass-making recipes dating from 1300–1100 BCE, which contain instructions for the astronomical timing of various procedures. See Pamela O. LONG, *Openness, Secrecy, Authorship: Technical Arts and the Culture of Knowledge from Antiquity to the Renaissance* (Baltimore: John Hopkins University Press, 2001), 79–81. For Zosimos's criticisms of different forms of propitious timing, see *Auth. Mem.* 1: *On Apparatus and Furnaces (Letter Omega)*.

some importance in this particular House of Life.

Culturally speaking, Panopolis was a very Hellenized city. Herodotus claims that in the fifth century BCE, the town of Chemmis (Khent-Min) had a statue of Perseus in their temple and that they celebrated Greek-style games in the hero's honor.[41] This is an exaggerated interpretation on Herodotus's part, but it is true that a couple of centuries later, during the period of Ptolemaic rule, there was an influx of Greeks migrating to Egypt. The first Greek pharaoh of Egypt, Ptolemy I Soter, established a new southern capital, Ptolemais, about twenty kilometers from Panopolis. Karolien Geens notes that Ptolemais was a Greek city, and that it had cultural tensions with Panopolis, yet also exerted cultural influence:

> Perhaps due to its location opposite this Greek centre, Panopolis came to the front in the revolts against the Ptolemies in the second century BC. On the other hand, thanks to the vicinity of Ptolemais, Greek culture was more easily accessible in Panopolis than in other cities of the Thebaid. Already in the late Ptolemaic and early Roman period, Egyptian culture apparently became influenced by Greek culture, and from the fourth century onwards, Panopolis became a stronghold of Greek literary culture.[42]

Under Greek rule, Hellenism became a mark of social status throughout the empire and continued to have cultural cachet throughout the Roman period. Greek remained the *lingua franca*, and in Panopolis the use of Hellenized names, like Zosimos, was on the rise.[43] The city had temples dedicated to Greek deities, such

---

41 HERODOTUS, *Histories* 11.91.
42 Karolien GEENS, "Hellenism as a Vehicle for Local Traditions in Third Century Egypt: The Evidence from Panopolis", in Peter Van NUFFELEN, ed., *Faces of Hellenism: Studies in the History of the Eastern Mediterranean, 4th Century BC to 5th Century AD* (Leuven: Peeters, 2009), 290.
43 Ibid, 307.

as Hermes, Persephone, Asclepius, as well as Egyptian gods.[44] Several bilingual mummy tags from the third century, written in demotic on one side and Greek on the other, have also been found in Panopolis.[45] Under Roman rule, intermarriage between Greeks and Egyptians was common; Greeks living in Egypt were legally classified as Egyptians, and "Greek" became more of a cultural identity than an ethnic one.[46] But Greek heritage and a Greek education were still markers of the elite class.

Some perspective on the elite Hellenized culture of Panopolis comes from a set of documents dating from the mid-to-late fourth century that were written by a *scholastikos* (lawyer) named Ammon, who comes from an elite priestly family and may have been a priest himself at one time.[47] He is writing a bit later than Zosimos, but it is likely that Ammon's father or older brother were high priests at the Temple of Min in Zosimos's day.[48] Peter van Minnen notes that Ammon's manuscripts, particularly a letter to his mother, are elegantly written by hand in a highly polished Greek prose, and bear the mark of an excellent Greek education.[49] Ammon's religious ideas focus on the role of Fate and divine providence, which is also emphasized in Zosimos's text *On Apparatus and Furnaces (Letter Omega)*. Van Minnen thinks that Ammon's discussions of the cycles of Fate might be inspired by the zodiacs and astronomical tra-

---

44 GEENS, "Panopolis, a Nome Capital in Egypt", 133.
45 Ibid, 86.
46 Christina RIGGS, *The Beautiful Burial in Roman Egypt: Art, Identity, and Funerary Religion* (Oxford: Oxford University Press, 2005), 23.
47 See Peter van MINNEN, "The Letter (and Other Papers) of Ammon: Panopolis in the Fourth Century AD", in *Perspectives on Panopolis: An Egyptian Town from Alexander the Great to the Arab Conquest* (Leiden: Brill, 2002), 182, 184. Ammon's brother was an *archiprophētes*, which is the highest-ranking priest that oversees all of the temples in a nome, equivalent to a bishop or archbishop. On this see WILLIS and MARESCH, eds., *The Archive of Ammon Scholasticus of Panopolis*, vol. 1, *The Legacy of Harpocration* (Weisbaden: Springer Fachmedien, 1997), 1–2.
48 His brother, Horion I, was *archiprophetes* in 299 CE. See van MINNEN, ibid, 187.
49 Ibid, 188-189.

ditions that flourished in Panopolis.⁵⁰ That could certainly be, but astral religion and ideas about Fate and Fortune were also quite popular throughout the Roman Empire. Fortune was personified as a goddess and was often merged with other goddesses, including Isis; temples and divine statues of Fortune can still be seen all over the Mediterranean. Zosimos talks about manufacturing statues of Fortune and Destiny, presumably for the local temples or to sell to private buyers.⁵¹ Therefore, Ammon's emphasis on the cycles of Fate could also be a sign of his Hellenism. His religious ideas are expressed in a rather generic Hellenized fashion; as van Minnen notes, he frequently refers to the gods, but he only mentions one by name—Agathos Daimon, who was a Hellenized version of the Egyptian god, Shai.⁵² We also see these tendencies toward a generic Hellenism in Zosimos's writings, though to a lesser degree.⁵³ This is probably due, in part, to his Hellenistic education and background, as well to long-standing social and economic pressures to

50   Ibid, 189-190.
51   CMA, Syr. II.6.31
52   van MINNEN, 182. On Agathos Daimon and Shai, see also DUNAND, "Book II: Ptolemaic and Roman Egypt", in DUNAND and ZIVIE-COCHE, *Gods and Men in Egypt*, 244.
53   Another example of this generic Hellenism can also found in the writings of the Christian monk, SHENOUTE (late 4th-early 5th c.), who was from the Panopolis region and wrote diatribes against "pagan" religions and rival forms of Christianity. Scholars have noted that Shenoute's writings, with a few exceptions, are lacking in detail about any Egyptian indigenous religions; instead, he writes about Greek myths and refers to gods by their Greek names instead of their Egyptian ones (Pan instead of Min, for example). As Mark SMITH has noted, when Shenoute is not specifically describing religion in Greek terms, the paganism that Shenoute presents is the sort of "bland, generic variety which might have been encountered almost anywhere". SMITH, "Aspects of the Preservation and Transmission of Indigenous Religious Traditions in Akhmim and its Environs During the Graeco-Roman Period", 242-245 (quotation from 244). Shenoute wrote in Coptic, but he was very well-versed in Greek and was most likely educated in Panopolis. See David BRAKKE and Andrew CRISLIP's introduction to *Selected Discourses of Shenoute the Great: Community, Theology, and Social Conflict in Late Antique Egypt* (Cambridge: Cambridge University Press, 2015).

assimilate to the higher status Greek culture. But Zosimos's writings also show signs of a conscious attempt to blend the teachings of different cultures in order to present them in a unified, more universal form.[54]

In the Roman period, temple scribes were interested in synthesizing different native theologies and myths in order to present a more universal account of Egyptian religion that transcended local and regional differences.[55] This universalism was not limited to Egyptian thought; the scribes were reading and translating texts from all over the Mediterranean and Near East and harmonizing ideas, expressing them in Greek, the *lingua franca* of their day. As David Frankfurter observes:

> The enterprise of interpreting old traditions was at the same time *archaistic*, in the sense of continually reinforcing the paradigmatic significance of ancient legends and their characters, and *synthetic*, in the sense of articulating the archaic models as contemporary propaganda of immediate historical relevance. This fundamental drive to synthesize was largely responsible for Egyptian priestly culture's tremendous capacity to assimilate foreign words, gods, and ritual methods like astrology, and ultimately to transform "Hellenism", its language, ideas, and mythologies, into a thoroughly Egyptian discourse.[56]

---

54 PHOTIUS, a ninth-century Patriarch of Constantinople, mentions Zosimos in his *Bibliotecha*, which is a digest of the books he had personally read. His name appears in a summary of a book by an unknown author, called *Precursors to Christianity*, who sought to harmonize Greek, Persian, Thracian, Egyptian, Babylonian, Chaldean, and Roman views that announce and support Christian doctrine. Zosimos appears to have been recognized by this author for his efforts to harmonize ancient teachings. Photius thinks that the inclusion of Zosimos is unusual enough to single him out for mention: "[H]e has not failed in taking even some from the alchemical writings of Zosimus (the latter was a Theban from Panopolis) to demonstrate the same propositions". See PHOTIUS, *Bibliotecha*, 170, trans. J. H. FREESE (London: SPCK, 1920); via www.tertullian.org.

55 DUNAND, op. cit., 234-235.

56 FRANKFURTER, *Religion in Roman Egypt*, 244.

The Hermetic literature that dates from the beginning of Roman rule is a good example of this synthetic tendency, blending Egyptian traditions with Greek and Jewish influences.[57] Zosimos, who was well versed in the Hermetic tradition, also exhibits this synthesis and universalism, at times intentionally trying to harmonize Greek, Hebrew, and Egyptian approaches to metallurgy and metaphysics.[58] His Hellenistic mode of expression can occasionally mask the Egyptian traditions that undergird his work, but it has the advantage of making his ideas more accessible to a broader audience, as well as bearing the marks of higher education, status, and prestige.

Egyptian language, customs, and religious traditions were still very much alive in Roman Egypt, particularly in the temples. One of the striking features of Egyptian temples is that they function like texts. The walls are covered with reliefs and hieroglyphic engravings—ritual instructions and prayers; names and gods and descriptions of their journeys through the worlds; lists of priests, kings, and notable citizens; lists of library holdings—these things and more are inscribed onto the temple walls and help preserve cultural memory, a need that became more acute with the ever-increasing multiculturalism in Roman Egypt.[59]

Phillipe Derchain coined the phrase "temple grammar" to refer to the integration of text, architecture, and iconography that went into the building and decoration of the temples; the temple grammar is unique to different temples, making each temple a world of its own.[60] Unfortunately, we know little to nothing of the temple grammar of the Temple of Min in Panopolis, but Derchain's work on the House of Gold at the Temple of Dendera (roughly 130 kilometers to the south) is pertinent to studies of

---

57   See Garth FOWDEN's discussion in *The Egyptian Hermes*, 27, 36–37.
58   *Auth.Mem.* 1.12–16.
59   Martina MINAS-NERPEL, "Egyptian Temples", in C. RIGGS, ed., *The Oxford Handbook of Roman Egypt* (Oxford: Oxford University Press, 2012), 374.
60   Ibid, 364.

alchemy.⁶¹ The temple has ascending and descending staircases that lead to the roof of the temple, where New Year ceremonies and Osiris rituals were performed.⁶² The ascending staircase is in the west, and a poem to the setting sun is inscribed on the wall. The poem is strategically positioned near a window so that the words become illuminated by sun's rays once it begins to set—a beautiful example of propitious timing and working in harmony with nature, which is important to Egyptian rituals and to Zosimean alchemy.⁶³ The entrance to a goldsmith's *atelier*, called the "House of Gold", is located on a landing off this stairway. Lower ranking artisans were forbidden to enter this room, where initiated priests finished making the cult statues and performed the "opening of the mouth" ceremonies that rendered the statues capable of receiving divine presence.⁶⁴ The deities that preside over this House of Gold are Thoth and his consort, Seshat; their images, along with other gods and depictions of the mystery of the birth of statues, are among the many engravings on the chamber walls.⁶⁵ As an artisan-priest, Zosimos would have been involved in these god-making rituals and immersed in this kind of temple grammar, which he had a role in interpreting. Derchain thinks that the origins of alchemy lie in these practices of making and consecrating divine statues, and I couldn't agree more.⁶⁶ Zosimos's *religious* approach

61   Phillipe DERCHAIN, "L'Atelier des Orfevres à Dendara et les origins de l'Alchimie", *Chronique d'Egypte* LXV (1990): 219–242. In 1981, two colossal royal statues were uncovered in Akhmim, which allowed archaeologists to determine the location of the entrance to the Temple of Min, but whatever remains of the grand temple lies buried beneath the modern city, making the temple grammar impossible to reconstruct. For a brief account of archaeological discoveries at Akhmim, see Jonathan Elias, "Akhmim", in *Encyclopedia of Ancient History*, ed. R. Bagnall, et al. (West Sussex, UK: Wiley-Blackwell, 2013), p. 263.
62   Miroslav VERNER, *Temple of the World: Sanctuaries, Cults, and Mysteries of Ancient Egypt* (Cairo: The American University in Cairo Press, 2013), 451.
63   DERCHAIN, "L'Atelier des Orfevres à Dendara et les origins de l'Alchimie", 219.
64   Ibid, 220–223.
65   Ibid, 222–223; see also VERNER, *Temple of the World*, 453–454.
66   DERCHAIN, 224.

to alchemy, in particular, seems to derive from (and elaborate on) the temple mysteries of god-making.

Temples were dependent on imperial funding, and during Ptolemaic and Roman rule, there was a significant amount of spending on temples in the Thebaid region. Funding for these building and renovation projects may have originally been done to quell rebellion and promote royal propaganda in the area; the Thebaid was notorious for rebelling against both Greece and Rome—Panopolis being one of the centers of these rebellions in the second century BCE.[67] Another reason is that Upper Egypt is home to most of the country's gold mines, and imperial rulers would have an interest in protecting that wealth. In addition to gold, the mountains of the Eastern Desert were a major mining center for precious metals and gemstones, and limestone used for building.

Panopolis, the capital city of the ninth nome of Egypt, was one of the gateways to the Eastern Desert, and in antiquity it was known for its craftsmanship in weaving, stonemasonry, and metalwork, particularly goldsmithing.[68] Its patron deity, Min, was known as the "Lord of the Eastern Desert" and was worshiped by miners and quarrymen.[69] Min was also the main deity of the city of Coptos, located at the same bend of the Nile River as Dendera, about 125 kilometers south of Panopolis. Shrines to Min, as god of the mines and quarries, have been found all throughout the Eastern Desert, along with shrines to Hathor, patron goddess of Dendera, who was worshiped as a goddess of gold, silver, lapis lazuli,

---

67 See DUNAND, "Book II: Ptolemaic and Roman Egypt", 206–213; J. ASSMANN and D. FRANKFURTER, "Egypt", in *Ancient Religions*, ed. S.I. JOHNSTON (Cambridge: Belknap Press, 2007), 159; and GEENS, "Hellenism as a Vehicle for Local Traditions in Third Century Egypt: The Evidence from Panopolis", 290.

68 See GEENS, "Panopolis, a Nome Capital in Egypt in the Roman and Byzantine Period", 301–302; and WILLIS and MARESCH, *The Archive of Ammon Scholasticus of Panopolis*, 5.

69 Geraldine PINCH, *Egyptian Mythology: A Guide to the Gods, Goddesses and Traditions of Ancient Egypt*, 164–165; see also GEENS, ibid, 301–303; and Sydney AUFRÈRE, *L'Univers Minéral Dans La Pensée Égyptienne*, Vol. 1, 137–139.

and turquoise.⁷⁰ These two gods were the principal metallurgical deities in the Thebaid.⁷¹ As an ithyphallic fertility god, Min would protect those who enter the mines and plumb the insides of the earth, whereas Hathor, a fertility goddess, was embodied in the subterranean passageways and beautiful treasures found therein.

Precious metals, of course, have great value as a source of material wealth, used since ancient times as a form of monetary currency, but Egyptians—particularly Upper Egyptian mining communities—also accorded them great spiritual value. Sydney Aufrère argues that theologies of the mineral world (which had local variations) are important sources for understanding alchemical traditions.⁷² The temple grammar of the theological and ritual use of metals at the Temple of Min at Panopolis is lost, but we can get a sense of its themes by looking more closely at the worship of Min. In addition to being a god of the mines, Min is also a patron deity of goldsmiths.⁷³ Therefore, gold likely had a theological place of prominence at Panopolis. Egyptians considered all precious metals and stones to be emanations of the divine, and gold, silver, electrum, copper, turquoise, lapis lazuli, carnelian, and jasper were often presented to the gods as ceremonial offerings.⁷⁴ Silver ore is rare in Egypt, occurring mostly in natural alloys of silver and gold ("aurian silver"), so much of it was imported.⁷⁵ Even though silver had a high market value—at times even higher than gold—Aufrère argues that gold was considered theologically superior because it was native to the sacred land of Egypt.⁷⁶ This idea may have been

70   AUFRÈRE, ibid, 133–136 (Hathor), 137–139 (Min).
71   Ibid, 133.
72   AUFRÈRE, *L'Univers Minéral Dans La Pensée Égyptienne*, Vol. 2, 803–804.
73   Ibid, 363, 366.
74   AUFRÈRE gives examples from the New Year ceremonies at the temples of Dendera and Edfu in *L'Univers Minéral Dans La Pensée Égyptienne*, Vol. 1, 161-169.
75   See Alfred LUCAS, *Ancient Egyptian Materials and Industries*, 245–248; and Jack OGDEN, "Metals", in *Ancient Egyptian Materials and Technology*, P. NICHOLSON and I. SHAW, eds. (Cambridge: Cambridge University Press, 2000), 170.
76   AUFRÈRE, Vol. 2, 423, 449. On silver having a higher market than gold up

especially promoted in Upper Egypt, where the majority of gold mines were located.

Astral metaphors were often used to describe gold; gold was compared with the sun and moon and the brilliance of the stars.[77] The morning hymn to the gods sung in most temples each day associates sunlight with gold: "Wake peacefully, wake beautifully, in peace! Wake to life, oh (god of this city)! [...] It is you who break the seal in the heavens and spread gold dust over the earth, who come to life in the east and vanish in the west and sleep in (your temple) each day".[78] This hymn includes the refrain, repeated at least forty-five times, "May you wake peacefully [...] and spread gold dust over the earth". [79] Because gold was associated with the sun and the solar deity (the primary creator god, Re) who descends each night into the Duat (underworld), gold was also associated with the mysteries of Osiris, god of the underworld.[80]

As the cult of Isis and Osiris spread and rose to prominence throughout Egypt, the god Min became increasingly assimilated with Osiris. At Panopolis, Min was worshiped in a triad with Isis (wife of Osiris) and Horus (their son), who were, in turn, assimilated with other prominent Panopolite deities: the fertility goddess Triphis, and the child god Kolanthis.[81] The cult of Osiris, which revolves around the death and resurrection of the god, undoubtedly influenced the metalwork practiced in the Temple of Min; it is certainly evident in Zosimos's writings, particularly his alchemical allegory, *On Excellence*, which includes a vivid, elaborate account of the death and resurrection of the metals in the underworld (see chapter 3).[82]

---

until the end of the Middle Kingdom (roughly 1600 BCE), see LUCAS, 247.
77   AUFRÈRE, 367.
78   SAUNERON, *The Priests of Ancient Egypt*, 79
79   Ibid.
80   AUFRÈRE, Vol. 2, 372–73; 389–390; 803.
81   GEENS, "Panopolis, a Nome Capital in Egypt in the Roman and Byzantine Period", 308–313.
82   See ZOSIMOS, *Auth. Mem.* X-XII.

Trade guilds and workshops

So far, temples and temple culture have been discussed. But when it comes to metalsmithing this is only part of the story, since not all metalsmiths were priests. Metalworkers were organized into trade associations (guilds), and Zosimos and his colleagues were undoubtedly affiliated with these groups—either as members or through trade networks. Historically, most Egyptian priests served only part-time, working month-long "shifts" at the temple four or five times a year; the majority of their time was spent working in occupations outside of the temple.[83] Craft guilds of the Roman period appear to have evolved out of trade networks that were attached to the temples.[84] These associations were usually founded by a master craftsman and typically numbered between ten and twenty-five members.[85] They exercised control over trade, both locally and regionally; they also regulated membership and local competition, and guaranteed the quality of members' products.[86] The associations played an important role in upholding and maintaining religious traditions; they typically honored a patron deity and helped support the cult of that deity as well as the local temple.[87] The temple, in return, would be an important source of

---

83 Sauneron, *Priests of Ancient Egypt*, 13; Teeter, *Religion and Ritual in Ancient Egypt*, 35.

84 See Richard Alston, "Trade and the City in Roman Egypt", in *Trade, Traders, and the Ancient City*, ed. Helen Parkins and Christopher John Smith (London: Routledge, 1998), 172.

85 See Philip Venticinque, "Family Affairs: Guild Regulations and Family Relationships in Roman Egypt", Greek, Roman, and Byzantine Studies 10 (2010), 278.

86 See Peter van Minnen, "Urban Craftsmen of Roman Egypt", in *Münstersche Beiträge zur Antiken Handelsgeschichte* VI (Ostfildern: Scripta Mercaturae Verlag, 1987), 57–58; Alston, "Trade and the City in Roman Egypt", 172; and the classic study by A.E.R. Boak, "The Organization of Gilds in Greco-Roman Egypt", *Transactions and Proceedings of the American Philological Association*, Vol. 68 (1937): 212–220.

87 Philip Venticinque, *Honor Among Thieves: Craftsmen, Merchants, and Associations in Roman and Late Roman Egypt* (Ann Arbor: University of Michigan Press, 2016), 114–121; Van Minnen, "Urban Craftsmen of Roman Egypt",

income for metallurgists, commissioning metal statues, ritual objects, temple decoration, and other goods. Zosimos's work in the temple, then, could have easily been contiguous with his work in a guild, both professionally and religiously speaking.

Data from Roman Egypt indicates that goldsmiths and silversmiths were organized into two distinct groups, each with its own guilds.[88] Goldsmiths (χρυσοχόοι, chrysochooi) had a close relationship with the temples, and some of their higher ranking members functioned as overseers who would contract with other metalsmiths and artisans to make goods and decorations for the temples and other public buildings, as well as for private clients.[89] According to Jack Ogden, they primarily worked in sheet gold, hammering and shaping it by hand, rather than casting; when casting was employed, it was usually for making statues or jewelry and was done in conjunction with hand-wrought work.[90] Silversmiths (ἀργυροκόποι, argyrokopoi) specialized in statuettes, jewelry, decorative items, and tableware.[91] Bronzesmiths (χαλκοτύποι, chalkotypoi) form a third category, but in a looser sense because gene-

---

52. See also P. O. LONG, Openness, Secrecy, Authorship, op. cit., 75–76; FRANKFURTER, Religion in Roman Egypt, 72–73 ; and ALSTON, The City in Roman and Byzantine Egypt, 207–218. In the first century of Roman rule, collegia were banned unless they had some religious purpose, including collections to help pay for burials for the members. See I. N. ARNAOUTOGLOU, "Collegia in the Province of Egypt in the First Century AD", Ancient Society 35 (2005), 197–216.

88 Fabienne BURKHALTER, «La production des objets en métal (or, argent, bronze) en Égypte hellénistique et romaine à travers les sources papyrologiques», in Commerce et artisanat dans l'Alexandrie hellénistique et romaine: Actes du colloque d'Athènes 11–12 décembre 1988, ed. J.-Y. EMPEREUR. (Athènes: École française d'Athènes, 1998), 125. See also Jack OGDEN, Ancient Jewellery (Berkeley: University of California Press, 1992), 58–59.

89 BURKHALTER, 130–132; van MINNEN, "Urban Craftsmen", 45, 57–58; and Thelma THOMAS, Late Antique Egyptian Funerary Sculpture: Images for this World and the Next, 30. Many of the statues in Egyptian temples were donated by private individuals. See Marsha HILL, "Lives of the Statuary", in Gifts for the Gods: Images from Egyptian Temples, ed. M. HILL and D. SCHORSCH (New Haven: Yale University Press, 2007), 153–155.

90 Jack OGDEN, "Metals", 165.

91 BURKHALTER, 125.

ric terms for bronze workers were applied to a diverse group of metalsmiths, whose products ranged from statues, crockery, amphoræ, weapons, tools, locks and keys, as well as metal for boats.[92]

Of all the metalsmiths, goldsmiths were the wealthiest group. According to the papyrus *P.Berl.Bork*, a topographical survey of Panopolis dating from the late third–early fourth century CE, there were seven goldsmiths registered as property owners in Panopolis: all of them owned one or more houses, and one owned as many as five homes.[93] There was also one silversmith, who owned one home, and three bronzesmiths, who owned either a home or a workshop, with one *bronzier* owning both.[94] The *P.Berl.Bork* survey is incomplete and not detailed enough to provide for a mapping of the city, but it can be gleaned that metalsmiths lived in proximity to one another, which is also the custom in other Egyptian cities.[95] In nearby Athribis, about ten kilometers southwest of Panopolis, metalsmiths and artisans lived in the northern quadrant of the city, near the sacred precinct in the northwest where many of the religious buildings were located.[96] Likewise, in Coptos, a guild of goldsmiths called the "goldsmiths of Min" lived and worked near the Temple of Min.[97] It is estimated that the *P.Berl.Bork* survey co-

---

[92] Ibid, 126, 128. *P.Berl.Bork* has separate listings for a locksmith (κλειδοποιός) and an unspecified metallurgist (μεταλλουργός; perhaps an overseer of mines?), but no blacksmiths/ironworkers are listed. This could be due to the fact that *P.Berl.Bork* is incomplete. In ancient Greek, variants of the term χαλκεύς (bronzesmiths) could be used to apply to all metalsmiths, including ironsmiths and goldsmiths. See Jack LINDSAY, *The Origins of Alchemy in Græco-Roman Egypt*, 226. See also Zbigniew BORKOWSKI's speculations about the term μεταλλουργός in *Une description topographique des immeubles à Panopolis*, 78–79.

[93] BURKHALTER, 126; GEENS, 220. GEENS' numbers differ from BURKHALTER's because she is including nearby homes belonging to the same family, and she notes that the fragmentary nature of the text, *P.Berl.Bork*, makes it difficult to get precise data.

[94] See BORKOWSKI's tables in *Une description topographique des immeubles à Panopolis*, 44–45; see also BURKHALTER, 126; and GEENS, 220.

[95] ALSTON, *The City in Roman and Byzantine Egypt*, 155, 175.

[96] GEENS, "Panopolis, a Nome Capital in Egypt", 25.

[97] AUFRÈRE, vol. II, 366.

vers at least ten-to-thirty percent of the city of Panopolis[98]: data is missing on the larger temple complexes and the properties and priestly residences that belong to them, so it is unknown whether the metalworkers in Panopolis lived and worked in proximity to the Temple of Min, but it is likely.[99] Incidentally, one of the goldsmiths who lived in Panopolis in Zosimos's day was named Agathos; he lived next to Agathos the youth (probably his son), and another neighbor named Askla, (son?) of Agathos Da[imonon]; these people were probably all related.[100] Zosimos mentions recipes and techniques of Agathodaimon in several of his texts.[101] Professions tended to run in the family, and sons tended to be named after their fathers, so perhaps the alchemical author Agathodaimon is related to this Panopolite family of goldsmiths.

Matteo Martelli has raised good questions about the work environment of early alchemists: we often use terms like "laboratory" or "workshop", but how are we imagining these places?[102] Alchemical workshops are not described in the Greco-Egyptian

[98] R. ALSTON and R. D. ALSTON, "Urbanism and the Urban Community in Roman Egypt", *Journal of Egyptian Archæology* 83 (1997), 212, n. 61.

[99] ALSTON, *The City in Roman and Byzantine Egypt*, 155-156. In more ancient times, artisan's workshops were located near the temple treasury, where they would obtain their precious metals, gems, tools, and other supplies, which were owned either by the temple or the state. Evidence from nearby cities cited above shows that this pattern hadn't changed, so it is likely that it held in Panopolis, as well. See Marianne EATON-KRAUSS, "Artists and Artisans", in *Oxford Encyclopedia of Ancient Egypt*, online ed. (Oxford: Oxford University Press, 2005).

[100] *P.Berl.Bork.* XII.22-25. Another neighbor is Kolanthis, a cosmetics maker, who might also be related since this profession involves minerals and dyes.

[101] Zosimos refers to the alchemical author Agathodaimon in *Auth. Mem.* II.4-5; IV.2; VII.3; VIII.3. Agathodaimon is also the name of a god, and Zosimos writes about a dream-figure with this name in his allegory, *On Excellence* (*Auth. Mem.* XI.2.). The figure of Agathodaimon in the allegory has multiple meanings (see my discussion in chapter 3), but Zosimos's references to the recipes of Agathodaimon seem more prosaic in nature, as if he were discussing a person of that name, and not a divine figure. Egyptians were commonly named after gods.

[102] See Matteo MARTELLI's article, "Greek Alchemists at Work: 'Alchemical Laboratory' in the Greco Roman Egypt", *Nuncius* 26 (2011): 271-311.

CHAPTER TWO

alchemical texts or the Leiden papyri, though different types of apparatuses are mentioned (stills and furnaces), as are different types of professions, like metalsmiths, dyers, and glassmakers. He gives a few examples of some of the Greco-Egyptian alchemical recipes that mention using equipment belonging to specialists,[103] including a goldsmith's melting pot,[104] a goldsmith's furnace,[105] a glass-blower's furnace,[106] and a potter's furnace.[107] As Martelli notes, these were all highly-specialized trades, yet alchemists seem to have expertise in all of these fields and appear to be sharing tools and workspaces with other craftsmen.[108] In my opinion, the most likely scenario for this kind of collaboration would be the temple, where teams of artisans worked in multiple media under the direction of one or more master craftsmen.

Temples in Egypt had artisans' workshops either on site or annexed to temple properties because the craftsmen needed to be in close proximity to raw materials like precious metals and gems, which were under control of the state and usually stored in temple treasuries, along with tools and equipment that belonged to the temple.[109] Some of these workshops could be quite extensive, like the well-documented aggregation of workshops near the temple complex of Karnak at Thebes, and appear to have served the needs of all the temples in town, or perhaps even several towns.[110] Although artwork in tombs and temples often depicts metalworkers, no ancient foundry was discovered until 1985.[111] This metalworking site, located at the funerary temple of King Seti I in the Theban necropolis, dates to the Ptolemaic period, and is probably similar

103   All of the examples listed here come from MARTELLI, ibid, 283.
104   P.Leid.x 68.2s.
105   CAAG II 305, 7–14.
106   CAAG II 307, 20–26; CAAG II 308, 6–10.
107   CMA II 51, 16–18 (Syriac text) and 92.23–93.2 (French translation).
108   Ibid, 288–289, 311.
109   EASTON-KRAUSS, "Artists and Artisans", Oxford Encyclopedia of Ancient Egypt, online ed.
110   Ibid.
111   Bernd SCHEEL, Egyptian Metalworking and Tools (Aylesbury: Shire Publications, 1989), 25.

to what Zosimos and his colleagues would have been familiar with a few centuries later.[112] Bernd Scheel gives a brief description:

> Four mud-brick structures of different lengths, each built of two parallel brick settings, were excavated. These served as hearths for the crucibles; the smaller hearths were 1.4 metres (5 feet) in length and the two larger ones 7 metres (23 feet). A small hearth had room for one crucible, a larger one was built to hold about five crucibles [...] It was possible, therefore, either to mass-produce many objects or to cast large ones at this site.[113]

This cast metal would have been further processed, shaped, or sculpted by artisans in separate workshops, like the cluster of workshops mentioned above near the Temple of Karnak in Thebes.

Workshops could also be owned by the state or by high-ranking government officials, and, beginning in the Greco-Roman period, by private individuals.[114] The *P.Berl.Bork.* data from Panopolis shows that there was one workshop for goldsmiths, and one for bronzesmiths; these were likely owned by the head of the trade guild for each group.[115] As we have seen, higher ranking goldsmiths were contractors and overseers for all kinds of artistic projects, including work for the temples and public buildings, so this group appears to have been the most versatile, able to work with many

---

[112] Ibid.
[113] Ibid, 25-27.
[114] SCHEEL, 59. Scheel notes that there were no private metalworkers in ancient Egypt, who had access to their own raw materials, equipment, and tools. Government officials and temples would release their workers to work for private individuals. As Jack OGDEN notes, this dynamic had changed sometime in the Ptolemaic period, which is when independent goldsmiths are first attested in Egypt. Guilds of metalsmiths begin to appear early in the Roman period. See OGDEN, *Ancient Jewellery*, 57-59.
[115] BORKOWSKI, 44-45. On master craftsmen as heads of trade guilds and workshop owners, see van MINNEN, "Urban Craftsmen of Roman Egypt", 57-58.

types of artists and sell metals other than gold.[116] Silversmiths and bronzeworkers seem to have been less involved as overseers of artisans outside of their own guilds (which might account for their lower income levels), and their ability to sell different metals may have been more restricted than that of goldsmiths.[117] The professional culture of Egyptian metallurgists is in need of much further study, but since the early alchemical recipes display a wide range of work with different metals, gems, dyes, and other materials, I surmise that the people who collected these varied recipes would most likely be high-ranking craftsmen, particularly goldsmiths, who served as temple overseers and/or contractors or supervisors within their guilds.

CRAFT KNOWLEDGE

Some understanding of how craft knowledge is attained and transmitted is essential to this discussion of temples and trade guilds; it is an important part of Zosimos's work as a scribe and interpreter of ancient recipes. But it is also an area prone to mystification, because it involves initiations and vows of secrecy as well as a belief that knowledge comes through divine revelation. I will therefore proceed with caution.

As we have already seen, access to temple knowledge and temple resources was restricted. One had to be initiated and of proper rank in order to be admitted into certain rooms of the temple, such as the House of Gold, for example, or the treasury. This was also the case for some trade guilds, whose membership was structured hierarchically, and one entered the guild and moved up in its ranks through a series of initiations; these initiations sometimes involved vows of secrecy for the transmission of trade

---

[116] For example, a second century goldsmith's receipt includes a charge for a silver statuette. See BURKHALTER, 131.

[117] Based on the data presented by BURKHALTER in *La production des objets en métal* (or, argent, bronze), op. cit.

secrets, though this was not always the case.[118]

In a long treatise called *Final Account*, Zosimos gives further details about alchemical traditions of secrecy. He attributes the origins of such practices to the fact that the kings of Egypt exercised strict control over mining, smelting, and other types of work dealing with precious metals; those who did not abide by the laws of secrecy were punished.[119] Zosimos claims that the ancient priests engraved cryptographic recipes and maps (i.e., locations of mines) onto *stelæ* and kept them hidden "in the darkness and depth of the temples [...] so that if anyone dared to confront the shadows of the sanctuary in order to obtain forbidden knowledge, he would not be able to decipher the characters, despite his audacity and trouble".[120] Zosimos also distinguishes between two types of metallurgical arts and the secrecy requirements for each: the treatment of mineral ores (ψαμμουργία, *psammourgia*), and the creation of timely tinctures (καιρικαι βαφαι, *kairikai baphai*). *Kairikos* means seasonal things, or opportune timing, and Zosimos uses this term to refer to tinctures created at astrologically opportune moments. He explains that the trade secrets of those who treat mineral ores are not as jealously guarded because this art is more public; it requires the use of furnaces, which "cannot be hidden away".[121] Whoever tried to treat mineral ores for their own profit, rather than the king's, would be easily detected. The timely tinctures, on the other hand, are created "out of view".[122] There is more opportunity for people to manufacture expensive goods secretly and independently, hence the need for stricter oaths to protect the trade secrets. It is possible that the production of timely tinctures involved the use of distillation methods, since distillatory equipment is more portable

---

118   Pamela LONG demonstrates that there is a lack of evidence for secrecy in ancient craft guilds. She claims that while the "lack of evidence does not mean it did not exist [...] the assumption that widespread craft secrecy prevailed is not justified". See LONG, *Openness, Secrecy, Authorship*, 74.
119   CAAG III.51.1.
120   CAAG III.51.5. My translation.
121   CAAG III.51.3.
122   Ibid.

and could be hidden—the Greco-Egyptian alchemical literature contains many illustrations of this type of equipment.[123] Zosimos relates that some alchemists have been critical of Democritus and other ancient authors for not mentioning these two arts. "Their reproaches are unjust", he says:

> They could not do it, these men who were the friends of the kings of Egypt and who gloried in holding the first rank in the class of prophets. How could they have openly, against royal orders, set out in public their knowledge and give others the sovereign power of wealth? Even if they could have done it, they would not, for they were careful of their secrets. It was possible only for Jews, secretly, to operate, write, and publish these things. Indeed we find that Theophilos, son of Theogenes, has described all the country's goldmines, and we have Maria's treatise on furnaces as well as other writings by Jews.[124]

In these passages, Zosimos locates the origins of alchemical secrecy in the Egyptian royalty's "jealous" guarding of their hoards of gold. This could be a reference to royal monopolies on gold working in the era of Ptolemaic rule.[125] Zosimos is sympathetic to

---

123 See MERTENS's discussion of the different types of distillatory apparatuses, along with the ancient illustrations, in *Zosime de Panopolis: Mémoires Authentiques*, cxiii–clxix.
124 CAAG III.51.2. LINDSAY's translation, based on FESTUGIERE's, 335.
125 FESTUGIÈRE, *La Révélation d'Hermès Trismégiste*, vol. 1, 276, n. 1. This increased control was likely due to the frequent revolts in the goldmining regions of Upper Egypt. See KLEMM, et. al., "Gold of the Pharaohs: 6,000 years of gold mining in Egypt and Nubia", *African Earth Sciences* 33 (2001), 656. Other scholars have argued that Zosimos could be responding to Emperor Diocletian's alleged banning of books dealing with *chēmia*, or the preparation of gold and silver, in the year 292. An entry for *chēmia* in the *Suda* states: "Diocletian, having sought out the books on this subject, burned them. Now, because of the revolutions, Diocletian treated the Egyptians harshly and cruelly and having sought out these books written by their forefathers on the chemistry of gold and silver, burned them lest wealth should accrue to the Egyptians through this art and lest they,

the ancient priests' need to protect the trade secrets out of loyalty to the king, but secrecy is undesirable, for it perpetuates envy and greed. Since the earliest alchemical texts date from around the time of the ascendancy of Roman rule in Egypt, it may have been the case that it was only possible to circulate these trade secrets once the Ptolemaic government had collapsed. Zosimos mentions that Jewish alchemists had disseminated some of these craft secrets, though he also notes that neither the ancient Egyptians nor the Jews or the Greeks had *ever* revealed the secrets of the timely tinctures.[126] "I have encountered no one among the ancients but Democritus making a clear allusion to this matter", he writes.[127] Some trade secrets were still closely guarded, but in Zosimos's day, this was probably due to increased competition as a result of the rising number of trade guilds in the Roman period, and more widespread dissemination of alchemical craft knowledge.

Zosimos, however, is critical of certain aspects of craft secrecy. He chastises Theosebeia for wanting to "hide the art", and for requiring oaths from the members of her group. "If mysteries are necessary", he says, "it is all the more necessary that everybody [initiates?] should possess a book of chemistry, which should not be kept hidden".[128] Zosimos claims that some of the well-known commentators on ancient texts have not only done a poor job of interpreting the ancient recipes, but they have also deliberately withheld pertinent information and have thus "spoiled the books

---

emboldened by riches, should in the future revolt against the Romans". (*Suda* entry translated by A. J. Hopkins, *Alchemy: Child of Greek Philosophy*, Appendix II.) Zosimos locates this "jealousy of the kings" in ancient times, however, and Diocletian's edict would have been a more current event (if it had even happened yet), so this is unlikely. Moreover, it is difficult to ascertain the context of Diocletian's banning of these books. Would this have impacted temple artisans like Zosimos, or other types of metalworkers, such as those who minted coins for the state? Diocletian did initiate a major currency reform in Egypt in 296. See Roger BAGNALL, *Egypt in Late Antiquity* (Princeton: Princeton University Press, 1993), Appendix II.

126   See CAAG III.51.3.
127   CAAG III.51.3. My translation.
128   CMA, Syr. II.8.1. My translation.

of chemistry".[129] He writes: "The Philosopher [probably Democritus] says that they have drowned in a great ocean the writings of the science of nature".[130] Zosimos accuses many commentators of seeking fame by attaching their names to the ancient recipes they have interpreted, and that "no one has prevented them. But they are scorned by the priests, by those that possess the books".[131] Zosimos also says that access to these books, which is the privilege of the higher-ranking artisan-priests, "must not become an object of envy, for this is also scorned by the priests".[132] Though Zosimos had achieved some renown for his interpretations of ancient recipes, he takes moral issue with certain fame-seeking colleagues (both past and present) who withhold information and require oaths of secrecy from their students in order to protect their privileged status as experts. These people are motivated by vanity, desire, and jealousy, Zosimos says, and he wants nothing to do with them or their books:

> Having seen the degree of their stupidity and poverty of mind, I diverted my face from all these writings, and I decided not to take them in hand anymore, and not to concern myself with the vows, the jealousies and the excessive malice; I refrain from interpreting them, without any jealousy on my part, because they are the product of passion.[133]

Zosimos's complaints against craft secrets revolve around two key issues. One is greed and egotism; as we have seen, Zosimos thinks some metallurgists posture as experts and use initiation and craft secrecy as a way to bolster and maintain their privileged status. The other is lack of understanding; to be a master craftsman

---

129 Ibid.
130 Ibid.
131 CMA, Syr. II.6.19. My translation.
132 Ibid.
133 CMA, Syr. II.6.4. My translation.

requires a great deal of knowledge, skill, and experience, and veils of secrecy can be a way of protecting this knowledge as well as feigning it. Zosimos tells Theosebeia that everyone in her group should possess a book of chemistry, because initiation is no guarantee that a person will have the requisite knowledge or experience to be able to interpret the recipes. Those that do will have a better chance of accurately explaining and preserving the methods if they are unencumbered by these mystifications.

Zosimos believes that craft knowledge and hermeneutics involves human intelligence, but he also believes that knowledge is divinely revealed. Therefore, jealousies and bad interpretations indicate that daimons (lesser, ambivalent spiritual entities) are at work, and this goes against the principles of the sacred art. In *Final Account*, he portrays the daimons as greedy, jealous beings, much like he portrays the Egyptian kings and certain priests as jealous guardians of the alchemical secrets. He writes:

> [T]he watchful daimons, once repelled by the powerful men of old, resolved to take control of the natural tinctures in our stead, so as to be no longer chased off by men, but to receive their prayers, to be invoked by them, and to be regularly nourished by their sacrifices. This, then, is what they did. They hid all the natural procedures, which acted through themselves, not only because they were jealous of men, but also because they were concerned with their own subsistence, so as not to be whipped, chased out, and killed with hunger through receiving no more sacrifices. [...] They hid the natural tincture (φυσικα) and introduced in its place their unnatural tincture (αφυσικα), and they handed these procedures on to their priests, and, if the townsfolk neglected the sacrifices, they prevented them from succeeding even in the unnatural tincture. All those [priests] then learned the so-called doctrine of the daimons of the time-fabri

cated waters, and, by reason of custom, law, and fear, their sacrifices multiplied.[134]

Zosimos is clearly a proponent of natural methods for making tinctures, and he claims that the unnatural methods are the invention of greedy daimons and will only work with their assent, which is gained through sacrificial offerings. According to this account, the priests who have been influenced by the greedy daimons must in turn persuade the townspeople to give offerings to these particular daimons, or else the priests will not be successful in their work. This is an unhealthy network in Zosimos's eyes, one that involves a corrupted form of religion as well as an inferior form of science, and this negatively impacts his industry and the religious life of the community. Zosimos claims that the natural methods he practices are more in line with the teachings of the great masters of old. They are based on understanding and working in harmony with natural forces, and require a different sort of piety, which includes appealing to a higher god and repelling the daimons through meditation. At the end of *Final Account*, Zosimos instructs Theosebeia to make the daimons disappear by calming her body and her mind. He writes:

> Remain seated at your hearth and God will come to you, who is everywhere and not limited to the lowest realm like the daimons. Rest your body, calm your passions, resist desire, pleasure, anger, grief and the twelve portions of death [i.e., the influences of the zodiac]. By righting yourself in this way, you will summon the divine to you, and it will come, that which is everywhere and nowhere.[135]

---

[134] Adapted from LINDSAY's translation in *The Origins of Alchemy in Græco-Roman Egypt*, 338. Lindsay's translation is based on CAAG II.51 and FESTUGIERE's rendering of the Greek text in *La Révélation d'Hermès Trismégiste*, vol. 1., 275–282 (French translation), 363–368 (Greek text).

[135] CAAG III.51.8. My translation.

The daimons stir the baser passions, like greed and egotism, and dispelling them is a way to maintain a solid moral grounding and openness to the wisdom of the divine, which will uplift the soul and deepen one's understanding of the work.

ZOSIMOS'S ASSOCIATES AND RIVALS

It will be easier to understand Zosimos's own work life if we look more closely at his colleagues. One of the few colleagues that Zosimos mentions by name is a female alchemist named Theosebeia, who leads and instructs a group of apprentices.[136] Many of his writings are addressed to her, instructing her about both religious matters and metalworking techniques. Later commentators refer to Theosebeia as a priestess, and also as Zosimos's "sister", which was a form of address used in both temple and trade guild contexts, though Zosimos doesn't refer to her in these terms in any of his surviving authentic writings.[137] He clearly respects Theosebeia a great deal, but at times he also teases her and criticizes some of her approaches, which implies a certain degree of familiarity between them.[138]

---

136   On Theosebeia and her circle, see CMA, Syr. VIII.1 (*On Tin*).
137   The *Suda* entry on Zosimos reports that he addressed his writings on chemistry to his sister, Theosebeia. This excerpt from the *Suda* is cited by M. MERTENS, *Zosime de Panopolis: Mémoires Authentiques*, xcvii. On Theosebeia as a priestess, see CMA, Syr. VII.19 (there are a few texts called Book VII—this one is on page 308, and it does not appear to be an authentic Zosimean text). On "brother" and "sister" as forms of address used in late ancient craft guilds, see James Malcolm ARLANDSON, *Women, Class, and Society in Early Christianity: Models from Luke-Acts* (Peabody, MA: Hendrickson Publishers, 1997), 87.
138   He teases her a couple times in *Final Account*, addressing her once as "Your Imperfection", and later with a more positive image of royalty: "lady of the purple robe". See CAAG III.51.9, 11. Jack LINDSAY comments on the ironic title, "Your Imperfection", in *The Origins of Alchemy in Greco-Roman Egypt*, 341. In CMA Syr. VIII.1 (*On Tin*), he is critical of her decision to require oaths of secrecy from her students.

Female goldsmiths are rarely mentioned outside of alchemical literature, but these were family businesses, and women were involved in production to greater or lesser degrees.[139] However, Theosebeia does not appear to be Zosimos's wife, or even a relative. He most often addresses her as γυνή (gynē, woman, wife, lady of the house) or δεσποινα (despoina, lady of the house), which are terms indicating matronal status.[140] Therefore, it is likely that Theosebeia was either married or widowed. My guess is the latter. One of Zosimos's letters gives some domestic details that provides a clue to their relationship:

> Once when staying in your house, lady, because of the attention you give me, I was admiring all the activities of the one you call *"strouktōros"*. I was quite impressed by his [or her?] work. I began to transport Paxamos [a 1st century CE author of books on the arts of cooking and dyeing][141] to the ranks of the gods, and I also felt that the deepest desire of every craftsman was, after having received some instruction from his predecessors, to apply himself to do even better.[142]

Zosimos says that this mood came upon him while watching the *structōr* (στρουκτωρος, *strouktōros*, is a rare word in Greek, which connotes something like a master chef or caterer)[143] steam poultry using an unusual cooking device, which inspired him to research books that might contain descriptions of similar devices.[144] Zosimos was a guest in Theosebeia's house and had not met her *structōr*

---

139 van MINNEN, "Urban Craftsmen in Roman Egypt", 51.
140 In CAAG III.27.7, Zosimos refers to another female alchemist as "the maiden (*parthenou*), Paphnutia". Paphnutia is a "miss", whereas Theosebeia is a "madam".
141 Paxamos was a popular writer of Egyptian origin, ca. 1st c. CE. See MERTENS, *Zosime de Panopolis: Mémoires Authentiques*, 197 n. 3.
142 *Auth.Mem.* VIII.1. Translation mine.
143 See MERTENS' French translation of *Auth.Mem.* VIII.1, n. 2.
144 *Auth.Mem.* VIII.2.

before, so it is doubtful that they were close relatives.

It is evident from this and other letters that Theosebeia was actively seeking Zosimos's advice. If she were married to a metalsmith, or if she were the daughter or sister of one, propriety would dictate that her male relative would be the one to contact Zosimos, since trade guilds had strict rules against the corruption of another member's home, including adultery or other forms of intrigue that might ruin reputations and interfere with relations between families.[145] This leads me to think that Theosebeia was living independently, and that she was either: (1) a rare case of a woman who had trained outside of the family profession and was now in a position to teach others;[146] or, more likely (2) a widow who had inherited her husband's (or father's) metalworking business; this would explain how she came to be in charge of a small group of apprentices, and also why she was seeking expert advice from Zosimos, as well as another artisan-priest named Neilos.[147]

It has been suggested that Theosebeia was Zosimos's spiritual partner, his *soror mystica*.[148] The idea of the *soror mystica*, which has been developed most fully in Jungian interpretations of alchemy, has its roots in alchemical emblems that depict chemical processes as a "wedding" of the king (sulfur) and queen (mercury), who are also represented as sun and moon.[149] Interestingly, Zosimos's relationship with Theosebeia has been depicted this way in an illustrated Arabic text from the thirteenth century, called the

---

145 See VENTICINQUE, "Family Affairs: Guild Regulations and Family Relationships in Roman Egypt", 285–288.
146 See van MINNEN, "Did Ancient Women Learn a Trade Outside the Home? A Note on SB XVIII 13305", *Zeitschrift für Papyrologie und Epigraphik* 123 (1998), 201–203.
147 Zosimos refers disparagingly to "this priest Neilos, your friend". See CAAG III.27.8.
148 See MERTENS, *Zosime de Panopolis: Mémoires Authentiques*, xvii–xviii, and Benjamin HALLUM, "Zosimus Arabus: The Reception of Zosimos of Panopolis in the Arabic/Islamic World", 246.
149 See L. PRINCIPE, *Secrets of Nature*, 74–79; and C. G. JUNG's classic work on this topic, *Mysterium Coniunctionis*, trans. R. F. C. HULL., 2nd ed. (Princeton: Princeton University Press, 1970).

FIGURE 6.

*Zosimos and Theosebeia conversing next to a furnace.
From the* TOME OF IMAGES *(Mushaf as-ṣuwar).
Arabic manuscript, thirteenth century.*

FIGURE 7.

Zosimos and Theosebeia depicted bearing the discs of the sun and moon on their heads. From the TOME OF IMAGES *(Mushaf aṣ-ṣuwar). Arabic manuscript, thirteenth century.*

Tome of Images (FIGURES 6–7).[150] Zosimos is painted with a solar symbol over his head, Theosebeia is crowned with the moon, and their interactions represent various aspects of the alchemical work. This is not an authentic Zosimean text, but a later development—a sort of *midrash* on Zosimos's authentic letters to Theosebeia that seeks to explain and elaborate on the nature of their relationship.[151] But the idea of an alchemical *soror mystica*, or even an allegorical marriage of substances, is seemingly not found in Greco-Egyptian alchemy.[152] Although Zosimos and Theosebeia

150 Theodore ABT, ed. *The Book of Images:Mushaf as-suwar by Zosimos of Panopolis, Edition of the Pictures and Introduction*. I follow B. HALLUM's dating of the manuscript to 1270, rather than Abt's date of 1211. See HALLUM, "*The Tome of Images*: An Arabic Compilation of Texts by Zosimos of Panopolis and a Source of the *Turba Philosophorum*", 77.

151 ABT argues that this is an authentic Zosimean text, but it clearly is not. HALLUM gives a good analysis and disputation of ABT's arguments in "The Tome of Images", 79–86.

152 There are descriptions of male and female substances. Zosimos's allegory, *On Excellence*, describes the ordeals of a copper man (*Auth.Mem.* X–XII), and in *Auth.Mem.* XIII.2, he describes the substance *kōmaris* as "the most highly honored feminine power". But these are not allegorized as a marriage of male and female substances. There were certainly religious and philosophical ideas in place in Roman Egypt that could provide fertile ground for imagining this type of soror mystica relationship. For example, Isis and Osiris were both sister and brother and wife and husband, and their religious drama of death, separation, union, and rebirth (at least with regard to Osiris) factors prominently in Zosimean alchemy. Zosimos is well-versed in Platonic philosophy, and Plato developed ideas about the eroticism of knowledge and taught about sublimating and transforming erotic energy into desire for universal truth, goodness, and beauty. Zosimos is also a devotee of Thoth, whose consort is Seshat, the goddess of wisdom and writing. In initiatory texts from the House of Life, which were in use during the Greco-Roman period, the male initiate imagines Seshat as both a mother and a lover: he is told to nurse from her breasts, drink from her well of flowing wisdom, and to enter her doorposts/vulva (this text puns on the Egyptian words for nurse, well, and vulva, which sound alike). Through these intimate forms of worship, Seshat nurtures, inspires, and brings insight to the initiate. Similar ideas, though not as overtly sexual, are also found in Hebrew wisdom literature, where Wisdom is personified as an ideal wife and mother, as well as a goddess-like figure—God's first creation—who works beside God like a "master worker", helping him create the world. Despite all of these possibilities, I don't see them being

have a close relationship based on a shared profession and spiritual interests, the nature of this friendship and their work together remains a mystery.

In addition to religious matters, Zosimos's letters to Theosebeia often express a grave concern that she is being influenced by alchemists who are practicing their art in ways that Zosimos thinks is misguided. As we saw in the last chapter, the rival alchemists he worries about most are those who use astrological and "unnatural" methods in their work, but these alchemists are not named.[153] Zosimos also warns Theosebeia not to follow the advice of a priest named Neilos, whom he paints as incompetent: he ridicules Neilos's failed attempt at whitening a lead-copper alloy, for example, and he says that he despises the spiritual ignorance of Neilos's disciples, who have no admiration for the maxim "Know thyself".[154] Zosimos is also dismissive of a young female colleague named Paphnutia, who appears to be studying with Neilos and other "uneducated men", and this has led to mistakes that have harmed her professional reputation; Zosimos is concerned that this will also happen to Theosebeia if she continues to listen to these people.[155] He tells her:

> But you, blessed one, renounce those vain elements that have disturbed your ears [...]. Renounce the company of those who have a blind mind and an overly inflamed imagination. We must pity these people and listen to the language of truth from the mouths of those who

---

employed by Zosimos and Theosebeia or discussed in the alchemical literature. On erotic imagery in the *Book of Thoth*, see JASNOW and ZAUZICH, *Conversations in the House of Life*, op. cit., 100–101, 112–113. On Wisdom as mother, wife, and co-creator in the Hebrew Bible, see *Proverbs* 1–8.

153 Zosimos rails against his rivals and their "unnatural" methods in *Auth. Mem.* 1 (*On Apparatus and Furnaces*) (*Letter Omega*) and CAAG III.51 (*Final Account*).

154 On Neilos's failed experiment, see CAAG III.27.8; on the ignorance of his disciples who fail to understand the saying "know thyself", see CMA, Syr. II.6.31.

155 See CAAG III.27.7–8.

are worthy. These people do not want help; they do not abide being taught by masters, yet they flatter themselves as masters. They claim to be honored for their reasoning, which is vain and void of sense. When we want to teach them the degrees of truth, they do not abide the knowledge of the art and they do not digest it. They desire gold rather than reason. Heated by an extreme madness, they become incapable of reasoning and impatient for wealth. If they were guided by reason, gold would accompany them and be in their power, because reason is the mistress of gold. Whoever attaches himself to reason, who desires and is united to it, will find the gold in front of him, in the midst of the diversions that hide it.[156]

It is uncertain whether all these rivals belonged to the same group, because Zosimos doesn't mention Neilos in conjunction with astrology or "unnatural methods" in either the Greek or Syriac texts.[157] However, Neilos is frequently mentioned in medieval Arabic alchemical manuscripts that appear to contain some authentic works by Zosimos.[158] Here are a few examples from a Zosimean text called *Keys of the Art*:

> As for the followers of Neilos, how far they are from the knowledge of the Art of gold, due to its difficulty for them.

---

156 CAAG III.27.7. My translation.
157 Zosimos rails against his rivals and their "unnatural" methods in *Auth. Mem.* 1 (*On Apparatus and Furnaces—Letter Omega*) and CAAG III.51 (*Final Account*), though none of them are mentioned by name, and in the Greek and Syriac texts where Neilos is mentioned (CAAG III.27.8 and CMA, Syr. II.6.31), there is no discussion of astrology.
158 Bink HALLUM has sufficiently demonstrated that there are sound reasons for thinking these are authentic writings, or that they are closely based on them. Some of the excerpts, which I did not include here, contain overtly Islamic interpolations. Hallum notes this and explains that the rest of the passage is likely to be authentic. See Hallum, "Zosimus Arabus", 220. I've omitted these examples because I think the Islamic overlay makes their authenticity more questionable.

How about Neilos and his followers, whose intellects—both his and his followers'—do not extend as far as reading either the books or the interpretations that were expounded by the sages who came before us?

As for the disciples of Neilos, who wanted us to grant them [knowledge of] the Art, with their lying about it and dissimulation [?], it would be necessary for Neilos to find a sitting place to which he could withdraw to read the books of the sages. For observe how much is collected in them and how far his understanding falls short of them.[159]

As Bink Hallum has shown, these medieval Arabic manuscripts also reveal that new traditions were being developed out of the figures of Neilos and Theosebeia. Neilos is given the role of an arch-nemesis figure, whereas the epistolary correspondence between Zosimos and Theosebeia is transformed into a Hermetic-style dialogue between teacher (Zosimos) and student (Theosebeia); in the *Tome of Images* (described above), their relationship is even used to illustrate aspects of the alchemical work itself.[160] Because we do not have the entire corpus of Zosimos's work, these later developments are of interest because they grow out of earlier, authentic layers. Based on the authentic Arabic fragments, where Neilos is mentioned several times, there is a good chance that Neilos and his disciples are the rival group of alchemists that Zosimos rails against in the Greek letters to Theosebeia, but does not name.

In addition to these colleagues and adversaries, Zosimos mentions other alchemical authors like Agathodaimon, and displays great reverence for past masters of the art like Democritus, Hermes, and Maria the Jewess (ca. second c. CE), who invented various apparatuses and developed advanced distillation tech-

---

159   Book 1, fol. 43b.9; Book 1, fol.47b.2-3; Book 1, fol.47a.10-13. All of these passages are B. HALLUM's translation; the interpolations in square brackets are also Hallum's. See HALLUM, "Zosimus Arabus", 224–225.
160   HALLUM, "Zosimus Arabus", 213–227.

niques.¹⁶¹ Zosimos is an admirer of "Hebrew" traditions of alchemy: there is no question that he was reading texts by Jewish and Christian authors, but it is uncertain whether he was interacting with Jewish or Christian colleagues. There is evidence of Jewish and Christian membership in trade associations in Roman Egypt, including guilds of gold and silversmiths, and in many cases these guilds were linked to particular synagogues.¹⁶² The Jewish population in Egypt had declined between 117–270 CE, in the aftermath of Jewish revolts against Rome, and I have not been able to find solid evidence of a Jewish population in Panopolis in Zosimos's day.¹⁶³ However, there were Christian communities in the Panopolis region. Some of them had been martyred during Diocletian's persecutions in 303; a cult of these regional martyrs is attested in the fourth century.¹⁶⁴ There was a Christian church in Panopolis in the early fourth century, and evidence of a Christian community in the Panopolitan nome circa 300 CE who were corresponding with another Christian community in the Great Oasis.¹⁶⁵ Mid-fourth centu-

161   On Maria the Jewess, see Jack LINDSAY, *Origins of Alchemy in Greco-Roman Egypt*, ch. 9; Raphael PATAI, *The Jewish Alchemists* (Princeton: Princeton University Press, 1994), chs. 5–6; and Naomi JANOWITZ, *Magic in the Roman World: Pagans, Jews, and Christians* (London: Routledge, 2001), ch. 4.
162   On Jewish and Christian participation in trade guilds in Roman Egypt, see Christopher HAAS, *Alexandria in Late Antiquity: Topography and Social Conflict* (Baltimore: John Hopkins University Press, 1997), 59, 236. On trade guilds as official subgroups of synagogues in Egypt, see Philip HARLAND, *Associations, Synagogues and Congregations: Claiming a Place in Ancient Mediterranean Society* (Minneapolis: Augsburg Fortress Press, 2003), 35.
163   See F. DUNAND, "Part II: Ptolemaic and Roman Egypt", in *Gods and Men in Egypt*, 253–260; and Andrew HARKER, "The Jews in Roman Egypt: Trials and Rebellions", in *The Oxford Handbook of Roman Egypt*, 282–286.
164   GEENS, "Panopolis, a Nome Capital in Egypt in the Roman and Byzantine Period (ca. AD 200–600)", 387–389.
165   An ἐκκλεσία is mentioned in *P.Berl.Bork.* III.27; this may be a church, but *ekklesia* can also mean a gathering place, and BORKOWSKI notes that the meaning is further complicated by the bad state of this line of the text (see BORKOWSKI, n.III.27, 72–73). Several people's occupations in this survey are listed as διάκονος, which could mean a deacon of the church; however, *diakonos* can also mean "servant". If this survey predates Constantine's Edict of Milan in 313, that decreases the likelihood that these are references

ry texts mention a Christian "camp" or quarter on the outskirts of Panopolis.¹⁶⁶ So it is indeed possible that Zosimos was in contact with Christians.

One way of identifying Jewish or Christian populations is through onomastic evidence, such as biblical names, or saints' names. When it comes to Greek names, names compounded with *theos* (god) can be indicators of monotheism, though this evidence is less reliable.¹⁶⁷ The name Theosebeia, for example, could point to Jewish or Christian parentage. There are several such names in *P.Berl.Bork.*; the name Maria also appears, which is likely a Jewish or Christian name.¹⁶⁸ If Theosebeia were Christian (and I think she was), this would help explain why Zosimos was so keen to incorporate Jewish and gnostic Christian concepts into his discussions of alchemy. But the fact that there were Christians in the area, and that Zosimos was a learned priest and scribe interested in harmonizing different religious teachings is enough to account for his interest in Jewish and Christian traditions. The influences of Hebrew metallurgy and religious traditions on Zosimos's work are important and complex, and will be discussed more fully in Chapter 4, along with the question of whether Theosebeia was Christian. Suffice it to say that he may have been interacting with Jewish or Christian people, and not just their books, and he is less worried about competition from them than he is from Neilos and his associates.

---

      to Christian buildings or clergy. On the communiques between Christian communities in Panopolis and Kysis in the Great Oasis, see Geens, "Panoplis, a Nome Capital", 391–392.
166 GEENS, "Panopolis, a Nome Capital", 390.
167 GEENS, "Panopolis, a Nome Capital", 371.
168 Ibid., 393–394. The name Maria appears twice in *P.Berl.Bork.*: in 11.29 and XIII.32.

Conclusion

As an artisan-priest, Zosimos's work with precious metals involves worldly and spiritual treasures of the highest value. He and his temple colleagues are making divine statues, ritual vessels, and other decorations for the temple, and their beauty and quality must be fitting for the gods. Panopolis, which is situated near the mines of the Eastern Desert, was a well-known center for goldsmithing and alchemy, and its patron deity, Min, was also a patron deity of goldsmiths and mines. Zosimos was also trained as a scribe and his main responsibilities included the translation and interpretation of ancient metalworking recipes. He indicates that this was difficult work due to the use of ancient and specialized writing systems (e.g., hieroglyphics, hieratic script) and the use of coded language known only to initiates, and it was further complicated by vows of secrecy or deliberate omissions to protect guarded recipes. Zosimos inveighs against those who have obfuscated the ancient recipes, as well as those who style themselves as masters even though they haven't studied the ancient scripts.

The Egyptian principle of *maat*—the natural, ethical and spiritual order of the universe—is strongly reflected in Zosimos's writings, from his advocacy of "natural methods" that work in harmony with nature, to his emphasis on moral behavior and spiritual discipline in alchemical practice. Indeed, upholding *maat* is the primary function of the Egyptian priesthood, expressed in their daily rituals intended to preserve divine cosmic order, and in the very design of the temple itself as a cosmos in miniature.

Although Zosimos's religious approach to alchemy appears to have originated in Egyptian temples, particularly in the practice of god-making, the temple was not the only employment avenue for metalsmiths. Trade guilds, which were gaining in popularity and economic influence in the Roman period, were another professional context where alchemical work could flourish. As we have seen, there was a considerable amount of overlap between metallurgy in temples and trade guilds. Since many priests worked part time, in month long shifts at the temples, it is likely that artisan-priests were also members of guilds. Although some guilds had their own workshops, the temple workshops had larger production sites and more capacity to work with different metals and materials. Since the recipes in the Greco-Egyptian alchemical corpus indicate use of a variety of metals, gems, and dyes, these recipes were likely collected by master craftsmen, either in the temple or the guilds. Research on trade guilds in Roman Egypt indicates that higher ranking craftsmen had the most freedom (particularly if they were goldsmiths) to contract with artisans who specialized in different media, like jewelers, dyers, and metalsmiths, and were also more involved in contract work with the temples.

Zosimos is writing at a time of economic uncertainty and rapid social change. During the first two centuries of Roman rule, the Egyptian priesthood, temples, and temple properties were under imperial authority, but due to economic hardships faced by the empire in the third century, Egyptian temples began to decline because of diminishing resources.[169] Not all temples declined at the same rate, however, and there is some evidence that the temples of Panopolis were holding steady in Zosimos's day.[170] But even so, this general decline was accompanied by other social changes, including increased multiculturalism. These dynamics are reflected in Zosimos's desire to preserve and protect certain Egyptian traditions, as well as to harmonize Egyptian teachings with Hellenistic philosophy, Hebrew metallurgical techniques, and Jewish and Christian religious ideas in order to have wider and more univer-

---

169   On temples declining in third century, see BAGNALL, *Egypt in Late Antiquity*, 267–268; FRANKFURTER, "Histories: Egypt, Later Period", in *Religions of the Ancient World: A Guide*, ed. Sarah Iles JOHNSTON (Cambridge: Harvard University Press, 2004), 160–161; FRANKFURTER, *Religion in Roman Egypt*, 27–30, 200; and ALSTON, *The City in Roman and Byzantine Egypt*, 272–273.

170   See FRANKFURTER, *Religion in Roman Egypt*, 200. P.Berl.Bork. indicates that five percent of Panopolitans were in the priesthood, which Frankfurter claims is a healthy number, but it is difficult to know for certain because this data is incomplete. See also M. MINAS-NERPEL, "Egyptian Temples", op. cit, 377.

sal appeal. Trade guilds, which were based in extended family and community networks, had more room for cultural and religious diversity, whereas the priesthood, for the most part, was a hereditary office and more firmly rooted in Egyptian religious culture. Therefore, Zosimos's synthesis of these different cultural traditions would have been socially and economically advantageous in an era when temple economies were waning and trade guilds were gaining economic power.

Alchemy as a
Spiritual Exercise

Whose right is it, O great gods, to create gods and goddesses in a place where men dare not trespass? […] Is it the right of deaf and blind human beings who are ignorant of themselves and remain in ignorance throughout their lives? The making of the gods and goddesses is your right, it is in your hands; so I beseech you, create, and in your exalted holy of holies may what you yourselves have in your heart be brought about in accordance with your unalterable word. Endow the skilled craftsmen whom you ordered to complete this task with as high an understanding as Ea, their creator.

PRAYER OF ESARHADDON, KING OF ASSYRIA
(upon ordering cult images to be made)
Seventh century BCE[1]

This Mesopotamian prayer raises good questions about the kind of knowledge one must have for so bold a task as the creation of gods. Zosimos, writing nearly a thousand years later in Egypt, echoes some of these sentiments. He says that the philosophers who have made the "preparation" (for the statues) have insisted that it is necessary to have right understanding, which leads him to complain about students who are full of "error and illusion" about these matters: "when the saying 'know thyself' is directed at

---

1   C. Walker and M. B. Dick, "The Induction of the Cult Image in Ancient Mesopotamia: The Mesopotamian *mīs pî* Ritual", in *Born in Heaven, Made on Earth: The Creation of the Cult Image in the Ancient Near East*, ed. M. B. Dick (Winona Lake, IN: Eisenbrauns, 1998), 64–65.

them", he writes, "they show no admiration for these words".[2] The translator of this Syriac Zosimean text, who was most likely Muslim or Christian, refers to the statues as idols and appears to have emended the text in places to condemn the folly of idol worship, making it difficult to discern Zosimos's original meaning.[3] But it is clear, at least, that Zosimos believes that philosophical insight, especially self-knowledge, is fundamental to the work. I think he would agree wholeheartedly with the Assyrian king that craftsmen engaged in the art of god-making should be self-aware and strive to partake in the divine knowledge of the creator.

Zosimos's approach to alchemy emphasizes virtue, purification, and contemplation of the divine and natural order, all of which are traditional components of Egyptian religion and philosophy, and demonstrate his strong commitment to upholding *maat* (the divine order that gives rise to cosmic and social order). But this approach also resonates more broadly with late ancient notions of the philosophical way of life. As Pierre Hadot explains:

> Several testimonies show that from the beginning of the second century A.D., philosophy was conceived of as an ascending spiritual itinerary which corresponded to a hierarchy of the parts of philosophy. Ethics ensured the soul's initial purification; physics revealed that the world has a transcendent cause and thus encouraged philosophers to search for incorporeal realities; metaphysics, or theology (also called "epoptics", because, as in the

---

[2] CMA Syr. II.7.30–31. Translations from the Syriac texts are mine, based on Duval's French, unless otherwise indicated.

[3] In CMA Syr. II.7.30, Zosimos praises an artist named Pabapnidos who invented a method for coloring metals blue. Yet there is a scribal note in the margins that says "all the passers-by admire the idol and praise the sculpted object, made by Pabapnidos, son of Sitos, the imposter". In 7.31, he seems to be talking about how people marveling at the vivid colors mistakenly think that they are due to supernatural causes, rather than the skill of the artist. I think this is the distinction he is trying to make, but there are scribal glosses to make it seem as if Zosimos is condemning idol worship.

Mysteries, it is the endpoint of initiation), ultimately entails the contemplation of God.[4]

Hadot has argued that for the ancients, philosophy involved a complete change of lifestyle, "a conversion of one's entire being", and included many kinds of spiritual exercises aimed at modifying and transforming the self.[5] This concept of spiritual exercises is a useful framework for understanding Zosimos's approach to alchemy, or as he often calls it, the sacred art (*hiera technē*). He teaches that the sacred art should be practiced in both a "corporeal" and "spiritual" manner, and along with his instructions for chemical recipes and techniques, he prescribes spiritual exercises for cultivating virtue, purifying the soul, and for facilitating the soul's ascent to the divine realms. Some of these exercises involve contemplating the ways that metals reveal the divine presence within nature and how they mirror human psychological states; others involve quietly examining the soul and quelling the passions. In his allegory, *On Excellence*, Zosimos gives a fascinating depiction of how the corporeal and spiritual aspects of alchemy intertwine in the art of god-making. Through a closer examination of his writings and the spiritual exercises he prescribes, Zosimos's philosophical approach to the sacred art will become more evident.

VIRTUE AND THE PURIFICATION OF THE SOUL

"In every art, there are ways to falsify pure things", Zosimos writes in *On Mercury*.[6] For example, artisans skilled in the coloration of metals can easily make adulterated gold pass for real gold. Zosimos says that there are tests for determining the quality or purity of all manner of things, and quips that "[a]ll craftsmen know how to use

---

4   Pierre HADOT, *What is Ancient Philosophy?* (Cambridge, MA: Belknap Press, 2002), 153–154.
5   Ibid, 3.
6   CMA, Syr. II.9.28.

them when they buy, but when they sell, they swear on their heads that they don't how to test them".[7] What is true for products is also true for philosophy: "the true philosophers and the corrupters are next to each other", he warns.[8] Zosimos complains in several of his writings that out of greed, spite, and jealousy, craftsmen have falsified or omitted pertinent information from the alchemical recipes.[9] Hence, it is necessary to examine things both corporeally and spiritually, so that one can more accurately assess product quality as well the quality of instruction one receives from books and teachers. As he writes in *On Iron*:

> If you are impure, you won't work well, you won't understand, and you won't hear others (teachers). Your whole heart will be enlightened by the knowledge of these words. A person, via easy work, can teach you the work of a child. One must understand, or listen to what others have said. A distinguished man understands something on his own. An excellent man has confidence in the teacher who teaches him well. But he who doesn't understand and who doesn't listen to what others tell him, is a lost man. Plato has stated these precepts in another way. Watch that Isdos (Petesis?) does not rebuke your idleness and stupidity, and after him, Plato. Know that you will be tested for spiritual and corporeal things until you attain perfection, acquiring patience with purity and love (of the art); when the corporeal arts are abandoned, then you will find (what you desire). Therefore, don't stop meditating and working, and you will understand. When you ask questions, listen to what you are told. Do not blaspheme when you don't know so-

---

7   CMA, Syr. II.9.29.
8   CMA, Syr. II.9.28.
9   See, for example, CAAG III.51 (*Final Account*); Auth.Mem. 1 (*On Apparatuses and Furnaces—Letter Omega*); CMA, Syr. II.6 (*On Copper*); and CMA, Syr. II.8 (*On Tin*).

mething, but confess your ignorance and have patience when you don't succeed.[10]

The quotation opens with a statement about how purity is necessary so that one can attain understanding of both corporeal and spiritual matters. Feigning understanding is akin to blasphemy; it is a form of self-deceit as well as an attempt to deceive others. Meditation is the key to practicing alchemy, or the sacred art (*hiera technē*) in a spiritual manner, for this purifies the soul of the passions that cloud understanding. In *Final Account*, Zosimos recommends a meditative exercise to Theosebeia that involves sitting quietly at home and calming the activities of the body and the passions of the soul, such as desire, pleasure, anger, and grief.[11] He says that through this exercise, the daimons will be repelled and the omnipresent divine will appear.[12] Divesting the soul of its passions is an exercise in self-awareness and self-mastery. The goal is to reach the passionless state of *apatheia*, where the higher, rational soul is free from material attachments and unmoved by the distracting impulses of the lower, irrational parts of the soul. Divine presence can be experienced more fully in this apathetic state.

As Hadot observes, in ancient philosophy "[t]he movement of concentration upon and attention to oneself turns out to be closely related to the opposite movement of dilation and expansion by which the "I" finds its place within the perspective of the All".[13] In some of the philosophies that influenced Zosimos—namely Platonism, Hermetism, and Gnosticism—the purification of the soul achieved through meditation is associated with the soul's ascent to the noetic realms beyond the cosmos; mastery of the self involves rising above one's own nature, rising above worldly concerns, and ultimately transcending nature altogether. In Plato's *Phaedrus*, for example, the purification of the soul is associated with the ascent

---

10   CMA, Syr. II.11.21.
11   CAAG III.51.8. See my discussion of this passage at the end of chapter 2.
12   Ibid.
13   HADOT, *What is Ancient Philosophy?*, 202.

of the soul through the heavens. The rational soul is described as a charioteer, whose mastery of the two horses, which are the passions and appetites of the soul, enables the soul to journey to the realm of the fixed stars where the gods reveal the divine reality beyond the cosmos.[14] As the soul ascends, it apprehends the divine more clearly, and this higher, holier vantage point brings new wisdom about the self and the world. In Zosimos's view, the end goals of corporeal alchemy will always fall short without the spiritual understanding that both illuminates and transcends the physical world. Only spiritual work can lead to perfection, and the rewards of virtue, self-control, and spiritual and scientific wisdom far exceed those of the corporeal work alone.

Contemplating nature as a spiritual exercise

Many ancient priests and philosophers devoted time to investigating the workings of nature. As Hadot argues, this type of research often had a spiritual dimension: physics was seen as a spiritual exercise. Citing passages from well-known thinkers from the major philosophical schools of the Greco-Roman period—Platonists, Aristotelians, Stoics, and Epicureans—Hadot demonstrates that across the board, philosophers believed that contemplating the natural world could lead to a type of mystical experience, where the soul expands beyond the limits of the self and comprehends the whole of reality at once.[15] Thinking about cosmic patterns and rhythms was part of the practice of soul-purification. For example, Marcus Aurelius, the second-century Stoic emperor, writes: "Survey the circling stars, as though you yourself were in mid-course with them. Often picture the changing and re-changing dance of the elements. Visions of this kind purge away the dross of our earth-bound life".[16]

---

14   See PLATO, *Phædrus* 246B–247E.
15   HADOT, *What is Ancient Philosophy?*, 205.
16   MARCUS AURELIUS, *Meditations* 7.47. Trans. Maxwell STANIFORTH.

The manner in which Zosimos contemplates the metals can be seen as a spiritual exercise that culminates in an experience of the One in All. Even in some of his more mundane recipes he expresses awe at the chemical reactions he observes and refers to these as "incommunicable mysteries".[17] In *On Lime*, he describes a whitening agent as "the stone that is not a stone, the one that is unknowable and known by all, the one that is unworthy of honor and most honored, the one that is not a gift while being a divine gift".[18] These paradoxes illustrate that even an inanimate and seemingly insignificant material substance partakes in divine reality. In the following passage, titled *On the Divine Water*, he reflects upon the properties of mercury and explains how this metal is an expression of the divine within nature:

> This is the divine and great mystery, the object of research, because this is the All. Two natures, [but] only one substance, because one attracts the other and one dominates the other. This is the silvery water, the hermaphrodite, which constantly flees, which hurries toward the proper realities; it is the divine water that all have ignored, whose nature is difficult to conceive. Indeed, it is not a metal, nor a water always in movement, nor a body [solid], because one cannot seize it. It is the universal in all things, because it at once possesses life and spirit, as well as a destructive power. The one who understands it possesses both gold and silver.[19]

Zosimos describes how the properties of mercury reflect the "universal in all things". This reflects a belief that the macrocosm is related to—and reflected in—the microcosm. He sees the whole of reality reflected in a particular substance, and views the metals

---

17 See, for example, *On Lime* (Auth.Mem. XIII.1)
18 Auth.Mem. XIII.1. He also refers to this substance, which is used to whiten pearls, as the "Mithraic mystery".
19 Auth.Mem. v. My translation.

as *synthēmata* ("signs"), or signatures, of the divine, which reveal the divine presence in the world. *Synthēmata* can be understood as visible properties of certain objects that reveal hidden sympathies to other objects and to the divine power that unites them as an interconnected whole.[20] For example, sunflowers, lions, roosters, and gold are all divine signatures of the sun, and of solar gods. One can contemplate these material objects and thereby gain access to the divine principle that unites them.

In *On Electrum*, Zosimos shows Theosebeia that by meditating upon electrum, one can travel a path of correspondences that leads through the cosmos and culminates in a vision of the divine mind. He begins with a story of how electrum, an alloy of gold and silver, was invented by Alexander the Great as a means of warding off thunderbolts that were plaguing the Empire to the point of near-destruction. Alexander had coins made from electrum and scattered them throughout the empire, which solved the problem, and that is why people to this day wear amulets made of electrum to protect them from lightning.[21] In alchemical writings, electrum corresponds to the planet Jupiter; Zosimos alludes to this by associating electrum with Zeus (Jupiter), god of the thunderbolt. He explains that people still wear talismans of electrum to ward off lightning, and that mirrors made of electrum are believed to ward off all pains. When one gazes into the electrum mirror, it gives him "the idea to examine and purify himself, from his head to the tips of his nails".[22] He then takes the symbolism of the mirror to a deeper level. The purpose of the mirror is not "for a man to contemplate himself materially", he says, but should be understood as a symbol of spiritual contemplation:

---

20   In FOUCAULT's discussion of pre-modern understandings of the universe as an "interplay of resemblances", he describes the role of signatures as visible signs of invisible similitudes. See Michel FOUCAULT, *The Order of Things: An Archaeology of the Human Sciences* (New York: Vintage Books, 1994), 26.
21   CMA, Syr. II.12.3
22   Ibid.

The mirror represents the divine mind; when the soul looks at itself, it sees the shameful things that are in it, and it rejects them; it makes its stains disappear and remains without blame. When it is purified, it imitates and follows the Holy Spirit as a model; it becomes a spirit itself; it possesses calmness and constantly returns itself to this superior state, where it knows (the divine) and where it is known. So having become stainless, it gets rid of its own bonds and those that are shared with the body, and it (rises) toward the Omnipotent. Indeed, what is the philosophical saying? "Know thyself". This is indicated by the spiritual and intellectual mirror. What then is this mirror, other than the divine and primordial Mind?[23]

Ultimately, one has to make the ascent through the cosmos in order to gaze into the mirror of the Divine Mind, because this mirror is located above the cosmos, where it serves as a mirror reflecting the divine presence within the universe:

This mirror is positioned above the Seven Doors [planetary spheres], toward the west, so that the one who watches there sees the east, where the intellectual light shines, which is above the veil. That is why it is also placed next to the south, above all the doors that are called the Seven Heavens, above this visible world, above the twelve houses [of the zodiac] and the Pleiades, which are the world of the thirteen. Above them exists the Eye of the invisible senses, the Eye of the spirit, which is present there and in all places. One sees in this perfect mind, in whose power everything is found, from now until death. We have reported this, because we have been driven there while talking about the mirror of electrum, that is to say the mirror of the mind.[24]

23 Ibid. Translated by Shannon GRIMES and Berekia DIVANGA.
24 Ibid.

In this meditation on electrum, Zosimos leads the reader from a popular mythical story of the metal's origins, to a discussion of how talismans and mirrors made of electrum are commonly thought to ward off disaster and pain, to a philosophical interpretation of the mirror as a means to "know thyself", and finally, to the noetic realm of the Divine Mind. These correspondences form a ladder of ascent, or a connecting bridge, between the material and spiritual worlds. For Zosimos, to deeply contemplate the nature of metals is to contemplate the divine mysteries that nature holds. Electrum is not only a substance used in making mirrors and talismans, it is a substance that reflects the divine presence in all things.

Zosimos also views letters of the alphabet as *synthēmata* that can reveal the cosmic mysteries.[25] In *Apparatuses and Furnaces (Letter Omega)*, he explains that omega (ω) has both a material and an immaterial significance:

> Round Omega is the bipartite letter, the one that in terms of material language belongs to the seventh planetary zone, that of Kronos. For in terms of the immaterial it is something else altogether, something inexplicable, which only Nikotheos the hidden knows. In material terms Omega is what he calls "Ocean...the birth and seed of all gods".[26]

In this same work, Zosimos discusses the mystical significance of the Hebrew name Adam:

---

25   *Synthēmata* do not have to be material "stuff" in the strict sense of the word. Divine names, music, images, and numbers could all be divine signatures. See Gregory SHAW's discussions of various kinds of *synthēmata* in the second half of *Theurgy and the Soul* (University Park: Pennsylvania State University Press, 1995).

26   *Auth.Mem.*1.1. Howard JACKSON's translation, from *Zosimos of Panopolis on the Letter Omega*, ed. and trans. Howard M. JACKSON (Atlanta: Scholar's Press, 1978). Nikotheos was a well-known Gnostic, mentioned (unfavorably) by Porphyry in his *Life of Plotinus*.

So, then, the first man among us is named Thouth, and among them Adam [...]. [T]he name they refer to him by is symbolic, composed of four elements from the whole sphere. For the letter A of his name signifies the ascendant east, and air; the letter D ‹...› signifies the descendant west, and earth, which sinks down because of its weight; ‹...›; and the letter M ‹...› signifies the meridian south, and the ripening fire in the midst of these bodies, the fire belonging to the middle, fourth planetary zone.²⁷

The alliteration of the first letters of these words and their associations (e.g., alpha/ascendant/air)—which are present in the original Greek—seems to be a mnemonic aid for contemplating the various correspondences. Adam is the cosmic man, and the letters of his name connect the human to the four elements and the four cardinal points of the zodiac. The letter M corresponds to the realm of the sun, the fire "in the midst of these bodies". Zosimos explains that Adam is the name of the flesh, the "visible outer mould", but that the "Man within him, the Man of spirit, has a proper name as well as a common one".²⁸ As is the case with the letter omega, only the initiates who perceive the immaterial reality within the divine signatures know this secret name. Zosimos says that the common name of the spiritual Adam is *Phōs*, or light; therefore the solar fire "ripening" in the midst of the cosmos is like the light of spirit ripening within the human being. In Stoic and Hermetic literature, the divine is described as an ethereal, fiery substance that permeates all things, so the fire "in the midst of these bodies" is also the divine fire. By reflecting upon these *synthēmata*,

27   *Auth.Mem.*1.9, trans. JACKSON. There is a lacuna in the text, so the interpretation of the second letter A is missing. This second A would be *arktos*, the northern point of the zodiac, which is associated with water. For an interesting study of various correlations between the name Adam and the four directions in late antiquity, see Dominique CERBELAUD, "Le nom d'Adam et les points cardinaux : recherches sur un theme patristique", *Vigiliæ Christianæ* 38.3 (1984): 285-301.
28   *Auth.Mem.*1.10, trans. JACKSON.

Zosimos makes connections between the human, the cosmos, and the divine, and in doing so, he experiences the divine power that is immanent in the world.[29]

This spiritual exercise of contemplating the metals and their symbolic correspondences appears to be one of Zosimos's methods for working in a spiritual and corporeal manner simultaneously. Observing the properties of metals and chemical reactions provides the alchemist with ample opportunity to reflect upon nature and the divine, and thereby elevate the human spirit. Some of these exercises are reminiscent of the ladder of ascent that Plato describes in his *Symposium*, in which Socrates conveys how the priestess, Diotima, initiated him into the mysteries of love. Diotima instructed Socrates to begin his meditations by focusing on physical beauty, and from there progress to the beauty of people's activities, and then move on to intellectual beauty, and finally, at the top of the ladder, one experiences the eternal source of all beauty.[30] Progression up the ladder involves a movement from the physical to the spiritual, from the particular to the universal. Zosimos exhibits a similar anagogic movement in his thought: every physical substance, every written letter, every household object has a spiritual essence and partakes of divine reality. He believes that one has to make an effort to go beyond one's everyday perceptions, including popular religious beliefs, in order to apprehend the noetic spiritual realities, which are in this world, but not of this world.

Zosimos wants his students to comprehend the divinity of nature, but there are also occasions when he expresses a negative, pessimistic view of materiality. This is a tension in his work, perhaps most evident in his famous allegory, *On Excellence*. I will turn now to a close reading of this text, in which technical and religious

---

29 Patricia Cox MILLER interprets these passages from Zosimos and comes to this conclusion in her chapter, "In Praise of Nonsense", in *Classical Mediterranean Spirituality*, ed. A.H. ARMSTRONG (New York: Crossroad, 1986), 496.
30 See PLATO, *Symposium*, 211C.

concepts are closely intertwined and expressed in violent images of sacrifice and death. Zosimos draws much of his imagery from Egyptian mortuary texts and traditions, which provides important context for understanding the vacillation between positive and negative portrayals of matter in this and his other works.

Alchemy and sacrifice in 'On excellence'

Zosimos's allegory of the alchemical opus, Peri aretē, is known by many names. Berthelot and Ruelle, the first to translate this work into French, use the traditional interpretation of αρετη (aretē) and call it "On Virtue". In English it is customarily referred to as "The Visions of Zosimos", the title given to it by F. S. Taylor, who was the first to translate it into English. Readers of C. G. Jung's interpretations of alchemy will know it as Zosimos's "Treatise Concerning the Art". But I prefer to follow Michèle Mertens's translation of aretē as "excellence", because I think it best captures both the spiritual and technical excellence that Zosimos emphasizes in his writings.[31]

This allegory is styled as a series of dreams in which a narrator is dreaming that he is inside the alchemical vessel with the metals, which are personified, and are undergoing a series of sacrifices and "punishments". The imagery is violent and grotesque, giving the impression that the narrator is trapped in a nightmare from which he cannot escape. But when the symbolism is decoded it becomes evident that this text is describing a spiritual purification, both for the metals and for the alchemist.

Alchemy is portrayed as a kind of sacrificial rite in this allegory. This violent sacrificial interpretation is found nowhere else in Zosimos's writings, so I think it is an important exegetical key.

---

31 See BERTHELOT and RUELLE, CAAG III.1; F. S. TAYLOR, "Translation of 'The Visions of Zosimos'", Ambix I (1937–38): 88–92; C. G. JUNG, Alchemical Studies (Princeton: Princeton University Press, 1967), 59; and MERTENS, Auth.Mem.x.

Although this text abounds in violent imagery, it was written at a time when the ritual killing of animals, once a mainstay of ancient religious practice, was beginning to wane in favor of more non-violent, spiritualized forms of sacrifice. This shift was a pan-Mediterranean phenomenon, fueled in part by changes in Jewish and Christian conceptions of sacrifice that began in 70 CE, after the destruction of the Second Temple. Prior to that time, it was customary for Jews to offer sacrifices at the Temple, but without the Temple, sacrificial rites could no longer be performed. These were replaced, in part, with a greater emphasis on scriptural study and doing good works as a means of atoning for one's sins and uniting with god. Early Christians, on the other hand, considered Jesus's death to be the fulfillment of sacrificial laws; Jesus offered himself as the ultimate sacrifice, and therefore temple sacrifices were no longer required. Sacrifice was viewed as adhering to the "letter" rather than the "spirit" of the law, although, as Guy Stroumsa has noted, Christianity in effect remained a sacrificial religion; their concepts of sacrifice just become more spiritualized and symbolized in the ritual of the eucharist.[32]

The spiritualization of sacrifice was also a trend among philosophers, who were promoting "intellectual sacrifices" such as contemplation and divesting the soul of its passions as the most appropriate offerings for the highest god. Porphyry (ca. 233–304 CE) is the most famous example of this. Porphyry rejected the practice of animal sacrifice, as did several philosophers before him, on the grounds that it is morally wrong to kill animate creatures.[33] In his treatise *De abstentia*, Porphyry delivers a series of arguments

---

32 Guy STROUMSA, *The End of Sacrifice: Religious Transformations in Late Antiquity* (Chicago: University of Chicago Press, 2009), 74.
33 Pythagoras, Empedocles, and Theophrastus are all cited by Porphyry. These philosophers also advocated vegetarianism for the same moral reason. Porphyry doesn't cite his teacher, Plotinus, as an example, though in his biography of Plotinus, he mentions that Plotinus was a vegetarian and refused to take medicines made from animal products. He probably objected to animal sacrifice as well. See Gillian CLARK's discussion in her introduction to PORPHYRY's *On Abstinence from Killing Animals* (Ithaca:

ALCHEMY AS A SPIRITUAL EXERCISE   129

against animal sacrifice along with thoughts on how one should substitute for this practice. He condones offerings of non-animate materials, such as grains and honey, to the local gods, but "to the god who rules over all", he says, "we shall offer nothing perceived by the senses, either by burning or in words".[34] Sacrifices should reflect the gifts given by the gods, so therefore it is appropriate for farmers to offer the first fruits of their harvests, but philosophers should offer their thoughts.[35] Porphyry says that philosophical sacrifice is "fulfilled in dispassion of the soul and contemplation of the god".[36] "For Porphyry", adds Stroumsa, "it is the philosopher who is the true priest of the supreme god. He serves this god, above all, by his temperance, his *sophrosyne*, which allows him to approach god with a pure body and soul. The real temple is the sage's thought; the sage transforms his heart into an altar upon which reigns the real statue of god, the sage's intellect".[37] Similar concepts are found in the Egyptian Hermetic literature, where thanksgivings and hymns of praise, as well as silent contemplation, are portrayed as sacrificial offerings to the divine.[38] Along with silent contemplation, Porphyry says that the objects of one's thoughts also make for a proper sacrifice. He claims that Pythagoreans offer numbers and geometrical figures to the gods, and the gods are so pleased by this that in return, they offer their divine help with anything that needs to be investigated.[39]

Zosimos appears to have adopted these philosophical notions of sacrifice.[40] The sacrificial offerings in Zosimos's allegory are polysemous, as I will demonstrate, but they ultimately repre-

Cornell University Press, 2000), 7–11.
34   *On Abstinence*, 2.34. Translated by G. Clark.
35   Ibid.
36   Ibid.
37   STROUMSA, 61
38   See *Corpus Hermeticum* 1.31 and XIII.17–21 (trans. Brian COPENHAVER). See also FOWDEN's discussion of Hermetic notions of intellectual sacrifice in *The Egyptian Hermes*, 147–148.
39   *On Abstinence*, 2.36
40   Zosimos refers to Porphyry in CAAG III.32, though here he discusses Porphyry's views on substances, not on sacrifice.

sent the act of meditation, the offering of one's *thoughts* to god, as well as one's *research*; Zosimos offers his metals in the same way that Porphyry describes the Pythagoreans offering up their numbers to the divine. This interpretation of sacrifice as meditation is consistent with the emphasis he places on meditative practices—such as sitting quietly and calming the passions, as well as the contemplation of metals as divine signatures that reflect and reveal the mysteries of creation, the One and the All. He imagines the purification of the soul as a spiritual ascent through the planetary spheres to the noetic realms beyond the cosmos. This is a journey in which materiality—including the passions, which are fueled by cosmic daimons and thus belong to the material realm—needs to be transcended. Just as the dross needs to be burned away in order to purify and transform the metals, so the appetitive and emotional attachments of the soul need to be transcended and transformed.

On Excellence is divided into three lessons, and the entire work is styled as a series of dreams, five in all. Upon awakening after each of the dreams, which are full of violent imagery, the narrator either understands some aspect of the chemical operations taking place, or arrives at a deeper understanding of nature. The dreams reflect the "violence" done to the metals as they are fired and treated with corrosive substances. References to the torture and suffering of the metals in Hades has precedents in Greco-Egyptian alchemical literature, and some of this likely derives from the Egyptian statue-making ritual called the Opening of the Mouth, in which the "violence" done to the statue during the manufacturing process—smelting, chiseling, engraving, and so forth—is acknowledged with horror by the artisan-priests, who promise to protect the divine statue from further harm and express hope that they will be forgiven.[41] But Zosimos amplifies the violent imagery

---

41 See David LORTON, "The Theology of Cult Statues in Ancient Egypt", 155–158; 174–178. Violence is an important theme in his ritual. The opening of the mouth ritual is performed by other ancient Near Eastern cultures, as well. See WALKER and DICK, "The Induction of the Cult Image in Ancient Mesopotamia: The Mesopotamian *mīs pî* Ritual", op.cit.

to a greater degree. He draws his sacrificial imagery explicitly from the Opening of the Mouth ritual and mortuary texts and rituals.[42] The narrative sequence in this allegory is chaotic, which is typical of dreams, but also meant to convey the fear and confusion of souls as they confront chaos and death in their journey through the underworld (the Duat). Since the metals are personified in this text and often change into one another and fuse with the identity of the alchemist, it can be difficult to keep track of the slippery cast of characters. For the sake of clarity, I will refer to the dreaming alchemist-narrator as "Zosimos".

'On excellence': lesson one

In the opening lines of Lesson One, Zosimos states his alchemical premises for the reader:

> The composition of waters, the movement, growth, removal, and restitution of corporeal nature, the separation of the spirit from the body, and the fixation of the spirit on the body are not due to foreign natures, but to one single nature reacting on itself, a single species, such as the hard bodies of metals and the moist juices of plants.
>
> And in this system, single and of many colors, is comprised a research, multiple and varied, subordinated to lunar influences and to the rhythms of time, which rule the end and the increase according to which the nature transforms itself.[43]

---

42 On the connection of alchemy to Egyptian mortuary traditions, see D. E. A. BURNHAM, "Explorations into the Alchemical Idiom of the Pyramid Texts", *Discussions in Egyptology* 60 (2004): 11–20.

43 F. S. TAYLOR's translation, *The Alchemists*, 57.

From a religious perspective, these opening lines evoke the transformative powers of death and regeneration that are responsible for the ongoing process of creation. In Egyptian religious thought, the gods create the world anew each day; every sunset is a death, and every sunrise a rebirth.[44] The science of nature, as Zosimos sees it, is essentially a study of the divine process of transformation. From a technical standpoint, the language of "spirits" (πνεύματος, *pneumatos*) and "bodies" (σώματος, *sōmatos*) refers to the separation of volatile substances from their metallic bodies, probably by means of distillation, and to fixing colors—which are also known as "spirits" in alchemical terminology—upon a substance. Zosimos insists that these processes are accomplished by a single nature acting upon itself, which is the fundamental nature, or primal matter, that manifests as the four elements and transforms in accordance with cosmic rhythms.[45]

At this point, Zosimos enters into a dream and sees a sacrificing priest (ἱερουργόν, *hierourgon*) presiding over an altar shaped like a phial (φιάλη, *phialē*), which is a technical term for the dome-shaped covers of various distillatory apparatuses, including the *kērotakis*.[46] He tells Zosimos that he had been sacrificed earlier that morning and has survived an "intolerable violence":

---

44   See HORNUNG, *Idea Into Image*, 49, 51.
45   PLATO argued that the four elements are not separate units, as EMPEDOCLES had proposed, because they easily change into one another; rather, they are four primary qualities of a single, fundamental nature (or primal matter). ARISTOTLE shared this view. See A.J. HOPKINS, *Alchemy: Child of Greek Philosophy*, 17–18, 22; and PLATO, *Timaeus* 49–50. Scholars of ancient alchemy often interpret concepts in terms of Greco-Roman scientific theories, but it should be noted that the idea of "one nature" had been a hallmark of Egyptian thought for millenia. See Henri FRANKFORT, et al, *Before Philosophy: The Intellectual Adventure of Ancient Man* (New York: Penguin Books, 1974 [1946]), 71–80.
46   TAYLOR translates this as a "bowl-shaped altar", but MERTENS preserves the technical term in her translation. See *Auth.Mem.* x, n. 6. In her footnote, MERTENS identifies the phial with the *kērotakis*, which is probably the device represented in this allegory, though in ancient alchemical illustrations, the covers or lids of several apparatuses are labeled as *"phialē"*. See the illustrations in BERTHELOT, CAAG, vol. 1, ch. 5, and in the introduction and appendix of MERTENS, *Zosime de Panopolis*.

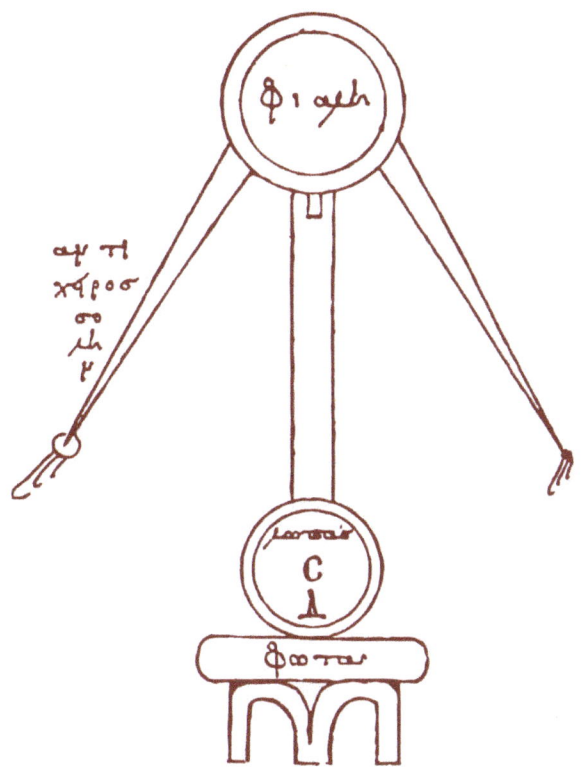

Figure 8. THE PHIALĒ

An alchemical apparatus from the
CHRYSOPOEIA OF CLEOPATRA *(Codex Marcianus 299)*
Greek Manuscript, tenth–eleventh centuries.

134   CHAPTER THREE

> For one came headlong in the morning, dismembering me with a sword, and tearing me asunder according to the rigor of harmony. And flaying my head with the sword which he held fast, he mingled my bones with my flesh and burned them in the fire of the treatment, until I learned by the transformation of the body to become a spirit.[47]

As the priest speaks these words, his eyes fill with blood and he begins gnawing off his skin and vomiting his own flesh. Clearly this is no ordinary sacrifice. Zosimos awakens from this terrifying vision and says, "Is this not the situation of the waters?"[48] The waters are later identified as white and yellow sulfurous (or divine) waters.[49]

He falls asleep again and dreams he is at the phial-shaped altar, where an endless number of people are submerged in boiling waters, wailing in pain. A little "razor-working man" (ξυρουργὸν ἀνθρωπάριον, *xyrourgon anthrōparion*) appears and explains to Zosimos that the spectacle that he is witnessing "is the entrance, the exit, and the transformation".[50] He continues: "This is the place of the operation called embalming (ταριχείας, *taricheias*). Those who wish to attain excellence enter here and become spirits, fleeing from the body".[51] Zosimos asks him if he is a spirit, and the man

47   TAYLOR, 57.
48   Ibid.
49   He identifies the white and yellow waters at the end of the second dream of Lesson 1. The frequent slippage in alchemical terminology between technical and religious ideas is at play here, for the Greek word for sulfur, *theion*, also means "divine".
50   TAYLOR omits the razor-working man's statement about the entrance, exit, and transformation, but it is present in the French translations by BERTHELOT and MERTENS.
51   Adapted from TAYLOR's translation, 58. He translates the word *taricheias* as both preserving and embalming. Compare with LIDDELL and SCOTT's *Greek-English Lexicon*, where *taricheia* refers to embalming as well as to methods of preserving food, such as pickling, salting, or smoking. BERTHELOT and MERTENS translate this term as *macération*, which means steeping or soaking, as well as mortification. Their translation fits well

replies that he is "a spirit and a guardian of spirits".[52] Then a copper man appears with a lead writing tablet in his hand, and counsels the people "under punishment" in the boiling waters "to calm themselves", and to "keep their eyes upward and their mouths open until their grapes are grown".[53] Zosimos then realizes that the copper man and the sacrificing priest are one and the same.

When Zosimos awakens from this second dream—the last in Lesson One—he understands cosmic unity, among other things. Before I address these revelations, it will be helpful to examine the technical and religious significance of the dream imagery encountered thus far in order to give a sense of how the corporeal and spiritual aspects of alchemy are overlaid in this text.

The technical procedure alluded to in this allegory is for coloring a copper-lead alloy, probably using a *kērotakis*. At the end of this lesson, Zosmius writes: "[T]he priest, the man of copper, whom you see seated in the spring and gathering his color, do not regard him as a man of copper; for he has changed the color of his nature and become a man of silver. If you wish, after a little time, you will have him as a man of gold".[54] Zosimos is probably referring to the *kērotakis* procedure for coloring alloys gold. This process effects a sequence of color transmutations—blackening, whitening, yellowing, and sometimes reddening—which agrees with Zosimos's statement that the copper-lead alloy is first colored silver (whitened), then gold (yellowed). In Lesson Two, the razor-working man is clothed in a red robe, which could indicate the reddening stage. According to A.J. Hopkins, the initial stage of the *kērotakis* process involves roasting a copper-lead alloy with sulfur. The sulfur vaporizes and "attacks" the metal, corroding it until it becomes a blackened, cinder-like mass.[55] The blackened alloy is

> with the imagery in the text, but I think that Zosimos's intent is to evoke the imagery of embalming practices, which of course are an important part of Egyptian mortuary traditions.

52 TAYLOR, 58.
53 Adapted from TAYLOR's translation, 58.
54 TAYLOR, 59.
55 A.J. Hopkins, "A Study of the Kerotakis Process as Given by Zosimus and

then purified by removing the excess sulfur with an agent known as "sulfur water", which is a solution of sulfur and lime powders dissolved in vinegar.[56] The whitening and yellowing of the alloy is then accomplished by treating it with various other ingredients, including mercury, or silver and gold leaf dissolved in an arsenic solution.[57] The white and yellow waters mentioned by Zosimos could refer to the "sulfur water", or to the silver and gold arsenic solutions, or both.

Many of images in this allegory are drawn from Egyptian depictions of the lowest levels of the underworld, a hellish region where condemned souls are bound, decapitated and dismembered, and then boiled alive in cauldrons until they are annihilated.[58] The violence in this realm can be likened to the turmoil of the embodied soul, which must be brought into order by controlling the soul's passions and appetites. The priest, as a copper man, tells those seated in the boiling waters to calm themselves, just as Zosimos recommends to Theosebeia that she should calm her body and mind in order to transcend the agitations of the passions. Thus the transformation of the base metals into a gold-colored alloy is likened to the transformation of the baser aspects of one's nature into spiritual "gold". As noted earlier (chapter one), gold, which is incorruptible in the sense that it does not tarnish or rust, was widely regarded in antiquity as a symbol of perfection and of the divine.[59] In Egypt, gold was known as the "flesh of the gods"; even though divine statues were polychromatic and made from several metals, gold had the highest symbolic significance because it is a

---

Later Alchemical Writers", 329–332.

56   Ibid, 335–336. Sulfur is yellow, and lime is white, though HOPKINS relates that when the mixture of these powders is dissolved in vinegar, the resulting solution has a blood-red color.
57   Ibid, 336–338.
58   These underworld images figure most prominently in the *Book of Caves*, a later addition to the New Kingdom collection of funerary texts known as the *Books of the Netherworld*. See Erik HORNUNG, *Idea Into Image*, 99–101.
59   See Dominic JANES's excellent study of the religious symbolism of gold in this period, *God and Gold in Late Antiquity* (Cambridge: Cambridge University Press, 1998).

divine signature of the solar creator god, Re, and of the divine light that permeates the cosmos.[60]

In some Egyptian funerary texts, the condemned souls in the underworld are guarded by knife-wielding demons who stoke the fires of the cauldrons of annihilation. They oversee the destruction of these souls, which prepares them for the state of non-being that is necessary for the creation of new life.[61] Zosimos's razor-working man, who identifies himself as a guardian of spirits, could be an allusion to the knife-wielding demons, though Zosimos paints him in a much friendlier light. He also puts a different spin on the condemned souls: he marvels at the fact that those in the cauldron are still alive.

The razor-working man mentions that the alchemical operation taking place is called "embalming", which links alchemy with Egyptian chemico-religious procedures for preserving corpses; this procedure was performed in order to enable the souls (or subtle bodies, the *ka* and *ba*) of the deceased to journey to the spirit world and to return to the body for nourishment. When a body is embalmed, many of the vital organs are removed, the bodily fluids are drained, and the corpse is placed in natrum, which dries and preserves it; the corpse is then wrapped tightly in linen so that it will remain intact.[62] Embalming rituals involved an Opening of the Mouth ritual similar to the one performed on divine statues, in which the priest spiritually animates the corpse and opens its eyes and mouth so that it will be serviceable to the soul in the afterlife.[63]

---

60 See chapter 1 for a discussion of how alchemy originated in the art of making polychromatic statues of the gods.
61 The knife-wielding demons are also found in the *Book of Caves*. In Roman-era versions of this text, the boiling of the souls in cauldrons is said to prepare them for the state of non-being, which is a prerequisite for new creation. See HORNUNG, *Idea into Image*, 100–101.
62 C. ZIVIE-COCHE, *Gods and Men in Egypt*, 167–168; see also A. ROSALIE DAVID's discussion of mummification procedures in different eras in "Mummification", in *Ancient Egyptian Materials and Technology*, ed. P. T. NICHOLSON and I. SHAW (Cambridge: Cambridge University Press, 2000), 373–375.
63 See Serge SAUNERON, *The Priests of Ancient Egypt*, 109; and Siegfried

CHAPTER THREE

According to Diodorus Siculus (1st c. BCE), the chief embalmer was known as the "ripper-up" of the body, and he was ritually punished by the embalmers for cutting into the body.[64] This is consistent with themes in the ritual performed for newly-made statues of the gods, in which the artisan-priests had to atone for violent acts inflicted upon the statues; these rites enabled the gods to animate the physical statue and to receive sacrifices and impart wisdom in that form.[65] The copper man in Zosimos's allegory alludes to these rituals when he tells the metallic people (future statues) in the boiling waters to "keep their eyes upward and their mouths open until their grapes are grown".[66] In the Opening of the Mouth ceremony for statues, a priest offers the statue a container of grapes, representing the Eye of Horus, and says, "O N., take the Eye of Horus, seize it; if you seize it, it will not pass by".[67] Jan Assmann explains that the grapes are not merely an offering of nourishment, but rather serve to open the mouth and eyes of the statue.[68] In Zosimos's allegory, the grapes have not yet been grown; the eye of Horus is sometimes associated with the moon, which is the alchemical symbol for silver and perhaps here refers to the anticipated whitening stage.[69]

MORENZ, *Egyptian Religion*, 155–158.
64 TEETER, Religion and Ritual in Ancient Egypt, 132.
65 See MORENZ, ibid.; R. BJERRE FINNESTAD, "The Meaning and Purpose of Opening the Mouth in Mortuary Contexts", *Numen* 25.2 (1978): 118–134; D. LORTON, "The Theology of Cult Statues in Ancient Egypt", 147–179; and Jan ASSMANN, *Death and Salvation in Ancient Egypt* (Ithaca, NY: Cornell University Press, 2005), 310–329.
66 TAYLOR, 58.
67 LORTON, 171; ASSMANN, *Death and Salvation in Ancient Egypt*, 316.
68 ASSMANN, ibid. The offering of grapes is followed by an offering of an ostrich feather (symbol of Maat) and a bowl of water, each of which are also accompanied by commands to "take the Eye of Horus".
69 MERTENS notes that "grapes" might also refer to protuberances that emerge on the surface of the metal as it is being treated. See *Zosime de Panoplis*, 221, n. 26. The Eye of Horus can represent both sun and moon. The right eye of Horus is solar, and also known as the Eye of Re; the left eye is lunar and also known as the Eye of Thoth. The divine Eye, or *udjat*, is a popular Egyptian symbol.

Many translators of *On Excellence* have rendered the *hapax* phrase *xyrourgon anthrōparion* as "barber".[70] The symbolism is not all that different from that of the embalming priest. In Zosimos's day barbers performed bloodletting surgeries, which were thought to release impurities from the blood and restore the humors to a healthy, balanced state.[71] The metals in this text are often described as either being drained of blood, or being filled with blood, so blood is synonymous with the "spirit" of the metals, either in the sense of the liquefaction of the solid bodies as they begin to melt and vaporize, or in the sense of a color being imparted to a metallic body. In Egyptian thought, blood was viewed as a connecting force, uniting the parts of the body together and making them come alive.[72] In a similar vein, Hermetists saw the spirit as an intermediary between the physical body and the immaterial soul, an animating force that connects the physical body via the bloodstream.[73] They envisioned the spirit as a sort of ethereal body or garment that serves as a vehicle for the soul as it journeys between the heavens and earth.[74] The barber, who heals the soul by ridding it of its material impurities, also signifies the release of

---

70 See, for example, the translations of BERTHELOT, F. S. TAYLOR, and C.G. JUNG. Zosimos does not use any of the standard Greek terms for barber, and the term ξυρουργὸν doesn't appear elsewhere in Greek literature. There are many *hapax legomena* and rare words in Zosimos's writings. See Mertens's discussion and a list of these words in *Zosime de Panopolis*, 220, 271–273.

71 Peter BRAIN, *Galen on Bloodletting* (Cambridge: Cambridge University Press, 1986), 6–14.

72 ASSMANN, *Death and Salvation in Ancient Egypt*, 28.

73 See also *Corpus Hermeticum* x.13–18, which describes the spirit as being united to the body via the bloodstream, where it "governs" and "moves" the human being.

74 See, for example, CH x.13–18, where the soul is the garment of mind (*nous*), and spirit is the garment of the soul. The purified mind eventually strips its spirit and soul garments and puts on a "fiery tunic" in which it ascends to the heavens. Compare with Neoplatonic concepts of the soul-vehicle (*ochēma pneuma*) in E. R. DODDS, *Proclus: The Elements of Theology* (Oxford: Oxford University Press, 1963), Appendix II.

the spirit from the body so that it may commence its ascent to the noetic realm.[75]

Whether the razor-working man is an embalmer or a barber, or meant to evoke both, he speaks of the spirit fleeing the body, yet he also stands for the preservation of the body. The metallic body is reduced to a blackened corpse, but this prepares it to receive the transforming spirit, or color. As the metal is resurrected, or transformed, more perfect "spiritualized" bodies emerge as silver and gold. The razor-working man, then, provides a sort of reassurance that even though the spirit is separated from the body, the vital links between spirit and body will remain, and when the spirit returns, the body—or one's experience of embodied existence—will be also be transformed by the spiritual ascent.

Indeed, Zosimos expresses a new understanding of embodiment when he awakens from these violent dreams. He has a revelation that nature is an interconnected whole and that all of life is based on reciprocity:

> And I found that I understood it well. And I said that it was fair to speak and fair to listen, and fair to give and fair to receive, and fair to be poor and fair to be rich. For how does the nature learn to give and receive? The copper man gives and the watery stone receives; the metal gives and the plant receives; the stars give and the flowers receive; the sky gives and the earth receives; the thunderclaps give the fire that darts from them. For all things are interwoven and separate afresh, and all things are mingled and all things combine, all things are mixed and

---

75   Compare with the following passage from the *Hermetica*, where reason is compared to a physician who heals the diseases of the soul: "As a good physician, using the cautery and the knife, causes pain to the body overtaken by disease, in the same way mind [reason] causes pain to the soul, withdrawing it from the pleasure that gives rise to every disease of the soul [...] Therefore, the mind that opposes this disease secures good for the soul, just as the physician secures health for the body". CH XII.3 (trans. Brian COPENHAVER).

all unmixed, all things are moistened and all things dried and all things flower and blossom in the altar shaped like a phial.[76]

The act of sacrifice is also based on reciprocity, in the sense that humans give offerings to the divine in thanks for the gift of life that they have received. Sacrifice is a means of honoring the ways in which earthly existence depends on divine grace, and for Zosimos, the sacrifice of metals and the offering of his own thoughts leads him to a deeper understanding of the interdependence of all things. He sees that earthly existence depends upon divine providence, and that all parts of nature depend on other parts for their existence. The cosmic rhythms of reciprocity are reflected in the microcosmic sacrifices occurring in the alchemical vessel, the phial-shaped altar.

The altar itself is another important symbol in this text. On one level it shows that Zosimos truly viewed his work as a "Sacred Art"; he represents the alchemical vessel as an altar in order to emphasize that this work needs to be performed in both a corporeal and a spiritual manner. The altar is always described as being shaped like the phial, or domed cap of the apparatus, which is where the vaporized "spirits" of the metals condense as they are sublimed. The altar also evokes the mixing-bowl of the Demiurge, the divine craftsman. In Plato's *Timæus*, the Demiurge creates the ordered cosmos out of disorderly, chaotic matter.[77] He fashions the divine World Soul in a mixing-bowl, and from the leftover ingredients he creates human souls.[78] In Hermetic literature, the Demiurge is identified as the craftsman of the cosmos and the son of the One God. He is often called the "Divine Mind" and is the equivalent of *nous* in Neoplatonic metaphysics. In the Hermetic text, *The Mixing Bowl*, the Demiurge creates all humans with reason, but not all of them have mind (νους, *nous*), which in this context means

---

76 Adapted from TAYLOR's translation in *The Alchemists*, 58.
77 *Timaeus* 30A.
78 Ibid., 41D.

knowledge of one's divine essence. The Demiurge puts mind in a mixing bowl and sends it down to humans, placing it "between souls", as a prize for them to win. He has a messenger announce the following proclamation: "Immerse yourself in the mixing bowl if your heart has the strength, if it believes you will rise up again to the one who sent the mixing bowl below, if it recognizes the purpose of your coming to be".[79] Those who immerse themselves in the mixing bowl containing the divine gift of mind become perfected; they become "immortal rather than mortal [...] for in a mind of their own they have comprehended all—things on earth, things in heaven and even what lies beyond heaven".[80] Zosimos alludes to this text in *Final Account*, when he tells Theosebeia to "spit on matter and, hastening towards Poimenandres [sic] and receiving baptism in the mixing-bowl, hasten up towards your own race".[81]

In Zosimos's dream, the altar first appears in the "temple of punishments", and the people immersed in the altar's boiling waters are suffering as their bodies are being transformed into spirits. There are fifteen steps that lead to this altar. When the sacrificing priest appears at the altar, a mysterious voice proclaims that he has "accomplished the descent of the fifteen steps of darkness and the ascent of the steps of light".[82] Throughout the rest of the allegory, Zosimos mentions only seven steps. He says he wishes to "ascend the seven steps and to look upon the seven punishments", which refers to the seven celestial zones ruled by the seven planets.[83] The fifteen steps, then, can be divided into seven descending steps and seven ascending steps; the remaining step is the ogdoad, or eighth region: the realm of the fixed stars.[84] The metal-men in the temple

---

79   CH IV.4 (trans. COPENHAVER).
80   Ibid., IV.5.
81   FOWDEN's translation, *The Egyptian Hermes*, 123. Poimandres is a divine being and revealer of wisdom in the Hermetic tradition.
82   TAYLOR, 57.
83   Ibid., 59.
84   MERTENS proposes that the numbers fifteen and seven refer to the number of days involved in performing certain aspects of the alchemical

of punishments are at the bottom of the descending steps; the goal is for them to become spirits and ascend the steps of light.

At the end of Lesson One, Zosimos (in a waking state) instructs his readers to build a temple "of one stone", that has "neither beginning nor end in its construction":

> Let it have within it a spring of pure water glittering like the sun. Notice on which side is the entry of the temple, and, taking your sword in hand, so seek for the entry. For narrow is the place at which the temple opens. A serpent lies before the entry guarding the temple; seize him and sacrifice him. Skin him and, taking his flesh and bones, separate his parts; then reuniting the members with the bones at the entry of the temple, make of them a stepping stone, mount thereon, and enter. You will find there what you seek.[85]

Serpents are often depicted in Egyptian iconography, and their symbolism is polyvalent. Serpents can be threatening forces: the gods, on their nightly journey through the underworld, encounter and slay the most dangerous of them all: Apophis, the serpent of chaos, who threatens orderly existence. Serpents can also be protective: the *uræus* symbol on the crowns worn by gods and pharaohs is an image of the mother cobra fiercely protecting her young. The Ouroborus, the tail-biting snake whose body encircles the cosmos, is another popular image which represents the regenerative powers of the universe. This cosmic serpent is frequently depicted in Greco-Egyptian alchemical literature, where it appears with inscriptions such as "the One is the All". It is associated with mercury, but also with the unity of matter, or what Zosimos calls the "one nature".[86] In Zosimos's allegory, the cosmic

---

       operation, which could also be the case. See *Zosime de Panopolis*, 226, n. 3.
85 Ibid., 58-59.
86 The *Chrysopoeia of Cleopatra*, for example, includes several drawings of the Ouroborus with inscriptions such as "One is All", "One is All and through

snake, symbolizing the ogdoadic realm of the fixed stars, appears as a sort of heavenly counterpart to the serpent of chaos below. It guards the temple without beginning or end, which is the infinite abode of the divine; the glittering spring of pure water represents the primordial waters that serve as a veil between the temporal cosmos and the infinite realms above.[87] To sacrifice the snake is to pass through the cosmic boundary and enter the noetic realm of the divine.

Zosimos's instructions for sacrificing the snake involve separating its parts and putting them back together again. Dismemberment and reconstitution are important themes in Egyptian religion—evident, for example, in the myth of the god Osiris, who was murdered and dismembered by his brother, Set. His wife, Isis, collected his scattered body parts, put them back together and resurrected him with magic spells. Osiris thereupon became Lord of the Underworld, where he judges souls to see if they are worthy of a blessed afterlife.[88] In tomb paintings and *Book of the Dead* imagery, the sun-god Re appears in the form of a knife-wielding tomcat, who hacks the serpent Apophis into pieces "on the night of making war and driving off the rebels".[89] In Zosimos's allegory, the sacrifice of the Apophis/Ouroborus snake evokes these mythic themes of death and salvation, but it also speaks to Zosimos's own research into the workings of nature, and how particular aspects of nature—metals and chemical reactions in this case—reflect the

---

it is All, and to it is All, and if it has not All, All is nothing". See H. J. SHEPPARD, "The Ouroboros and the Unity of Matter in Alchemy", *Ambix* 10.2 (1962): 83–96.

87 The primordial cosmic waters are found in many mythologies, including Egyptian funerary texts, the creation myth in the Hebrew Bible, and in several Gnostic and Hermetic texts. In addition to serving as a veil, they can also represent the flow of creation.

88 As Jan ASSMANN explains, "In mythic thought, there is no such thing as a natural death. Each death was a violent assault, and to the Egyptians, who thought in terms of dismemberment and connectivity, it represented a tearing of limb from limb". He goes on to explain that the act of dismemberment and reconnection are mythic expressions of death and salvation. See *Death and Salvation in Ancient Egypt*, 31 ff.

89 PINCH, *Egyptian Mythology*, 107–108.

workings of nature as a whole. Once the cosmic parts are reconstituted, or the vision of nature as whole is attained, this deep understanding of the "one nature" becomes a stepping-stone to the noetic realm beyond the cosmos. As the alchemist transcends the material cosmos and arrives at the divine temple of the infinite, the phial-shaped altar becomes the mixing-bowl of the Demiurge. The people immersed in the mixing-bowl, transforming their bodies into spirits, will attain the divine gift of mind and acquire knowledge of "things on earth, things in heaven and even what lies beyond heaven".[90]

Zosimos's alchemical work imitates the creative work of the Demiurge in that it involves bringing the "chaotic matter" of the base metals into a new ordered form.[91] According to Plato, the Demiurge brought chaotic matter, which has no qualities in and of itself, into order by giving it form, resulting in an indissoluble unity that manifests as the four elements.[92] This is the "one nature", which continuously acts and reacts upon itself. When Zosimos awakens from these dreams, he understands that his alchemical work is an extension of the creative powers of the universe:

> [I]t is by method, by measure and weight of the four elements, that the interlacing and dissociation of all is accomplished. No bond can be made without method. It is a natural method, breathing in and breathing out, keeping the arrangements of the method, increasing or decreasing them. When all things, in a word, come to harmony by division and union, without the methods being neglected in any way, the nature is transformed. For the nature being turned upon itself is transformed; and it is the nature and the bond of the excellence of the whole world.[93]

90 CH IV.5
91 Gregory SHAW argues this point regarding Iamblichus's views of theurgy in *Theurgy and the Soul*, 15.
92 PLATO, *Timaeus* 30A and 32C.
93 Adapted from TAYLOR's translation, 58.

In order to understand the method by which the one nature organizes and transforms itself, one not only has to experience the "one nature" from a spiritual perspective, which is accomplished by "turning upon oneself" in the act of meditation, but one also has to transcend nature and behold the divine mind of the Demiurge, the creator of the universe who devised this "method" of organization.

The entire purpose of the alchemical work is encoded in the symbolism of Lesson One: the corporeal transformation of metals into a divine image, a receptacle for the divine, and the spiritual transformation of the alchemist into the same. Both are accomplished by performing sacrifices that enable the spirit to flee the body. The remaining lessons are much shorter. In these, Zosimos describes the whitening and yellowing stages of the metal alloy, and also addresses issues regarding the art of spiritual discernment.

'ON EXCELLENCE': LESSONS TWO AND THREE

In Lesson Two, Zosimos gets lost. He writes, "Again I wished to ascend the seven steps and to look upon the seven punishments, and, as it happened, on only one of the days did I effect an ascent. Retracing my steps I then went up many times. And then on returning I could not find the way and fell into deep discouragement, not seeing how to get out, and fell asleep".[94] In his dream he encounters the helpful razor-working man, who is now clad in red, royal garments, hinting at the gold that is to come. The razor-working man offers to show him the way to the "place of punishments", meaning the altar, but once they draw near, he is cast into the punishment and consumed by fire. "On seeing this I fled and trembled with fear", says Zosimos.[95] Zosimos awakens and realizes that the razor-working man is the copper man dressed in red, and that it is necessary to cast him into the punishment. The message of this

---

94   TAYLOR, 59.
95   Ibid.

ALCHEMY AS A SPIRITUAL EXERCISE 147

dream is to return one's wandering thoughts to the meditation and to the alchemical work, which is not yet complete.

Zosimos falls asleep, and finds himself once again "losing sight of the path, wandering in despair".[96] This time he meets Agathodaimon, "a white-haired old man of such whiteness as to dazzle the eye".[97] Agathodaimon fixes Zosimos's attention by staring at him "for a full hour".[98] When Zosimos asks him to reveal the way, Agathodaimon suddenly hastens toward the correct path and quickly reaches the altar. By the time Zosimos arrives, Agathodaimon has been cast into the punishment, just as the razor-working man was before him. At this sight, Zosimos exclaims,

> O gods of heavenly natures! Immediately he was embraced entirely by the flames. What a terrible story, my brother! For from the great strength of the punishment his eyes became full of blood. And I asked him, saying, 'Why do you lie there?' But he opened his mouth and said to me 'I am the man of lead and I am undergoing intolerable violence'.[99]

Upon awakening, Zosimos understands with great clarity that one must "cast out the lead".[100] Casting out the lead will cleanse the metal of its impurities, and it also implies that the lost Zosimos will find his way again when he returns his attention to the task of cleansing his soul of its material stains.

Technically speaking, these dreams refer to the whitening stage of the *kērotakis* process, as Agathodaimon's dazzling white appearance suggests. In an anonymous ancient commentary on this passage from *On Excellence*, the author connects Agathodaimon with the waning moon, which is the alchemical notation

---

96 Ibid.
97 Ibid.
98 Ibid. Compare with Poimandres' long stare in CH 1.7.
99 Ibid, 59–60.
100 Ibid, 60.

for mercury.¹⁰¹ The author explains (not too clearly, I might add) that Agathodaimon is the whitened or silver-colored alloy, which he calls "lunarized magnesia".¹⁰² The silver color is imparted to the alloy by treating it with volatized mercury, and the author says that the metallic body is fixed, or amalgamated, as the active principle (mercury?) falls away.¹⁰³ Zosimos associates this fixing of the metal with the fixing of his attention, which helps him regain his focus and reunite with his goal of accomplishing spiritual ascent.

As Michèle Mertens notes, Agathodaimon is a complex figure and it is difficult to determine exactly what he represents in this text.¹⁰⁴ Agathodaimon, "the good daemon", was a popular deity in Greco-Roman Egypt, worshiped as a god of good fortune and also as the ruler of the cosmos.¹⁰⁵ He is often depicted as a man-headed snake and connected with the Ouroborus, the celestial serpent whose body encircles the cosmos.¹⁰⁶ In Hermetic literature, Agathodaimon is portrayed as a revered sage and quasi-divine figure who reveals the wisdom of the universe. According to some genealogies, he is the son of the god Hermes/Thoth, and the father of Hermes Trismegistus.¹⁰⁷ Zosimos also refers to the works and

101   On the waning moon as a symbol for mercury, see TAYLOR, 51. The commentary on this passage from *On Excellence* comes from a collection of alchemical commentaries written by various authors from different eras (CAAG III.6). The title of this particular commentary is "The Divine Zosimos on Excellence and its Interpretation", but this is somewhat misleading. The author only discusses a few passages from *On Excellence*, and his interpretations are purely technical. Most of the commentary is a comparison of the technical writings of various alchemical authors, such as Democritus, Ostanes, Hermes, and Stephanus (7th c. CE). Zosimos is included as one of these great alchemists, but he is not the main subject of the commentary.
102   See CAAG III.6.9.
103   BERTHELOT's note on this passage explains that the volatization with mercury amalgamates and unites the metals (the copper and lead alloy), and gives the alloy a silver color. Ibid, n.1.
104   MERTENS, *Auth.Mem*.XI, n. 11.
105   See David FRANKFURTER, *Religion in Roman Egypt*, 63, 99; also Brian COPENHAVER, *Hermetica* (Cambridge: Cambridge University Press, 1992), 165.
106   See COPENHAVER, ibid.; and BERTHELOT, CAAG vol. I, 18.
107   COPENHAVER, ibid., XV, 164-165.

techniques of an alchemist named Agathodaimon, so perhaps he learned this technique of amalgamation from Agathodaimon the alchemist. Any or all of these understandings of Agathodaimon could be operating in this text.

In the late antique imagination, the cosmos was densely populated with daimons and angels. While Zosimos warns against the folly of invoking daimons, he nevertheless encounters them as he ascends through the planetary spheres; they are part of his religious network of relationships. He portrays the razor-working man and Agathodaimon as helpful daimons; they appear without being summoned and offer their assistance as the lost and despairing Zosimos attempts to resume his spiritual ascent. Once Zosimos regains his focus, signified here by his proximity to the altar, the beneficent daimons are cast into the punishment. Though this is terrifying to Zosimos in the dream, when he awakens he realizes that it is necessary to cast them into the flames. In *Final Account*, Zosimos advises Theosebeia to offer meditative sacrifices that "repel and destroy the daimons" rather than entice them. Casting the helpful daimons into the fire is consistent with this view: even though daimons can be helpful, they are merely cosmic entities, and their "material" status can hinder the soul's ascent to the immaterial realms if one becomes attached to them.

At the beginning of Lesson Three, Zosimos sees the sacrificing priest dressed in white, presiding over the phial-shaped altar, and for the first time in this allegory, the altar is described as "divine" and "sacred", and not as a place of punishment.[108] Zosimos mounts the fourth step—which corresponds to the realm of the sun, and to the metal gold—and there he sees three men approaching from the east. One is holding a sword, and he is followed by another man who is bringing "someone with his arms bound behind his back, clothed in white and of a gracious aspect, whose name was 'culmination of cinnabar' (μεσουπάνισμα κινναβάρεως, *mesoupanisma kinnabareōs*). *Mesoupanisma* is an astrological term

---

108 TAYLOR, 59.

for the meridian, or southern point of the zodiac, which is directly overhead.[109] Since cinnabar is associated with the sun in alchemy, the name of the bound man can be interpreted in cosmic terms as the meridian of the sun, or the sun at noon—a "gracious aspect" because the sun is at the height of its journey through the sky.[110] The solar imagery and the redness of cinnabar indicate the final stages of the work, the yellowing and reddening. The silver-white alloy is about to become golden. The sword is handed to Zosimos, and he is told to sacrifice the man clothed in white: "Cut off his head and sacrifice his meat and muscles by parts, to the end that his flesh may first be boiled according to the method and that he may then undergo the punishment".[111] Zosimos awakens, but the two dream characters are still present. They most likely represent the copper-lead alloy that has now been treated and colored gold. The one with the sword says, "You have fulfilled the seven steps beneath".[112] And the second man, at the same moment that the lead is cast out, proclaims: "The work is completed".[113]

The vision of the man arriving from the east, with another man following close behind, bringing the meridian of the sun, is reminiscent of the passage in Zosimos's *On Electrum* where the mirror of the mind is placed in the west so that it may reflect the eastern and southern points of the cosmos, where the "intellectual light shines". The east is the ascendant, where the sun and all the planets first appear on the horizon; their ascent culminates at the meridian (south), and thereafter they begin to descend. Zosimos uses this cosmic imagery to convey the onset of his divine revelation. He must take the sword in hand and sacrifice the solar man, who represents the revelatory peak, the height of heaven, the attainment of gold. The solar man clad in white is the sacri-

---

109   See MERTENS, *Auth.Mem.*XII, n. 11.
110   This is TAYLOR's translation of the phrase, 60. MERTENS explains that in some versions of this text (manuscripts A and L), the symbol for the sun is used rather than the word "cinnabar". See MERTENS, ibid.
111   Taylor, 60.
112   Ibid.
113   Ibid.

ficing priest, because when Zosimos first encounters the priest in Lesson One, the priest claims that someone had dismembered him with a sword, cut off his head, and burned his bones and flesh in the fire of the treatment. Zosimos is instructed to do the same. This priest, who presides over the divine and sacred altar, can be read here as an image of the soul as it is about to merge with the Divine Mind. The image itself is tainted by materiality; the priest appears with his hands bound, and his "flesh" needs to be cut away and boiled in the treatment. Therefore, the final sacrifice is made in order to repel the final image, which, being an image, is an object of thought and not pure thought itself. The goal is to attain union with the divine mind, and therefore this image, which represents self-consciousness, is the last thing to be slain in this philosophical sacrifice.

Conclusion

Zosimos is a priest and maker of divine statues, and his emphasis on purity and self-understanding is the proper mindset for god-making, purging the soul of its baser qualities so that spiritual and technical excellence can be achieved. As we have seen, Zosimos recommends spiritual exercises like quelling the passions, which helps purify the soul, and contemplating nature and tracing divine signatures in order to understand the relationship between matter and spirit, or the One and the All. As Hadot argues, philosophy was a way of life for ancient philosophers, but they also saw it as an "exercise of death" in which the philosopher aims to separate soul and body by freeing the soul of all its worldly passions and attachments; this results in a transformation of the self, a death and rebirth.[114] Zosimos's allegory illustrates this quite well; its sacrificial imagery and allusions to Egyptian mortuary traditions embroil the reader in religious contexts for preparing body and soul for the

---

114   HADOT, *What is Ancient Philosophy?*, 190.

destruction that necessarily precedes new life. The sacrificed characters are dismembered, boiled alive, consumed in the fire, and reappear again to undergo further torturous treatment until they become perfected, or made "gold". I have argued that the sacrifices in this text are "intellectual sacrifices" that were being promoted in Zosimos's day, whereby philosophers offered their thoughts and research to the gods in lieu of animal sacrifices, with the aim of separating the soul from the body so that it can be purified of its material stains and attain divine union.

Although it is evident that Zosimos views materiality as an impurity, as something from which we need to be liberated, he also exhibits a deep appreciation of nature and a desire to penetrate nature's mysteries. This tension in his work is common in ancient religion and philosophy: the contemplation of nature can bring one closer to the divine, yet the material world is imperfect and can also lead one astray. In late antiquity there was a wide spectrum of positions regarding the relationship between the spiritual and material. Some thinkers, including Manicheans and some Gnostics, were quite anti-cosmic, and their oppositional dualism between matter and spirit could express a real disenchantment with the world. But this does not seem to be the case with Zosimos. Egyptian thought is pantheistic and exhibits a more complementary type of dualism: there is no day without night, no life without death, no union without division. As Erik Hornung explains, "[C]reation is not a single, completed occurrence, in the Egyptian view; it is in need of continued repetition and confirmation. Form can be defined only against that which is formless; and regeneration cannot occur without a journey through non-being".[115] The separation of spirit from the body echoes the primeval separation of heaven and earth at the time of creation, and the mythic victory of light over darkness celebrated daily in Egyptian temples. In the House of Life, where Zosimos was most likely a priest, the death and resurrection of Osiris was commemorated in daily rituals, and an initiation text refers to this institution as the Chamber of

---

[115] HORNUNG, *Idea Into Image*, 49.

Darkness, and uses underworld imagery to describe the initiate's passage from darkness to light.[116] In *On Excellence*, Zosimos's harsh descriptions of materiality as a "place of punishments" are better understood in light of Egyptian beliefs and initiations into the spiritual life. Zosimos is not an anti-cosmic thinker: the divine does not exist apart from the world, because the world itself is divine.

In the sacred art, the transformation of matter (corporeal arts) and the transformation of the inner self (spiritual arts) go hand in hand, and ultimately, the goal of each is the union of matter and spirit. The artisans who produce divine statues must purify themselves, perform rituals, and meditate so that their creations are fit for the gods. In doing so, they can realize their own divine nature. As Zosimos advises his students, "Don't stop meditating and working, and you will understand".

---

[116] JASNOW and ZAUZICH, *Conversations in the House of Life*, 23–24, 43.

ON GNOSIS
AND NATURAL METHODS

*Jewish and Christian Influences
in Zosimos's Work*

ZOSIMOS'S EMPHASIS ON JEWISH THOUGHT is unmatched in early alchemical literature. He is one of the few ancient alchemists to write about Hebrew metallurgical techniques, which he praises highly, and he incorporates Jewish ideas into his writings to such a degree that some medieval Arab alchemists referred to him as "Zosimos the Jew".[1] His works exemplify the religious borrowing that was occurring in Roman Egypt between Egyptians, Greeks, Jews, Christians, and others, examples of which can be seen in magical papyri, philosophical works, Gnostic texts, and in the Hermetic philosophical and technical writings that serve as a major source of inspiration for Zosimos.[2] In his discussions of Hebrew and Egyptian traditions of metallurgy and religion, Zosimos acknowledges the distinct contributions of each, yet he also highlights their commonalities in order to demonstrate that these two sacred "races"—the Hebrews and the Egyptians—have been promulgating the same universal truths regarding science and religion since ancient times. By grounding his approach to alchemy in these ancient, universal truths, this helps to legitimize his "natural"

---

[1] On medieval Arab references to "Zosimos the Jew", see Raphael PATAI, *The Jewish Alchemists* (Princeton: Princeton University Press, 1994), 56. In *Tabula smaragdina* (1929), Julius RUSKA proposed that Zosimos may have been Jewish, but scholars generally agree that there is not enough evidence to support this claim. See PATAI, *The Jewish Alchemists*, 56.

[2] For an overview of Jewish influences on Hermetic and other Egyptian writings, see Fabrizio LELLI, "Hermes Among the Jews: *Hermetica* as Hebraica from Antiquity to the Renaissance", *Magic, Ritual, and Witchcraft* 2.2 (2007): 112–117.

methods of alchemy and denounce the "unnatural" methods of his rivals.

This chapter begins with a brief discussion of Jewish metallurgy and its relation to alchemy, but the majority focuses on the way that Zosimos uses certain Jewish religious ideas in his polemics against the unnatural methods practiced by other metallurgists. In fact, in almost every instance where Zosimos expounds on Jewish religious thought, it is in the context of his concerns over proper scientific and spiritual methodologies. These polemics are examined here in detail, focusing particularly on his use of themes from two Jewish apocryphal works, *Testament of Solomon* and *Book of Enoch* (1 Enoch), which were influential among early alchemists, as well as on Zosimos's text, *On Apparatus and Furnaces (Letter Omega)*, in which he draws upon Hermetic, Gnostic, and Greek mythologies in order to present a universal doctrine of the Anthropos, or primal man, and uses this to teach his colleague, Theosebeia, about the difference between material and spiritual forms of knowledge.

Hebrew metallurgy and alchemy

Hebrew metallurgy has a long and illustrious history. The Hebrew Bible contains numerous references to metalworking, where it is often associated with the construction and decoration of the Tabernacle and the Temple.[3] Diaspora metallurgists living in Ptolemaic and Roman Egypt formed guild communities, which were often officially associated with synagogues.[4] The Babylonian Talmud, compiled between the third–fifth centuries CE, mentions that Jewish metalworkers in Alexandria exercised a great deal of control

---

3   See Oded BOROWSKI, *Daily Life in Biblical Times* (Atlanta: Society of Biblical Literature, 2003), 34–35.

4   On Jewish and Christian participation in craft guilds in Roman Egypt, see Christopher HAAS, *Alexandria in Late Antiquity: Topography and Social Conflict* (Baltimore: John Hopkins University Press, 1997), 59, 236. On craft guilds as official subgroups of synagogues in Egypt, see Philip HARLAND, *Associations, Synagogues and Congregations*, 35.

over their craft and trade.⁵ Zosimos's writings support the Talmudic description: he speaks of Hebrew metallurgy as a distinct and highly respected tradition, and claims that they carefully guard their trade secrets and initiatory formulas; though he also says that in the past, Jewish metallurgists in Egypt could publish craft texts more freely than the Egyptian temple artisans, who were restricted by governmental and temple legislation.⁶

Writings by ancient Hebrew metallurgists are nearly absent from the historical record. In the collection of alchemical texts that date from Zosimos's time or earlier, there are writings by only two alchemists who are identified as Jewish. The first and most influential is Maria the Jewess (ca. second century CE), who is quoted extensively by Zosimos and other alchemists, though none of her original texts survive. There are also a few alchemical recipes attributed to Moses, which are difficult to date,⁷ but some were circulating in Zosimos's day because Zosimos refers to a text called the Maza of Moses.⁸ The biblical Moses was the pseudepigraphical author of many Jewish and "pagan" texts in the Greco-Roman pe-

5   See Christopher HAAS, *Alexandria in Late Antiquity*, 97.
6   On Jewish metallurgists guarding their formulas, see CAAG III.51.5, especially FESTUGIÈRE's translation in *La Révélation d'Hermès Trismégiste*, vol. 1, 278, or Jack LINDSAY's English translation, based on FESTUGIÈRE's, in *Origins of Alchemy in Græco-Roman Egypt*, 336. On Jewish freedom to publish alchemical texts, see CAAG III.51.2.
7   There are two Mosaic recipes in the Greco-Egyptian alchemical literature: a lengthy recipe entitled *Chemistry of Moses* (CAAG IV.22), and a short recipe called *Diplōsis (Doubling) of Moses* (CAAG I.18). Scholars typically assign an early date to these Mosaic recipes, between the second and third centuries CE, but there are reasons to believe they are from a later period. See BERTHELOT, CAAG VOL. III, 287, n. 7; and F. S. TAYLOR, "A Survey of Greek Alchemy", 12. TAYLOR notes some of the problems in dating the Mosaic recipes in "The Origins of Greek Alchemy", 38–39.
8   According to medieval commentators, *maza* is a synonymous term for alchemy; in Greek, *maza* can refer to a lump of something—for alchemists it probably referred to a "lump" of metal, or an amalgam. For Zosimos's reference to the Maza of Moses, see CAAG III.24.4-5, and also BERTHELOT's note to CAAG III.43.6. Alchemical definitions of the term *maza* can be found in CAAG I, 209. See also John GAGER's discussion of this text in *Moses in Greco-Roman Paganism* (Nashville: Abingdon Press, 1972), 153–155.

riod; he was widely renowned as a holy man, a magician, and a great inventor.[9] Since the alchemical recipes attributed to Moses follow the same literary conventions as the recipes attributed to the ancient, legendary figures of Hermes, Ostanes, and Democritus, who were also popularly regarded as wise men and magicians, it is possible that Ps.-Moses wasn't a Jewish alchemist at all, but that Egyptian alchemists were simply capitalizing on Moses's fame by using his name. Maria the Jewess's name has also been used in this fashion, though most scholars, myself included, are inclined to think that she was an historical alchemist and not a legendary figure. Medieval alchemists, though, associate her with Moses's sister, Miriam, and also with the Virgin Mary.[10] However, these portrayals of Maria do not appear until the ninth century, and Zosimos gives no indication that she has any relation to these biblical figures.[11]

The writings of Ps.-Moses and Maria are technical works, and therefore it is difficult to determine whether these texts represent a Jewish tradition of alchemy, religiously speaking.[12] The Mosaic

---

9 For a thorough study of how Moses was perceived in late antiquity and portrayed in pagan literature, see GAGER, *Moses in Greco-Roman Paganism*. On Moses as an inventor, see Louis FELDMAN, *Jew and Gentile in the Ancient World* (Princeton: Princeton University Press, 1993), 286–287. On Moses and Egyptian thought, see Jan ASSMANN, *Moses the Egyptian: The Memory of Egypt in Western Monotheism* (Cambridge: Harvard University, 1998).
10 PATAI, *The Jewish Alchemists*, 75.
11 As PATAI notes, E. O. von LIPPMAN, an influential scholar of early alchemy, claims that Zosimos identifies Maria with Miriam, the sister of Moses, but there is no evidence of this in the Greek or Syriac versions of Zosimos's works. See PATAI, *The Jewish Alchemists*, 74.
12 Scholars are divided over whether or not there was such a thing as Jewish alchemy. As PATAI notes, scholars have come to wildly different conclusions about Jewish alchemy: some claim that Jews invented alchemy and played a major role in its development throughout history, while others argue that Jewish participation in alchemy was either insignificant or non-existent. See PATAI's discussion in *The Jewish Alchemists*, 7–17. John GAGER, whose work on Moses is cited above, argues that these "Jewish" alchemical authors may not have actually been Jewish, because their writings were not preserved in Jewish circles, and non-Jewish alchemists may have used these names as pseudonyms—particularly that of Moses—in

recipes include a few sparse religious references that point to a Jewish origin. *The Chemistry of Moses*, for example, opens with a paraphrase of *Exodus* 31:2-5: "And the Lord said to Moses, 'I have chosen the priest, Beseleel by name, of the tribe of Judah, to work gold, silver, copper, iron, all workable stones and wooden artifacts, and he will be master of all trades'".[13] Another recipe, the *Diplōsis (Doubling) of Moses*, contains only a generic reference to God, and is therefore less convincing as evidence of a Jewish tradition: "Melt while narrowing the funnel and you will find, with the help of God, the whole to be gold".[14] There are no religious remarks in the excerpts of Maria's writings preserved by Zosimos, but there is one in a fragment cited by the alchemist Olympiodorus (ca. fifth or sixth century): "Maria says again: 'Do not touch it with your hands; you are not of the race (*genos*) of Abraham; you are not of our race'".[15]

Hebrew metallurgical traditions undoubtedly included the written transmission of recipes and techniques, even if only a few of these were collected in the surviving Greco-Egyptian alchemical literature. Zosimos refers to several books of Hebrew techniques. In a letter to Theosebeia, he says that while he was visiting her at her home, he was watching her servant steam some poultry and this led him to wonder if a similar technique could be applied to the cooking and coloring of metals. He thought that the "an-

order to give their writings an aura of antiquity and authority. See GAGER, *op. cit.*, 155. More recently, Gabriele FERRARIO has summarized these positions and argued that while there is a lack of evidence of uniquely Jewish approaches to alchemy, and therefore no Jewish alchemical tradition *per se*, there is evidence (dating from medieval times forward) of Jewish interest in alchemical works. See FERRARIO, 'The Jews and Alchemy: Notes for a Problematic Approach", in *Chymia: Science and Nature in Medieval and Early Modern Europe*, M. LÓPEZ PÉREZ, D. KAHN, and M. R. BUENO, eds. (Newcastle upon Tyne: Cambridge Scholars Publishing, 2010), 19–25.

13   GAGER's translation, 153.
14   Ibid.
15   CAAG II.4.54. On the dates of Olympiodorus, see C. VIANO, "Olympiodore l'alchimiste et les présocratiques : une doxographie de l'unité", in *Alchimie : art, histoire, et mythes*, ed. Didier KAHN et Sylvain MATTON (Paris: S.É.H.A., 1995), 99–102.

cients" might have described an apparatus for this, and he found the description he was looking for in "the Jewish books".[16] In *On Electrum*, Zosimos mentions another Hebrew craft text, telling Theosebeia that she can find information on "the mixture, weight, and the treatment of each of the bodies and precious stones in the Jewish writings, mainly those by Apilis, son of Gagios".[17] He also claims that a Jew named Theophilus, son of Theogenes, wrote a book describing Egypt's goldmines.[18] But of all the Jewish authors mentioned by Zosimos, none is referred to as frequently or with greater respect than Maria the Jewess. He regards her as a great ancient master of the craft, on a par with Democritus, whom he also cites extensively.[19]

Maria's contributions to the metallurgical arts include her alleged invention of particular distillatory apparatuses, including the double boiler (or water bath), which the French still refer to as a *bain-Marie*, as well as important distillation techniques like the *kērotakis* process, which Zosimos describes in religious language in his allegory, *On Excellence*.[20] Maria emphasizes distillation more than any of the other early alchemical writers, and F. Sherwood Taylor has postulated that Maria and Democritus represent two distinct schools of alchemical theory and practice: the Marian school, which focused on distillation and sublimation methods (vapors), and the Democritean school, which emphasized cementation and

---

16   See *Auth.Mem.*VIII.1–2. The apparatus in question is the *tribikos*, a distillatory device; in another text, which he must have written at a later date, Zosimos gives Maria's technique for working copper using a *tribikos*. Michèle MERTENS comments that Zosimos usually refers to Maria by name, so the "Jewish books" where he found the description of the *tribikos* were probably not the writings of Maria. See MERTENS, *Zosime de Panopolis: Mémoires Authentiques*, 197–198, n. 5.
17   CMA, *Syr.* II.12.5.
18   See CAAG III.51.2.
19   Zosimos proclaims Maria to be an "ancient" author in CAAG III.24.3.
20   PATAI rightly points out that there is an ambiguity in Zosimos's writings as to whether Maria actually invented the devices and processes she describes. See PATAI, *The Jewish Alchemists*, 60.

fusion methods (powders).²¹ Zosimos, in Taylor's assessment, belongs to the Marian school.²² But as Robert Multhauf points out, it appears as though Zosimos is actually trying to synthesize the two schools:

> The materials mentioned by Zosimos are virtually identical to those in the earlier Egyptian sources, but the method of manipulating them is quite different. Zosimos tends to convert (Bolos) Democritus' cementation processes into distillatory processes, using apparatus associated with Maria, and although Democritus mentioned distillation briefly in *Physica et Mystica*, with a claim to have written on it more extensively elsewhere, we not only lack any such work but find that where Zosimos refers to (Bolos) Democritus in connection with distillation he usually does so in an attempt to show him to be in agreement with Maria.²³

Zosimos regards the Egyptians and Hebrews as metallurgists par excellence, and Maria's distillatory techniques undoubtedly factor into his great respect for the Hebrew tradition. In a work titled *The True Book of Sophe the Egyptian and of the Divine Lord of the Hebrews and the Powers of Sabaoth*,²⁴ Zosimos extols Maria's *kērotakis* methods along with "Egyptian" doubling (*diplōsis*) methods for yellowing copper, and claims that Jewish and Egyptian alchemists

---

21 See F. S. TAYLOR, "A Survey of Greek Alchemy", 114–118.
22 Ibid., 119.
23 R. MULTHAUF, *The Origins of Chemistry*, 104.
24 The name Sophe here derives from the Egyptian king Souphis, the second king of the fourth dynasty, ca 2600 BCE. Herodotus calls him Cheops. See F. DAUMAS, "L'alchimie a-t-elle une origine Egyptienne?" *Römisch Byzantinische Ägypten. Akten des internationalen Symposions 26–30 September 1978 in Trier* (Mainz am Rhein: P. von Zabern, 1983), 113. MERTENS adds that Julianus Africanus claimed to have obtained a sacred book written by Cheops on a voyage to Egypt, which shows that books were circulating in Egypt in the third century CE that were attributed to this king. See MERTENS, *Zosime de Panopolis: Mémoires Authentiques*, LXVII–LXVIII.

are united by a common spiritual philosophy that represents the best of their science and wisdom:

> There are two sciences and two wisdoms, that of the Egyptians and that of the Hebrews, which are stronger in divine justice: Indeed, this science and wisdom of the most excellent things comes from the depths of the ages—no master has produced it, it is autonomous—and it is immaterial and does not seek a body plunged in matter and entirely perishable,[25] because it operates without undergoing any change itself (ἀπαθῶς). Now you have it as a free gift. Indeed, for those that save and purify the divine soul enchained in the elements, or rather the divine spirit mingled with the dough of the flesh, the symbol of chemistry is drawn from the creation of the world by means of example, because just as the sun, flower of fire, is the celestial sun and the right eye of the world, so copper, if it becomes a flower by purification (i.e., takes the color of gold), is a terrestrial sun, which is a king on earth just as the sun is king of the sky.[26]

The spiritual goal of transcending materiality and uniting with the divine in the spiritual realms beyond the cosmos is a common theme in both Egyptian Hermetism and in Jewish and Christian gnostic literature. The language of spirits fleeing their bodies is also technical language, used predominantly in descriptions of

---

25   Probably a reference to divine statues. The divine is greater than the material "body" of the statue. Idolatry is prohibited, of course, in Jewish religion, and Zosimos might be acknowledging that the Hebrew and Egyptians are in agreement that the divine is not dependent on matter, but rather the other way around.
26   The surviving versions of this text are in a corrupt state and difficult to translate. I have consulted the Greek as well as the French translations by BERTHELOT and RUELLE (CAAG III.42.1) and FESTUGIÈRE (*La Révélation d'Hermès Trismégiste* vol. 1, 261). My translation is largely based on Festugière's.

distillatory processes. The linking of divine signatures through cosmic sympathy (copper → sun → celestial eye of the world, i.e., Eye of Re/Horus) is prominent in Egyptian alchemical writings, and is an important meditative technique in the natural methods practiced by Zosimos; there are also theories of cosmic sympathies found in Jewish pseudepigraphical literature, and Zosimos demonstrates that these "Jewish" theories of cosmic sympathy were widely read and applied in alchemical circles.[27] Therefore, it seems that Zosimos is synthesizing these predominant features of Hebrew and Egyptian science and wisdom, and presenting this as a unified "spiritual" theory of metallurgy, which ultimately describes his own vision of alchemy.

Zosimos's familiarity with certain Hebrew metallurgical writings indicates that not all of their craft secrets were closely guarded. Zosimos thought that craft secrets should be shared openly, and apparently he had encountered Jewish or Christian metallurgists who felt the same way.[28] As John Barclay points out, Jews living in the Mediterranean diaspora had varying degrees of social integration with the Gentile communities in which they lived, with some becoming so assimilated into pagan culture that they abandoned their Jewish heritage altogether, while others had minimal contact with Gentiles and strictly adhered to their ancestral traditions.[29] There are also levels of integration that fall somewhere in the middle. Barclay identifies employment as a potential arena for mid-level assimilation: Jews could work and do business with Gentiles, and ideas could be exchanged, but they still remained committed to preserving their Jewish identity.[30] I suspect that the Jewish alchemists that Zosimos refers to in his writings had attained middle to high levels of assimilation with Gentile culture. First of all, the

---

27 Zosimos credits Egyptians for being the first to allude to the secret "natural" methods for preparing timely tinctures in *Final Account* (CAAG III.51).

28 CMA, *Syr.* II.8.1. See my discussion of Zosimos's opposition to craft secrecy in chapter 2.

29 See John M.G. BARCLAY, *Jews in the Mediterranean Diaspora* (Berkeley: University of California Press, 1999), ch. 5.

30 Ibid., 112–116.

Jewish authors he mentions by name—Apilis, son of Gagios; and Theophilus, son of Theogenes—all have Hellenized names, as do their fathers, so it is likely that these families were more socially integrated with Gentiles. Secondly, the Jewish religious texts and ideas that Zosimos references come from Jewish/Christian Gnostic traditions and from Solomonic and Enochian pseudepigraphical literature, all of which are highly syncretic.[31] So while Zosimos refers to Jewish/Hebrew traditions of metallurgy, and there is evidence of Jewish guilds in Egypt (though not in Panopolis, as far as I can tell)[32], it is also likely that only the more culturally assimilated Jewish metallurgists were working in Gentile guilds, sharing Hebrew techniques with Egyptian or Greek colleagues, and vice versa.

31   The term "Gnostic", which I use here to refer to Jewish and Christian forms of Gnosticism popular in the first few centuries of the common era, is problematic for several reasons. Zosimos is commonly labeled as a "Gnostic" by scholars in the earlier twentieth century, and while they seem to be implying that Zosimos exhibits Jewish/Christian forms of Gnosticism, they could be using this term in a broader sense, since in that time the term "Gnosticism" was also commonly used to describe Hermetism and esoteric knowledge in general. See, for example, M. BERTHELOT, *Les Origines de l'alchimie* (Paris: G. Steinheil, 1885), 2, and BERTHELOT and RUELLE, CAAG vol. 1, 9; C.G. JUNG, *Alchemical Studies*, 59; and J. R. PARTINGTON, *A History of Chemistry*, vol. 1, part 1 (London: MacMillan & Co., 1970), 267. After the publication of the Nag Hammadi library in the late 1970s, more nuanced discussions of Gnosticism have emerged and are still being debated; see Michael A. WILLIAMS, *Rethinking "Gnosticism": An Argument for Dismantling a Dubious Category* (Princeton: Princeton University Press, 1996); and Karen KING, *What is Gnosticism?* (Cambridge: Belknap Press of Harvard University Press, 2003). Daniel STOLZENBERG and Kyle FRASER have more recently argued that Zosimean alchemy was a type of Gnostic ritual for purifying the soul, and they draw upon Jewish/Christian forms of Gnosticism to illustrate their points; they are using "Gnosticism" in the same sense that I am. See STOLZENBERG, "Unpropitious Tinctures: Alchemy, Astrology, and Gnosis According to Zosimos of Panopolis"; and FRASER, "Baptized in Gnōsis: The Spiritual Alchemy of Zosimos of Panopolis", *Dionysius* XXV (Dec. 2007), 33–54.
32   See my discussion of Jewish and Christian communities in Panopolis in chapter 2.

Although cultural assimilation makes it possible for Jews and Gentiles to work together and share ideas, the blending of traditions can be problematic for people in either camp because new worldviews are created, which can threaten old traditions. This problem comes up again and again in Zosimos's writings. Although Zosimos is clearly an integrator, blending traditional Egyptian thought (both religious and scientific) with Greek philosophy and Jewish and Christian teachings, he also clings to an ideal purity of ancient traditions and laments that these traditions are being corrupted.[33] This is most evident in his diatribes against alchemists who practice "unnatural" methods, as opposed to his "natural" methods, which are more in line with traditional Egyptian teachings. As I mentioned earlier, Jewish religious ideas are almost always invoked in these debates, particularly the more "magical" forms of Judaism that incorporate daimonology. Zosimos's interpretations of Jewish texts and ideas are interesting for the ways in which he reads them against some of the more marginal Jewish ideas and reinforces traditional viewpoints, and tries to harmonize them with "ancient" Egyptian and Greek traditions.

Zosimos never clearly delineates what he means by "natural" (φυσικα, *physika*) and "unnatural" (αφυσικα, *aphysika*) methods, though he does associate them with particular ideas. Natural methods, which involve creating alchemical tinctures in accordance with seasonal and celestial patterns, are associated with the purification of the soul and meditating upon divine signatures, or *synthēmata*, in order to trace cosmic sympathies and pathways of spiritual ascent; whereas he associates the unnatural methods of his rivals with daimonology and particular approaches to astrology. He frames these as opposing methods for the preparation of "opportune tinctures" (καιρικαὶ βαφαί, *kairikai baphai*).[34] Several scho-

---

33 See, for example, CMA *Syr.* II,12.5, cited later in this chapter.
34 In *Auth.Mem.*I (*On Apparatus and Furnaces, Letter Omega*), Zosimos uses the term καταβαφαί, possibly meaning "deep tinctures", instead of βαφαί, which might refer to more superficial colorings. See MERTENS, *Zosime de Panopolis: Mémoires Authentiques*, 62, n. 9. Stolzenberg notes that in another text attributed to Zosimos (CAAG III.37), the school of Agathodaimon

lars have argued that Zosimos's polemics are targeted at alchemists who use astrology in their work, and that he is against astrological determinism.³⁵ While this is true to some extent, this argument needs to be more nuanced, because Zosimos believes that the planets, which were considered by many ancients to be "cosmic" gods or daimons, *do* have an influence on terrestrial activities. In *On Excellence*, for example, he states that all alchemical research, though it is "multiple and varied", is nevertheless "subordinated to lunar influences and to the measure of time".³⁶ Zosimos also gives instructions for gold coloring techniques that are best performed in the summertime, when the sun is at its peak; and he recommends that the heliacal rising of Sirius, which corresponds to the annual flooding of the Nile, is the best time to extract mercury from cinnabar.³⁷ It therefore appears that Zosimos *does* use a type of astrology in his alchemical practices, but that it *differs* from that of his rivals.³⁸ Unfortunately, Zosimos does not explain his approach in detail, though it seems to be based on ancient horological methods that were used by temple priests (ὡρολόγοι, *hōrologoi*) for determining proper times for cultic activities.³⁹ All forms of astrology in

uses these terms to refer to coloring metals gold (καταβαφαί) or silver (βαφαί). See STOLZENBERG, "Unpropitious Tinctures: Alchemy, Astrology, and Gnosis According to Zosimos of Panopolis", 5, n. 4.

35 See, for example, LINDSAY, *The Origins of Alchemy in Graeco-Roman Egypt*, 326–327, 337; Jean Letrouit, "Hermetism and Alchemy: Contribution to the Study of Marcianus Graecus 299 (=M)", in *Magia, Alchimia, Scienza dal '400 al '700: L'influsso di Ermete Trismegisto*, vol. I, ed. C. GILLY and C. van HEERTUM (Florence: Centro Di, 2002), 87, 89 (Letrouit's article is in both French and English, and as the French and English texts are printed side by side, the pagination is the same for both); and Daniel STOLZENBERG, who, gives the most thorough treatment of the subject in "Unpropitious Tinctures".

36 *Auth.Mem.* x.1(b, ms.M). F. Sherwood TAYLOR's translation.

37 On favorable positions of the sun, see CAAG III.15.2. On the preparation of cinnabar in conjunction with the heliacal rising of Sirius, see CMA, *Syr.* II.9.18.

38 This position is also taken by MERTENS, *Zosime de Panopolis*, 66–67, and FRASER, "Zosimos of Panopolis and the Book of Enoch: Alchemy as Forbidden Knowledge", 138–141.

39 See Sauneron's discussion of the difference between the *hōrologoi*

this period are based upon theories of cosmic sympathy, but these theories were by no means uniform. I contend that debates over certain understandings of cosmic sympathy and how knowledge of the cosmos is best attained are at the heart of Zosimos's polemics; these debates include astrology, but are by no means limited to it.

KING SOLOMON THE EXORCIST

In *Final Account*, Zosimos claims that "unnatural" methods were devised by daemons who were greedy for sacrificial offerings, and that these methods could only work with their assent. Natural methods, on the other hand, "act by themselves", and involve repelling the daimons, who are jealous of these methods.[40] Zosimos sometimes refers to these daimons as *ephoroi*, and in late antiquity this term, which means "guardians" or "overseers", was used to designate planetary gods, gods of polytheistic pantheons (e.g., the Greek gods, Egyptian gods), as well as other cosmic beings that preside over various domains of human and terrestrial life.[41] Zosimos contrasts these cosmic daimons, who are "confined in the lowest places", with God, "who is everywhere".[42] At the end of *Final Account*, Zosimos tells Theosebeia to "offer sacrifices to the

---

      (astronomer-priests who determined the appropriate moments for cultic activities) and the *hōroskopoi* (calendrical priests who determined lucky and unlucky days and cast natal horoscopes) in *The Priests of Ancient Egypt*, 64–65. The difference between them sounds similar to the difference that Zosimos describes between his methods and the astrological methods of his competitors.

40   CAAG III.51.7. See STOLZENBERG's translation of this passage in "Unpropitious Tinctures", 10–11.

41   STOLZENBERG notes that *ephoroi* denotes different types of gods, but he stresses their role as planetary gods and identifies them with the Archons of Gnostic literature in order to show that Zosimos was against astrology and held a "Gnostic" view that the planetary powers are evil. I will be arguing along different lines. See STOLZENBERG, "Unpropitious Tinctures", 22–24.

42   CAAG III.51.8. My translation.

daimons", not the ones that "nourish and please them", he warns:

> but rather the sacrifices that chase them away and make them disappear, such as the formulas given by Membres to Solomon, king of Jerusalem, and better yet, those that Solomon himself has written, according to his own wisdom. By doing so, you will obtain the genuine timely and natural tinctures.[43]

Solomon was renowned in late antiquity as a magician, exorcist, and astrologer. Several late ancient texts attributed to Solomon contain elaborate daimonologies in which the daimons are mapped in astrological terms, as planetary daimons, governors of the decans of the zodiac, and rulers of particular hours of the day.[44] Zosimos appears to be familiar with several books of Solomon, but his allusion to the writings that "Solomon himself has written" is most likely a reference to the *Testament of Solomon*. Many versions of this ancient text survive today, but the basic storyline is the same in all of them: An angel gives Solomon a magic ring that he uses to conjure legions of daimons. Each daimon resides in a specific cosmic location and has its own particular powers. Solomon compels the daimons to reveal the nature

---

43   Ibid. "Membres" is most likely a reference to Mambres (also known as Jambres), who, according to Jewish lore, is one of two Egyptian magicians who opposed Moses in Exodus 7–11. The other is named Jannes, and the two are mentioned in 2 Timothy 3:8 and in other late antique literature. Though these magicians are mentioned in books of Solomon, Zosimos's reference to Mambres as Solomon's teacher is obscure, and not found in any of the surviving texts of Solomon. See D. C. DULING's introduction to his translation of *Testament of Solomon*, in *The Old Testament Pseudepigrapha*, vol. 1, ed. J. H. CHARLESWORTH (New York: Doubleday, 1983), n. 94.

44   See Pablo TORIJANO's excellent study of these Solomonic texts in *Solomon the Esoteric King* (Leiden: Brill, 2002). Egyptian astrologers invented the concept of decans, which were originally a group of 36 constellations led by the constellation Sirius; by the Greco-Roman period, they had come to refer to a ten-degree segment of the zodiacal circle; each of the twelve signs of the zodiac therefore has three decans. See Tamsyn BARTON, *Ancient Astrology* (London: Routledge, 1994), 20.

of their meddlesome, evil powers, and to reveal the names of the angels who have the ability to thwart them. For example, when Solomon invokes the planetary daimons, they respond as follows:

> 'I am Deception. I plot deception and I devise the most evil heresies. But there is one who thwarts me, the angel Lamechiel'. The second said, 'I am Strife. I cause strife by making available clubs, pellets, and swords, my implements of war. But I have an angel who thwarts me, Baruchiel'.[45]

With this knowledge, Solomon gains power over the daimons and commands them to help him build the Temple. Most versions of this story end badly, however, when Solomon falls in love with a "Shummanite" woman who persuades him to offer sacrifices and build temples to foreign gods. Solomon does as his beloved requests, and the glory of God departs from him and he falls into ruin.[46]

This tale of Solomon, who conjures daimons and forces them to build the Temple, resonates with what Zosimos calls "unnatural" methods of practicing alchemy, which involve summoning cosmic daimons in order to enlist their help with the production of tinctures. But Zosimos appears to be interpreting this in support of his natural methods, which involve appealing to a higher divine source in order to understand the nature of cosmic powers and attain scientific and spiritual mastery: Zosimos tells Theosebeia to emulate Solomon's exorcisms, not his conjurations, and in *Testament of Solomon*, Solomon exorcises the daimons in the name of God and the holy angels. Likewise, in Zosimos's allegory, *On*

---

45 *Testament of Solomon* 8:5–6, trans. D. C. DULING, ibid. This text will hereafter be abbreviated as *TSol*.
46 See *TSol* 26. DULING includes some variant endings of the story in his notes to this section, and he also notes that the "Shummanite" woman could be a reference to Abishag, the Shunammite woman brought to comfort King David in 1 Kings (1:1–4, 15; 2:17–22), or that it may be a derivative of "maid of Shulam" (Song of Solomon 6:12; 7:1).

Excellence, the alchemist receives instruction from the daimons he encounters in his chemico-religious work, but then they are banished or destroyed, allowing him to continue his spiritual ascent toward the divine realms.⁴⁷ Of course, Zosimos always insists that one should remain focused on the divine, a message that is also expressed in the *Testament of Solomon*, because Solomon falls into ruin when he begins worshiping the daimons and loses sight of God.

In *On Electrum*, Zosimos refers again to a book of Solomon, in which an angel instructs Solomon to make seven bottles out of electrum and to trap daimons within them. He indicates that this book may not be Jewish in origin, but rather an Egyptian adaptation of a Jewish text. He writes:

> Among the Egyptians, there is a book called *The Seven Heavens*, attributed to Solomon, against the demons; but it is not correct (to say) that it is by Solomon, since these bottles had been brought at another time to our priests [...]. After these writings were spread everywhere, still unfinished, they were corrupted. It is he (Solomon) who composed them, as I have said above. But Solomon only wrote a single book about the seven bottles, while some person invented and composed commentaries at different epochs to explain what this work contained; but in these commentaries there is some deception. All or almost all agree concerning the function of the bottles directed against the demons. These bottles acted like the prayer and the nine letters written by Solomon: the demons cannot withstand them.⁴⁸

---

47 There are other allusions to *TSol* in Zosimos's allegory. He instructs his reader to build a temple with the mind, as a means of contemplating the infinite abode of the divine. Zosimos says that this temple has a spring of pure water within it. Compare with *TSol* H 9: "And the Temple of the Lord God, in which a river has its source under his throne, was completed". See DULING, 987, n. f (9).

48 CMA Syr. II, 12.5. P. TORIJANO's translation, *Solomon the Esoteric King*, 180.

Though *The Seven Heavens* has not survived, the theme of trapping daimons in jars is also found in several versions of the *Testament of Solomon* and in other texts from the first few centuries CE.[49] Specific references to the seven jars of Solomon can be found in *Testament of Solomon* E XI.3, though in this text the jars are made of bronze, not electrum.[50] Two Christian collections of exorcisms that date from approximately the fourth century mention that Solomon trapped the daimons in jars made of bronze, and a reference to the seven jars of Solomon is also found in the Christian Gnostic tractate, *Testimony of Truth*.[51]

The Egyptian book that Zosimos is discussing, *The Seven Heavens*, appears to be a metallurgical text in which the seven jars of Solomon are associated with the seven planets:

> The corrupted book that we have entitled *The Seven Heavens* contains, in summary, the following: The angel ordered Solomon to make these bottles. It adds: Solomon made the seven bottles according to the number of the seven planets, in conformity with the divine prescriptions for the working of stone, for the mixing of silver, gold, and copper of Cyprus with the substance called *orichalkos* and copper of Marrah [?] [...].
>
> The wise Solomon also knows how to evoke the daimons; he gives a formula of conjuration and mentions the electrum, that is, the bottles of electrum, on the surface of which he inscribed this formula.[52]

---

49   See DULING's discussion of the various versions of *TSol* in *The Old Testament Pseudepigrapha*, vol. I, 937–939. In the version that DULING has translated, there are references to Solomon imprisoning daimons in jars at 15:8–11, and 16:7.
50   TORIJIANO, *Solomon the Esoteric King*, 181–182.
51   Ibid, 182, and NHC IX, 3: 69.31–70.30.
52   CMA, *Syr.* II.12.5. Translated from DUVAL's French by Shannon GRIMES and Berekia DIVANGA.

Zosimos has a negative opinion of the altered, "corrupted" books that are based on Solomon's original, noting that they "contain some deception", and he refers Theosebeia to different works, including those of the Jewish metallurgist, Apilis, son of Gagios, where she can find proper instructions for the preparation and treatment of the nine necessary ingredients for making electrum. Elsewhere in this text, Zosimos rails against the deceptions found in alchemical books inspired by the daimons.[53] Even though *The Seven Heavens* is written "against the daimons", and therefore may not be representative of "unnatural" methods, Zosimos seems to believe that any alchemical work that contains faulty information is inspired by daimons.

The kind of knowledge granted by daimons is inadequate because daimons are limited to specific cosmic locations and specific forms of knowledge and power; they do not possess an understanding of nature as a whole. Some of the astrological texts attributed to Solomon contain extensive tables of the propitious angels and daimons that govern every hour of each day of the week, along with specific prayers to the planets that must be recited before the cosmic spirits are summoned. In the *Hygromanteia of Solomon*, Solomon instructs his son, Rehoboam, in these methods of propitious timing:

> I impress upon you a method so that you, very dear Roboam [sic], may know that it is completely necessary to know the hour in which you want to accomplish your will: first, utter the prayer of the planet that is found in that hour; afterwards, adjure the angel and the servant, that is the daimon.[54]

Zosimos rejects this form of cosmic understanding, which was very popular in his day. Solomon is wise because he knows

---

53 See CMA, *Syr.* II.12.1.
54 From the *Hygromanteia of Solomon*, trans. TORIJIANO, *Solomon the Esoteric King*, 243.

the names, locations, and powers of all the daemons, and how to manipulate these cosmic sympathies and antipathies. Zosimos, however, usually refers to cosmic sympathies in natural terms, as the influence of moon, sun, and stars, never as the influence of angels or daimons who reside in the thirteenth degree of Aquarius, for example, or who govern the second hour of the third day of the week. Zosimos also insists upon appealing to the Divine Mind (a common Hermetic term for God), creator of the cosmos, as the preeminent source of scientific and spiritual wisdom. Why bother with the daimons when one can go straight to the source? This appeal to the Divine Mind for scientific wisdom is an important component of Zosimos's universal approach. The daimons have very particular knowledge, and the books that describe the daimons and their powers are often inconsistent and disagree with each other. Particularity and inconsistency do not reflect universal truths. Zosimos finds more uniformity and agreement in teachings that appeal to God, or the One, as the creative source of the All.

The Book of Enoch and the Origins of Alchemy

In a treatise entitled *On Tin*, Zosimos recounts for Theosebeia a myth concerning the origins of alchemy:

> The holy writings, Madam, say that there is a race of daimons who have intercourse with women and lead them. Hermes also mentions them in his book *On Natural Things*; and the entire book offers a meaning both manifest and hidden. He mentions it in these terms: The ancient and divine books say that certain angels were taken with passion for women. They descended to earth and taught them all of the works of nature. It is about them [the angels] that our book says that those who became proud were driven from heaven, because they had

taught to men all things evil, which do not serve the soul. They were the ones who composed the works, and from them came the first tradition of these arts. Their book is called *Chema* [*koumou*], and it is from this that chemistry [*koumia*] received its name.

The book is composed of twenty-four sections; each has its own name, or letter, or treatise. This is explained by the voice of the priests. One of them is called "Imous", another "Imout", and one has for its title, "Face". One section is called "Key"; another, "Seal"; another, "Manual" [ἐγχειρίδιον]; another, "Time" [ἐποχή]. As I have said, each has its name. One finds in this book the arts exposed in thousands of words.[55]

This myth is based upon the tale of the fallen angels in the *Book of Enoch* (1 Enoch), in which the angels, who lust after human women and mate with them, unleash much sin and evil upon the world by teaching the women sorcery, including spells, the cutting of roots and plants, and the auguries of the earth, sun, moon, and stars.[56] Interestingly, metallurgy, jewelry making, and the fabrication of cosmetics, precious stones, and tinctures—all of which are alchemical arts—are also included in the Enochian list of offensive teachings.[57]

---

[55] CMA, *Syr.* 11.8.1. My translation, based on DUVAL's French. George SYNCELLUS (9th c.) also cites and paraphrases this fragment from Zosimos in *Ecologa Chronographia* 14.4–11. See FRASER, "Alchemy as Forbidden Knowledge", 125, n. 1.

[56] See 1 Enoch 6–8, trans. Matthew Black (Leiden: Brill, 1985). This myth is based on Genesis 6:1-5.

[57] E. ISAAC, in his translation of this text, adds "alchemy" to this list, but notes that this is his rendering of the Ethiopian phrase, *tawaleto ʻalam*, which he translates more literally as "transmutation of the world". BLACK, on the other hand, translates this phrase as "varieties of adornments", which makes much more sense given the context. See ISAAC's translation of 1 Enoch 8:2, in *The Old Testament Pseudepigrapha*, vol. 1, ed. J.

Kyle Fraser has addressed the ambiguity in Zosimos's appropriation of this myth: Zosimos appears to be endorsing the "unwholesome" view that the alchemical arts were taught by lustful fallen angels, but given his negative opinion of daimons (or fallen angels), this seems strikingly out of character.[58] Fraser notes that the Enochian myth's polemics against occult sciences and technology reflect broader cultural suspicions of magic and illicit religious practices, and he argues that Zosimos uses this myth strategically to condemn the "profane" or unnatural alchemy of his competitors and thereby legitimize his own "spiritual" form of alchemy.[59] I agree with Fraser's assessment, but I also think that the polemics against magic in both the *Book of Enoch* and in Zosimos's appropriation of the Enochian myth need to be understood primarily as competing truth claims about proper relations between humans, the divine, and the natural order.

Zosimos thinks highly of the book, *Chema* (probably *Chēmia*, in Greek), which supposedly contains the alchemical teachings of the fallen angels, but he adds that there are numerous commentaries on this text, which "contain nothing good". He regrets that the commentators have not only "spoiled these books on chemistry, but they have made them into mysteries".[60] These "false philosophers", as he calls them, are trying to instruct Theosebeia, but Zosimos reminds her that she has more wisdom than they do, since she knows the difference between "body and soul".[61] He opens this letter to Theosebeia with the Enochian myth of the fallen angels, who seduce women and teach them the alchemical arts, in order to

H. CHARLESWORTH, n. 8d.
58 See Fraser, "Alchemy as Forbidden Knowledge", 125, 131–132.
59 Ibid., 131–132, 145.
60 CMA, *Syr.* II.8.1. By "mysteries", Zosimos apparently means that mystery schools, requiring oaths of secrecy, have grown up around these corrupt interpretations of alchemy. In this text he criticizes Theosebeia for requiring oaths of secrecy from her students, and for restricting access to certain books.
61 Ibid. In his letters, Zosimos frequently warns Theosebeia not to fall prey to these false teachings; it appears to be an ongoing concern of his.

show her that she, too, is being seduced by false philosophers who want to instruct her in their techniques.

It seems odd that Zosimos would approve of the chemistry books attributed to the fallen angels, who are disparaged for disobeying god in the Enochian version of this myth. However, a different rendering of this fallen angels story is found in a Hermetic alchemical text called *Isis the Prophetess to Her Son Horus*, which Zosimos most likely read and admired, because many of the ideas espoused in this text are similar to his own.[62] This text contains some hermeneutical clues as to how Zosimos may have understood the Enochian myth. Isis explains to Horus that "by the permission of a favoring season and according to the necessary movement of the spheres", an angel from "the first firmament" spied her and wanted to mate with her, but she refused his advances, demanding that he must first reveal the mysteries of the preparation of gold and silver.[63] The angel was not able to explain them, but a superior angel named Amnael, who did know the mysteries, appeared and he, too, was seized by desire for Isis. He repeatedly tried to seduce her, but Isis states that she did not succumb: "I triumphed over his lust until he was ready to show me the sign on his head and reveal to me, generously and without hiding anything, the sought-for mysteries".[64]

Due to her persistent rebuffing of the lustful angel, which

---

62   OLYMPIODORUS preserves a fragment from a lost book of Zosimos (*On Energy*) in which Zosimos quotes a passage from *Isis to Horus*, and cites Hermes as the author. The alchemical author, Hermes, may have been the author of *Isis to Horus*, or perhaps Zosimos simply means to imply that this is a Hermetic work. See CAAG II.4.32.8.

63   There are two extant versions of this text, "A" and "E", and they have been translated into French by BERTHELOT and RUELLE (CAAG I.13), and by FESTUGIÈRE. I am using Jack LINDSAY's English translation, which is based on Festugière's. Lindsay synthesizes the two versions, using E as the base text, and placing his insertions from manuscript A in brackets. The quotation I have used here is from text A. See FESTUGIÈRE, *La Révélation d'Hermès Trismégiste*, vol. I, 256–260; and LINDSAY, *The Origins of Alchemy in Græco-Roman Egypt*, 194–195.

64   LINDSAY, 195. Quotation is from text E.

Zosimos would surely applaud, Isis was able to gain mastery over Amnael, and he revealed to her the alchemical knowledge. It appears that she did not have to mate with him in return, because the moral lesson of this story, which she imparts to Horus, centers on the notion that like begets like:

> So go then, my child, to a certain laborer [Achaab] and ask him what he has sown and what he has harvested, and you will learn from him that the man who sows wheat also harvests wheat, and the man who sows barley also harvests barley. Now that you've heard this discourse, my child, learn to comprehend the whole fabrication, *demiourgia*, and generation of these things, and know that it is the condition of man to sow a man, of a lion to sow a lion, of a dog to sow a dog, and if it happens that one of these beings is produced against the order of nature, he has been engendered in the state of a monster and cannot subsist. For one nature rejoices in another nature, and one nature conquers another nature.[65]

In the Enochian myth, which is based on Genesis 6:1–4, the angels mate with human women and beget a race of giants called the Nephilim. Isis's claims that such breeding is "against the order of nature" and "engenders monsters" are in full agree-

---

65 Ibid. In the fragment preserved by OLYMPIODORUS (see n. 57 above), Zosimos refers to the laborer Achaab. He writes: "For the truth of my words, I take Hermes to witness. He declares: Go to Achaab the laborer and learn that he who sows wheat brings wheat to birth. Similarly I too have told you that substances are tinctured by substances as it is written: as to the tincturing, it is divided into two kinds, the bodily and the incorporeal. The Art limits itself to these two kinds". Trans. LINDSAY, *The Origins of Alchemy*, 196. This distinction between corporeal and incorporeal alchemy is consistent with his comment to Theosebeia in *On Tin*, about knowing the difference between body and soul. Corporeal and incorporeal alchemy could also refer to cementation methods (powders) as opposed to distillation (vapors, "spirits").

ment with the sentiments of the Jewish scriptures. Her point is that it is unnatural to love the daimons, or cosmic spirits, and Zosimos may have understood this as a polemic against unnatural alchemical methods.

Isis to Horus also promotes concepts that Zosimos associates with natural methods. It teaches that alchemists can acquire knowledge from cosmic spirits (angels and daimons), but should also resist their influence. It also describes a type of astrology in which the activities of cosmic spirits are subordinate to natural cycles: the angels appear only "by permission" of a favorable season and planetary alignment. The (false) belief that daimons govern natural forces, or can override them, seems to be a target of Zosimos's critiques of "unnatural" forms of astrology and alchemy.

Zosimos's emphasis on spiritual ascent and divine revelation as a superior means of understanding nature is not found in *Isis to Horus*, but these themes do appear in *Book of Enoch*. After Enoch hears the myth of the fallen angels and how daimonic revelations of nature and technology lead to sin and wickedness, Enoch is then taken to heaven where he witnesses the punishment of the fallen angels, and the divine majesty of God's creation is also revealed to him. Nature and divine power are dominant themes in this text, and, to use Martha Himmelfarb's phrasing, nature "serves as testimony to God's greatness and to the order of the universe".[66] This is evident in the homily on nature that immediately precedes the myth of the fallen angels, in which the contemplation of God's creation is encouraged as a sort of spiritual exercise:

> Consider all [his works] and observe the works (of creation) in heaven, how the heavenly luminaries do not change their paths in the conjunction of their orbits, how each of them rises and sets in order, at its appointed

---

66   See Martha HIMMELFARB's discussion of the theme of nature in the *Book of Enoch* and other Jewish apocalyptic texts, in *Ascent to Heaven in Jewish and Christian Apocalypses* (New York: Oxford University Press, 1993), ch. 4; quotation is from p. 72.

time, and at their fixed seasons they appear, and do not violate their proper order [...]

Consider all trees; in all of them green leafage appears and covers them; and all their fruit appears in glorious splendor. Examine and consider all these works (of creation) and reflect that the God who lives forever and ever has created all these works. And all his works which he has made forever attend on him year by year; and all his works serve him and do not change, but all perform his commands.[67]

The stability and reliability of the natural order are emphasized, along with the notion that God controls and directs the course of nature. The governing forces of the universe, particularly the role of Fate, were a topic of much philosophical debate in antiquity. The *Book of Enoch* presents a biblical view of God's omnipotence in the context of these wider debates, stressing that God alone governs the universe, and that the natural order, which never strays from God's will, is a model for moral order.

In the Enochian myth of the fallen angels, divine revelation is contrasted with daimonic revelation as a source of knowledge of nature. The "magical" arts taught by the fallen angels—astrology, botanical medicines, and auguries of natural omens—are all sciences of nature, but this knowledge is portrayed as improper and "unnatural" because it comes from angels who have transgressed the natural order by mating with human women. The critiques against these "magical" sciences are leveled at practitioners who believe that daimonic powers will grant them knowledge of nature. They err in their failure to recognize that God alone is the master of nature.

The metallurgical and tinctorial arts seem to be placed in a different class than the magical arts. These technologies are associated with weaponry, but greater emphasis is placed on the "va-

---

[67] 1 *Enoch* 2:1 and 5:1–2, trans. M. BLACK. See also my previous discussion, in ch. 3, of the contemplation of nature as a spiritual exercise.

rieties of adornment" produced by these technologies, such as cosmetics, jewelry, and colorful dyes, which are condemned because they perpetuate vanity and lust. In Greek, the word *kosmos* can means both "universe" and "adornment", and this dual meaning seems to be operating in this text.[68] Adornment and vanity signify a superficial orientation toward the world, in which the artificial beauty created by humans (with the help of daimons) is glorified to a greater degree than God's majesty and his wondrous creation.[69]

This critique of metallurgy and the tinctorial arts in *Book of Enoch* was undoubtedly one of the reasons that this myth of alchemical origins became popularly known among alchemists, though neither Zosimos nor the author of *Isis to Horus* respond to its charge that their arts lead to vanity. Instead, they both address the Enochian claim that their arts are revealed by daimons. The author of *Isis to Horus* responds by portraying Isis as a victor over the daimons' lust, and therefore her methods of obtaining alchemical wisdom are in accordance with the natural order (like begets like). Zosimos, whose theories of the divine and natural order (*maat*) are very similar to those expressed in the *Book of Enoch*, uses the fallen angels myth as a polemic against his competitors, who wish to seduce Theosebeia with their false teachings. His approval of the ancient books of *Chema*, which were allegedly revealed by the fallen angels, makes sense in light of the Hermetic re-working of the Enochian myth. He can condone these books because according to Egyptian alchemical tradition, Isis, one of the women whom the angels desired, acquired this scientific knowledge not through

---

68 1 *Enoch* was originally written in Aramaic and translated into several languages, including Greek and the Ethiopian version which I am citing here. The Ethiopian word for "world" appears to be synonymous with adornment, as it is in Greek, because scholars have translated the Ethiopian phrase *tawaleto 'alam* as both "transmutation of the world" and "varieties of adornment". See n. 57 above.

69 In Hellenistic philosophy, particularly in Platonic thought, artifice is often opposed to divine creation.

lust or unholy alliances, but through her skillful employment of natural methods.

THE ANTHROPOS, OR PRIMAL HUMAN

I have shown how Zosimos uses certain themes from Jewish texts to argue against the "unnatural" methods of his competitors, which are based on daimonic revelation. In this last example, taken from Zosimos's *On Apparatus and Furnaces (Letter Omega)*, I will discuss his use of Jewish/Christian Gnostic teachings on the Anthropos, or primal human, which he uses to instruct Theosebeia on the difference between corporeal and incorporeal knowledge and how each is obtained.[70] He draws upon Hermetic and Gnostic myths, as well as Hesiod's myth of Prometheus and Epimetheus, in order to present a universal doctrine of the Anthropos, but he focuses particularly on Gnostic views of the Anthropos. Though Christian themes figure prominently in his discussions, Zosimos always refers to these ideas as "Jewish" or "Hebrew", never as Christian.[71] This designation appears to be related to his portrayal

---

70 "Gnosticism" is a problematic category for several reasons, including its use as an umbrella term to describe a broad range of ideas (including Hermetic thought). Neither Hermetism nor Jewish/Christian Gnosticism should be understood as uniform doctrines. For a fuller treatment of problems with the term "Gnosticism", see Michael WILLIAMS, *Rethinking "Gnosticism": An Argument for Dismantling a Dubious Category* (Princeton: Princeton University Press, 1996); and Karen KING, *What is Gnosticism?* (Cambridge: Belknap Press of Harvard University Press, 2003). See also Garth FOWDEN, *The Egyptian Hermes* (esp. ch.1), and Brian COPENHAVER's introduction to *Hermetica*, for discussions of the diverse doctrines within Hermetic literature and problems with categorization.

71 There are Gnostic texts which appear to be of Jewish origin and make no mention of Christ, whereas others are clearly Christian, and still others in which Jesus is mentioned, but plays a minor role. I will not attempt here to identify which types or schools of Gnosticism Zosimos is identifying with, but rather how he presents his own version of Gnostic ideas, which seems to me to be an eclectic mix, including oral traditions or unknown texts as well as Sethian and Valentinian Gnostic texts. For other comparisons of alchemical and Gnostic texts, see Daniel STOLZENBURG's discussion of Zosimean alchemy and Gnosticism in "Unpropitious Tinctures", 18–19,

of these beliefs as the "ancient" wisdom of Jewish metallurgical traditions; the term "Christian" may have seemed out of context in light of the topic, or may not have carried the same prestige given that Christianity was relatively new. It is also possible that Zosimos was being cautious due to imperial persecutions of Christians; the last of these, issued by Diocletian in 303 CE, swept through Upper Egypt, and several Christians from the Panopolis area were martyred.[72]

Zosimos opens *On Apparatus and Furnaces* with a discussion of how his competitors have been ridiculing an old alchemical book that he holds in high regard.[73] This book likely contained "natural" astrological methods for preparing tinctures, because Zosimos in turn ridicules his rivals for using a daimonic form of astrology in their alchemical operations. He says that their formulas—by which he probably means their tables for determining the propitious appearances of daimons—yield inconsistent results, and when their operations fail, they admit there might be some truth to the older methods (i.e., those respected by Zosimos), but when they succeed, they forget "the former clear proofs" and credit their daimons for granting them success.[74] These alchemists, he says, are driven by Fate. Their personalities are as inconstant as the daimons, who, as they are "transformed in the course of the changing times of their

---

where he links Zosimos's text to Nag Hammadi writings like *On the Origin of the World*, the *Apocryphon of John*, and *Hypostasis of the Archons*. See also Régine CHARRON, "The Apocryphon of John and the Græco-Egyptian Alchemical Literature", *Vigiliæ Christianæ* 59.4 (2005): 438–456; and, more recently, Kyle FRASER's argument that Zosimean alchemy can be interpreted as a Sethian-gnostic inspired baptismal ritual in "Baptized in Gnōsis", 43–49.

72 See Karolien GEENS, "Panopolis, A Nome Capital in Egypt in the Roman and Byzantine Period", 387–388.
73 This book is called *On Furnaces and Apparatus*, but it is not the same as Zosimos's similarly titled text.
74 *Auth.Mem.* 1.2-3. I am working with the Greek and with MERTENS' French translation of this text, as well the English translation by Howard JACKSON, which is incomplete. Quotations here are from JACKSON, *Zosimos of Panopolis on the Letter Omega*.

fate", are beneficent one moment and maleficent the next.⁷⁵ Such men, he writes to Theosebeia, have "no conception of anything incorporeal, and [...] no understanding of Fate herself, who conducts them justly. Instead they insult the instruction she gives through corporeal experience, and imagine nothing beyond the good fortune she grants".⁷⁶

Zosimos then proceeds to tell Theosebeia a story about the Anthropos, in which he upholds the primal human, who is a divine mediator between heaven and earth, in contradistinction to the daimonic mediators invoked by his rivals. Myths of the Anthropos are found in several Hermetic and Jewish/Christian gnostic texts.⁷⁷ This literature is quite diverse, and therefore there are differences in the way the primal human is conceived, but he is typically portrayed as a divinely created entity, the "Son of God", or "Son of Man", who is created in God's image and becomes the archetypal model for the creation of human beings. In some versions of the story, including the one presented by Zosimos, the primal human falls into matter, and thus becomes associated with the spiritual principle concealed within nature, and with the divine spirit (or divine image) trapped within the human body.⁷⁸ The Anthropos also has a soteriological function in that he bestows spiritual knowledge upon creation, which enables humans to return to their divine source. The various emanations of the Anthropos

75 *Auth.Mem.* 1.2. JACKSON's translation.
76 *Auth.Mem.* 1.4. JACKSON's translation.
77 The Anthropos also figures prominently in Manichean literature, but Zosimos is drawing particularly on Hermetic and Gnostic versions of the myth. Examples of these myths can be found in the Hermetic texts, CH I (i.e., *Poimandres*, which contains the most detailed account of the Anthropos), and CH VIII; and in the Gnostic texts, *On the Origin of the World* (NHC II, 5), and *Apocryphon of John* (NHC II, 1). This is by no means a comprehensive list, but a representative one.
78 For detailed comparisons of the Anthropos myth in Hermetic and gnostic literature, see Jonathan PESTE, "The Poimandres Group in Corpus Hermeticum: Myth, Mysticism, and Gnosis in Late Antiquity", 49–83. See also Kurt RUDOLPH's summary of the basic features of Anthropos myths in *Gnosis: The Nature and History of Gnosticism* (San Francisco: HarperSanFrancisco, 1987), 92–94.

as he appears in the divine and cosmic realms can be seen as series of sympathetic links that unite the human spirit with the divine.[79]

Zosimos explains that the doctrine of the primal human is known to many cultures: the Egyptians call him Thoth, the "interpreter of all things", and the Jews, Chaldeans, and other Near Eastern peoples call him Adam, or "earth".[80] Thoth and Adam are the names of the "man of flesh", but the Anthropos is also composed of an inner "man of spirit", whose name is Phōs, or light.[81] Zosimos reads Hesiod's myth of Prometheus and Epimetheus as the Greek version of the Anthropos myth.[82] He identifies the spiritual man with Prometheus, who brought heavenly fire to humankind and warned his brother Epimetheus not to accept the gifts of Zeus, or Fate.[83] Epimetheus, who accepts Fate's gift of Pandora, and thus indirectly brings evil into the world, is the man of flesh. Zosimos says that Prometheus and Epimetheus are to be understood as "a single man, according to the allegorical explanation, that is to say, a soul and body".[84]

---

79   The emanations of the Anthropos are specifically described as sympathetic links in Hermetic texts, for example, in CH VIII: "According to the father's will, and unlike other living things on earth, mankind, the third living thing, came to be in the image of the cosmos, possessing mind as well as a relation not only of sympathy with the second god but also of thought with the first god". Trans. B. COPENHAVER.

80   *Auth.Mem.* 1.8. Zosimos lists several etymological renderings of the name Adam, including "blood-red earth", and "fiery earth". Of course, in Genesis 2:19–23, Adam is also an "interpreter of all things" in that he names all the living creatures.

81   *Auth.Mem.* 1.10. Zosimos uses the more gender-neutral term *anthrōpos* when referring to the beings of flesh and spirit, but JACKSON translates this as "man". Since Zosimos uses male figures as representatives of the various manifestations of the Anthropos, I will follow JACKSON's gendered translation in order to avoid confusion and cumbersome prose.

82   HESIOD's *Theogony and Works and Days* contain the earliest extant versions of the Prometheus and Epimetheus myth. In later versions, Prometheus and Epimetheus are said to be the creators of humankind, and their stories become more assimilated with themes in Genesis. Prometheus's son, Deucalion, is identified with Noah, for example.

83   Zosimos explicitly identifies Zeus with Fate. See *Auth.Mem.* 1.6.

84   *Auth.Mem.* 1.12. My translation, based on MERTENS'.

Zosimos gives a "Hebrew" account of how the man of spirit became flesh. In Paradise, Phōs, who was "innocent and unactivated", was persuaded by the agents of Fate to "clothe himself with their Adam, who comes from Fate".[85] The sinister agents of Fate rejoiced that they had deceived Phōs and enslaved him. A similar theme is found in several Gnostic texts, where Adam's body is created by the cosmic creator and his minions, the planetary archons, but Adam's spirit is created by a divine source. The notion of two different creators for the spirit and body of the Anthropos, one good and one evil, is not found in Hermetic literature, and Zosimos apparently uses the Gnostic version to underscore the difference between corporeal and incorporeal knowledge, since he plays upon the distinction between flesh and spirit throughout the text.[86]

Zosimos refers to the man of spirit in Hermetic terms as the Son of God, one of the divine beings of the "triad which cannot be named".[87] In Hermetic thought, the divine is often conceived as a trinity consisting of the divine Father and his two "sons", Mind (*nous*) and *logos* (also called Will).[88] Mind and *logos* are understood

85 *Auth.Mem.* I.11. JACKSON's translation.
86 In Hermetic literature it is strongly emphasized that God is the sole creator. See, for example, CH XI, in which debates about two creators are addressed, and it is insisted that there is only one creator: "Clearly, there is someone who makes these things, and quite evidently he is one, for soul is one, life is one, and matter is one. But who is this someone? Who else but the one god? To whom, if not to god alone, might it belong to make ensouled living beings? God is one, then. {How entirely absurd!} Since you have agreed that the cosmos is always one, that the sun is one, the moon one, and divinity one, do you propose to number god himself among them?" Trans. B. COPENHAVER.
87 *Auth.Mem.* I.7. My translation, based on MERTENS.
88 My account of Hermetic notions of the trinity is largely taken from *Poimandres* (CH I), a text which Zosimos was familiar with, but these trinitarian ideas can be found in several Hermetic texts. See also J. PESTE's discussions of these divine entities in "The Poimandres Group in Corpus Hermeticum", 49–54. H. JACKSON also discusses the Hermetic trinity, but I do not fully agree with his interpretations. He speculates that the trinity consists of the Father, *logos*, and either the material cosmos or man possessing mind, and therefore overlooks the Demiurge, or the second Mind.

as aspects of the one ineffable God, but they are also personified as distinct entities with their own specific, yet interrelated, functions. Mind (also called the second Mind) is the Demiurge, who creates the cosmic framework and the seven planets that govern the cosmos; the planetary government is called Fate. The third aspect of the trinity, *logos*, also called the Son of God, is the will and word of God; he is a co-creator of the cosmos, and the divine presence within nature. The Son of God is also the Anthropos, the divine being who becomes flesh, and the savior who awakens humans to their divine nature.

Zosimos presents the following Hermetic view of the Son of God as a savior figure:

> [C]ontemplate the Son of God, who becomes all for the love of holy souls, in order to draw the soul out of the realm of Fate into the realm of the incorporeal. See him becoming All—god, angel, man subject to suffering; for, being omnipotent, he becomes everything he wills. And he obeys the Father; insinuating himself through every body, illuminating the intellect of each soul and spurring it into the realm of bliss, where it was already before the corporeal elements came to be. The intellect follows after him, and under his action, tends to itself and is guided into that light.[89]

The Son of God, who is the personification of divine will, has the qualities of omnipresence and also the ability to appear at will. Zosimos associates this aspect of the Hermetic trinity with Jesus Christ. Like the Hermetic Son of God, Jesus is a divine savior who

---

As Jackson notes, there are many triads in Hermetic literature, and this can result in confusion. See *Zosimos of Panopolis on the Letter Omega*, 44–45, nn. 26–27 and 30. See also MERTENS' discussion of the triad, and how it has been interpreted in various ways, in *Zosime de Panopolis: Mémoires Authentiques*, 76–80.

89   *Auth.Mem.* 1.7. My translation, based on MERTENS and JACKSON.

has the ability to appear whenever and to whomever he wills, and to take on different forms:

> Adam was attached to Jesus Christ, who made him ascend to where those named *phōtes* had sojourned before. He even appeared to men quite helpless by becoming a man who suffered and was beaten with rods; while in secret, he carried off his own *phōtes*, he who did not suffer at all, but instead showed that death could be trampled underfoot and repelled. And to this day—and (he will do it) until the end of the world—he comes to carry off his own, both secretly and openly, counseling them secretly and through their intellect to get rid of their Adam.[90]

At first glance, Zosimos seems to be giving a docetic account of Jesus, in which Christ only *appears* as a man of flesh and does not actually suffer at the hands of man. Gnostic christologies are often noted for their docetic doctrines, which have been (problematically) used to support claims that Gnostic teachings are radically dualistic and utterly devalue the cosmos and the flesh.[91] But elsewhere Zosimos says that the man of light—Prometheus, in this case—inhabits body, mind, and soul.[92] Likewise, the Hermetic Son of God is said to pervade all bodies. The appearance of the Son of God in the material realm, or in physical form, does not diminish the divine in any way. Zosimos *does* make sharp distinctions between the flesh and the spirit in this text, but it is not his intention to denigrate the physical world, which he believes is essentially divine. In antiquity, the terms "flesh" and "spirit" were used to

---

[90] Auth.Mem. 1.13. In *On Electrum*, Zosimos refers to the Son of God as the "Holy Spirit", and "the Word", which underscores the conceptual and terminological slippage between Hermetic and Christian notions of the Trinity. See CMA, *Syr.* II.12.3–4.

[91] On the problematics of docetism in interpretations of Gnostic theologies, see KING, *What is Gnosticism?*, 208–213, and WILLIAMS, *Rethinking "Gnosticism"*, 126.

[92] Auth.Mem. 1.12.

signify spiritual ignorance (or worldliness) and spiritual wisdom, and this is the sense in which Zosimos is using them. His emphasis on the manifold appearances of the spiritual man is meant to show that the divine is omnipresent, but that this is only *apparent* to those who are spiritually aware. Zosimos calls those who are saved by Jesus Christ *phōtes*; they are enlightened human beings who recognize their true spiritual nature and have shed their "Adam", or their ignorance.[93] They have transcended Fate, and therefore death, by realizing the immortal spirit within. Zosimos indicates that this spiritual knowledge is available to all humans who make the effort to understand their divine nature, because he says that Epimetheus, the man of flesh, had a "change of mind" and became enlightened, and that he "explains all...for those who have ears of the mind. But those who have only bodily ears belong to Fate, for they neither grasp nor confess anything else".[94]

Zosimos contrasts the Son of God with the Mimic Daimon (ἀντίμιμος δαίμων, *antimimos daimōn*), who guides the "Adams", the men of flesh.[95] The Mimic, who blasphemously calls himself the Son of God, has an ugly body as well as an ugly soul; he is jealous of the men of light and wishes to deceive them.[96] The Mimic resembles the Gnostic Demiurge, the cosmic creator who is often portrayed as ugly and ignorant or jealous of the spiritual realities above.[97] But given that Zosimos views the Demiurge as the

---

93 Auth.Mem. 1.10.
94 Auth.Mem. 1.16.
95 The concept of a Mimic Daimon is not found in the extant Hermetic literature.
96 Auth.Mem. 1.14.
97 JACKSON, *Zosimos of Panopolis on the Letter Omega*, 53, n. 67. See also MERTENS, *Zosime de Panopolis: Mémoires Authentiques*, 104–106, n. 89. Jackson and Mertens both note that in the Gnostic texts *Apocryphon of John* and *Pistis Sophia*, there is mention of a "counterfeit spirit" created by the cosmic rulers (i.e., the Demiurge and the planetary archons), which they impart to humans in order to keep them ignorant of divine reality. The ignorance and false guidance of the counterfeit spirit is also a feature of Zosimos's text, and he is probably familiar with these Gnostic ideas, but he uses them in a way that does not conflict with Hermetic beliefs.

Mind of God, and as one of the holy trinity, it is certainly not his intention to compare the Mimic to the Demiurge. In Zosimos's myth, the Mimic is not the creator of the world, but is described as one who has not yet appeared; therefore, the Mimic is more comparable to the Antichrist.[98] Zosimos says that before the Mimic Daimon appears, he will send a forerunner from Persia who tells "fabulous, deceptive tales and lead[s] men on about Fate".[99] Similar predictions, that forerunners of the Antichrist will appear and deceive the people with false teachings, are found in the New Testament.[100] Zosimos does not say what will happen when the Mimic Daimon comes. His main point is that the "men of flesh" (namely his competitors, who know only Fate) are guided by daimons and deceived by false teachings, whereas the "men of light" have the Son of God as their guide.

Zosimos includes a puzzle that, if solved, would reveal the name of the forerunner of the Mimic Daimon: "The letters of his name are nine, if the diphthong is preserved", he writes, "in accordance with the pattern of Fate".[101] The word he uses for Fate is *heimarmenē* (εἱμαρμένη), which has nine letters and includes a diphthong. The name of the forerunner, then, will have a similar pattern. Scholars including Reitzenstein, Festugière, and Jackson have all proposed that the answer to this riddle is Mani, the famous third-century prophet and founder of the Manichæan religion. His name was often rendered Manichæos (Μανιχαιος) in Greek, which includes nine letters and a diphthong. Mani was also from Persia, and Zosimos mentions that the forerunner of the Mimic Daimon will come from there. Howard Jackson argues that the seer Nikotheos, whom Zosimos mentions earlier in this text, could

---

98 This is also FESTUGIÈRE's assessment. See *La Révélation d'Hermès Trismégiste*, vol. I, 271, n. 3.
99 *Auth.Mem.* 1.14.
100 See, for example, Mark 13, 2 Thess. 2, and Rev. 13.
101 *Auth.Mem.* 1.14. Thanks to Michael WILLIAMS, who was a respondent at a 2008 Society of Biblical Literature conference panel at which I delivered a paper on Zosimos and the Anthropos myth, for suggesting that I further pursue this riddle. Unfortunately, a riddle it remains.

have been a prophet from the Elchasaite sect, which Mani broke with early on, and that Zosimos's Gnostic sources or associates could therefore be anti-Manichæan.¹⁰² While this is an interesting and plausible speculation, it is very difficult to prove. Zosimos does not mention Mani elsewhere in his teachings, and it does not make sense that the rivals whom he criticizes in this text would be Manichæans, because Manichæans were generally opposed to the summoning of daimons and other kinds of "magical" practices.¹⁰³ While I do not want to rule out the possibility of Mani, I am not convinced that he is the answer to this riddle. In other writings, Zosimos mentions two different riddles dealing with a nine-lettered name. In *On Electrum*, cited earlier in this chapter, he claims that wise Solomon knows of a nine-lettered name that gives him power over the daimons.¹⁰⁴ There is also a riddle of the nine-lettered name of God found in the *Sibylline Oracles*.¹⁰⁵ Zosimos makes another reference to nine letters in the text *On Mercury*: "Just as the mystery of the nine letters is the common key of visible things, as it says in the *Book of Names* and in the *Book of Amulets*, so the letter *theta* contains the whole key of the visible art, the key that resides in all species of mercury".¹⁰⁶ In this last reference, the nine letters unlock the mysteries of the visible world, as opposed to the

FIGURE 9.

The Greek letter Theta, which "contains the whole key to the visible art".

---

102   JACKSON, *Zosimos of Panopolis on the Letter Omega*, 54, n. 72.
103   Theoretically they were opposed to this. As Paul MIRECKI points out, there is evidence that some Egyptian Manichæans were practicing forbidden forms of magic. See P. MIRECKI, "Manichæan Allusions to Ritual and Magic: Spells for Invisibility in the Coptic Kephalia", in *The Light and the Darkness: Studies in Manichæism and its World*, P. MIRECKI and J. BEDUHN, eds. (Leiden: Brill, 2001), 173-174.
104   CMA *Syr.* II, 12.5
105   See *Sibylline Oracles*, 1.175.
106   CMA *Syr.* II, 9.1.

spiritual world. He goes on to say, "this book is about mercury, but it needs another to complete it".[107] The riddle of the nine letters thus appears to be somewhat common in the literature that Zosimos was reading, whether it stood for the name of God or another entity that could grant one power over the daimons, or whether it signified the key to the mysteries of the visible world, or Fate. I would not be surprised if Zosimos has a more mundane solution that would be obvious to Theosebeia: the nine letters plus the diphthong might simply spell the name of a rival alchemist, temple, or guild; one of the "men of Fate", who are misleading Theosebeia with their false teachings and unnatural methods.

Although Zosimos creates an opposition between the man of spirit and the man of flesh in his Anthropos myth, he is also careful to note that they are one being, the body and soul of every human. The cosmic struggle of good and evil forces is essentially a contest of wisdom and ignorance. The message of Zosimos's myth is that people must activate the "man of light" within and overcome the deceptions of Fate, which keep them ignorant of their true spiritual nature. He also intends this as a lesson in cosmic sympathy.[108] The human spirit is sympathetically linked to the Son of God because the human spirit contains his divine image. The Son of God is also the divine presence within nature, and Zosimos believes that by contemplating the natural order (*maat*, the divine will manifest in creation), one can penetrate the mysteries of creation.[109] By contrast, the Mimic Daimon is sympathetically linked to the daimons, the ambivalent powers of Fate, and to ignorance. Daimonic methods of cosmic sympathy yield false understandings of the cosmos, in Zosimos's opinion, and this includes the notion that the cosmos is ruled by Fate. He believes that it is a mistake to think

107 Ibid.
108 This is reinforced by his demonstration of how the letters of the name Adam correspond to the cardinal directions, and that by tracing a series of divine signatures, or sympathies, one can perceive the divine presence within self and cosmos. See my previous discussion of this passage in chapter 3.
109 This is a prominent theme in Hermetic literature.

that the world is solely governed by Fate and its daimonic agents, because the divine presence, which is all-powerful, is everywhere. Fate is the guide of the ignorant "men of flesh", whereas the "men of light", who are spiritually aware, perceive Fate in another way, as divine providence revealed in the natural order.

Jewish/Christian colleagues

After this analysis of Zosimos's use of Jewish texts, the question remains as to whether or not Zosimos was working with actual Jewish/Christian colleagues, or just reading their works. While there were Christians, and perhaps also Jews living in the Panopolis area in Zosimos's time, there is not enough evidence to establish whether any of them were metallurgists.[110] However, I think it is reasonable to assume that Theosebeia was Jewish or Christian. Greek names with the compound *theos* (God) are often indicators of Jewish or Christian parentage.[111] And in almost every instance where Zosimos elaborates on Jewish/Christian religious ideas, it is in works addressed to Theosebeia.[112] However, not all of Zosimos's works are addressed to her. His allegorical work on statue-making, *On Excellence* (discussed in chapter 3), appears to have been written for other Egyptian priests because his religious references are overwhelmingly Egyptian and would likely have required some degree of priestly initiation in order to understand.[113]

---

110   See my discussion of this in chapter 2. There is evidence of Jewish/Christian names in Panopolis in the late third or early fourth century, which comes from the partial topographical survey *P.Berl.Bork.*

111   Geens, "Panopolis, A Nome Capital in Egypt in the Roman and Byzantine Period", 371.

112   The one exception is CAAG III.42, *The True Book of Sophe the Egyptian and of the Divine Lord of the Hebrews and the Powers of Sabaoth*, which is in a partial and corrupt state.

113   Some artisans who didn't have the proper initiation were excluded from the Opening of the Mouth rites that animated divine statues, which Zosimos alludes to in this text. See, for example, Derchain, "L'Atelier des Orfevres à Dendara et les origins de l'Alchimie", 220.

There is a *locus desperatus* in this text that contains an unflattering reference to Jews. It begins with an account of how nature, having taken the *visage* of the All, now has to return to particularity, and it experiences this as a death; the next line reads "whenever, having to express itself in a barbarous language, (nature) imitates, for example, the Jewish language against its will".[114] H. D. Saffrey explains that this "death" might be more painful or disappointing if it occurs by way of a magical formula recited in a foreign language, and that in this passage one can see traces of "well-known Egyptian anti-semitism".[115] Zosimos seems a far cry from an anti-Semite, but this odd passage underscores the notion that some of Zosimos's writings were meant to instruct other Egyptians, and that his letters to Theosebeia are probably intended for a multi-religious audience, including Theosebeia as a Jew/Christian, and her students or guild members, who were may have been a mixed group of Jews/Christians, Egyptians, and Greeks.[116]

Conclusion

Zosimos is clearly a champion of Hebrew metallurgical techniques, especially the distillatory methods and equipment invented by Maria the Jewess. There is a lack of evidence that Hebrews had a particularly religious approach to metallurgy, and given the religious content of his letters to his friend, Theosebeia, it appears that she is curious about this aspect of metallurgy as practiced in the Egyptian temples. In his letters to her, Zosimos articulates a Jewish/Christian approach that is in agreement with his temple traditions, often making use of the very same Jewish texts (*Testa-*

---

114   My translation of H. D. SAFFREY's, in "Mort et transformation de la matière : à propos d'un *locus desperatus* des *Mémoires Authentiques de Zosime de Panopolis* (x 6.130) », in *L'Alchimie et ses racines philosophiques : La tradition grecque et la tradition arabe*, ed. C. VIANO (Paris: Vrin, 2005), 110.

115   Ibid, 111.

116   These three religious/cultural approaches are harmonized in *Auth.Mem*.1 (*On Apparatus and Furnaces, Letter Omega*).

ment of Solomon, or *Book of Enoch*, for example) to uphold certain Jewish teachings while condemning others. His hermeneutical style reveals his adroitness at finding shared truths upon which to build agreement, as well as his universalism, which was shared by many philosophers in his era.[117] Ancient philosophy involves both theological and scientific speculation, and it is one thing to have different techniques and different traditions of worship, but when it comes to theories about the natural order, inconsistencies and diverse opinions are less acceptable, because the natural order is the epitome of consistency and universality, a reflection of the divine mind and divine providence. This emphasis on universality is one sense in which alchemy can be seen as a precursor of modern science.

The religious ideas that Zosimos promotes, especially the upholding of the universal creator-God as the force and the wisdom that directs all of nature, and his disdain for "magical" forms of daimonology and astrology, represent two competing approaches to metallurgy in his day, both of which were being promoted by temple priests. Theosebeia, who is seeking advice from Zosimos, is also consulting other priests, and Zosimos is worried that she is being corrupted by the astrological methods of his competitors. He finds ways to reach her through his skillful interpretations of Jewish texts, which illustrate the underlying harmony that his traditional "natural methods" approach has with Jewish/Christian and Greek teachings.[118] His syncretism shows that his approach

---

117 This is especially true in Neoplatonic philosophy, and is evident in the works of Porphyry and Iamblichus, who were near contemporaries of Zosimos.

118 Zosimos's explicit inclusion of Greeks in his universalizing efforts is in contrast to some anti-Greek sentiments in the philosophical *Hermetica*. In CH XVI, for example, there is a desire to protect Egyptian language and Hermetic books in particular from Greek translators, who will corrupt the meaning and spiritual power of the words: "For all the Greeks have [...] is empty speech, good for showing off; and the philosophy of the Greeks is just noisy talk. For our part, we use not words, but sounds full of energy". See FOWDEN, *The Egyptian Hermes*, 36–37; and Jan ASSMANN's discussion of ways in which Hermeticism and other late period Egyptian texts rein-

to the sacred art is not just for temple artisans who make divine statues, but a path to divine and cosmic understanding shared by philosophers from different cultures, all seeking and reflecting the same universal truths.

forced cultural boundaries between Egyptians and Greeks in *The Mind of Egypt*, 393–398.

Spirits in the Material World

Alchemy, Theurgy, and the Divine Cosmos

Zosimos's spiritual approach to alchemy is very much aligned with the "grand theme" of late ancient philosophy: the soul's liberation from the bonds of Fate (or matter), and its return journey to the divine source.[1] Metaphysical speculations on the relationship between spirit and matter—e.g.: How did the One become the All? What is the relationship between the noetic intelligibles and the sensible world? Is the material world good and holy, or a prison for the soul?—were particularly prominent in the Platonic, Hermetic, and Gnostic philosophies in which Zosimos was immersed. In the previous chapter we saw how Zosimos reinterpreted Jewish and Christian texts to answer similar questions and articulate his distinctions between the spiritual "man of light", who is aligned with divine providence and the will of God, and the "man of flesh", who trusts in daimons and follows only Fate. This chapter further investigates Zosimos's ideas of spirit and matter by comparing the Egyptian and Hermetic philosophies embraced by Zosimos with the theurgical Neoplatonism of Iamblichus, who was Zosimos's contemporary.[2]

---

1   Garth Fowden's phrase. See *The Egyptian Hermes*, 88.
2   Iamblichus died around 325 CE, and Zosimos flourished sometime between 270 and 325 CE. For issues regarding the dating of Iamblichus and his work, see the introduction to *Iamblichus: De Mysteriis*, trans. and ed. Emma Clarke, John Dillon, and Jackson Hershbell (Atlanta: Society of Biblical Literature, 2003), xviii-xxiv. Unless otherwise noted, all quotations from Iamblichus's surviving work on theurgy, *De Mysteriis* (abbreviated DM), are from this translation, which is based on the Budé edition of Édouard Des Places.

Alchemy and theurgy have long been considered compatible practices.³ In recent years, scholars have claimed that Zosimean alchemy is a form of "Gnostic theurgy", or that it bears a close resemblance to Iamblichean theurgy, but without offering any detailed comparisons or justifications for these claims; I aim to provide a more substantial comparison in this chapter.⁴ Iamblichus is

3   An internet search on "alchemy and theurgy" will reveal numerous examples of this linkage, which is particularly prominent in contemporary magical or esoteric communities. Until very recently, scholars commonly referred to alchemy and theurgy as "irrational", "bizarre", and "obscurantist" magico-religious practices that contributed to the decline of rational science and philosophy in late antiquity. E. R. DODDS is perhaps the most famous and influential example, in *Greeks and the Irrational*, Appendix II, 284, 287, and 295; arguing along similar lines, see also Samuel SAMBURSKY, *The Physical World of Late Antiquity* (Princeton: Princeton University Press, 1962), 47, 59. Sambursky wrongly claims that Iamblichus was a practicing alchemist. There is an alchemical text attributed to Iamblichus in the Greco-Egyptian alchemical literature (CAAG IV.19), but Sambursky does not take into account the alchemical tradition of pseudonymous authorship. Other scholars have been more sympathetic to alchemy and theurgy, such as Antoine FAIVRE, who views them as important currents of western esoteric thought and classifies them as forms of "white magic". See FAIVRE, *Access to Western Esotericism*, 36. In all of these cases, however, alchemy and theurgy are viewed as forms of magic. Although some practitioners of these arts in different times and places might consider their practices to be magical, Zosimos and Iamblichus would firmly reject this label (as we shall see).

4   Garth FOWDEN notes that there are similarities between Zosimos's allegory, *On Excellence*, and Iamblichean theurgy, and suggests this as an area for further study. See FOWDEN, *The Egyptian Hermes*, 153, n. 43. Daniel STOLZENBERG claims that Zosimean alchemy is a type of "Gnostic theurgy", in "Unpropitious Tinctures: Alchemy, Astrology and Gnosis According to Zosimos of Panopolis", 4, 29–31. Kyle FRASER also suggests that Zosimean alchemy is a form of late ancient theurgy in "Zosimos of Panopolis and the Book of Enoch: Alchemy as Forbidden Knowledge", 131, n. 22. To my knowledge, the scholars who have gone the farthest to establish Zosimean alchemy as a type of Iamblichean theurgy include Aaron CHEAK in "The Perfect Black: Egypt and Alchemy", *Alchemical Traditions From Antiquity to the Avant-Garde*, ed. A. CHEAK (Melbourne: Numen Books, 2013), and myself, in earlier iteration of this chapter from my dissertation, S. GRIMES, "Zosimus of Panopolis: Alchemy, Nature, and Religion in Late Antiquity" (PhD diss., Syracuse University, 2006).

of particular interest because he writes his exposition of theurgy, *De Mysteriis*, in the guise of a Hermetic priest named Abamon and frames theurgy as ancient Egyptian hieratic art.[5] By venturing further into these Neoplatonic and Hermetic currents, we can better situate Zosimos's writings in some of the philosophical developments of his day, focusing particularly on theories of divine presence in nature and in material objects (like statues), and the goal of divinization, or becoming god.

What is theurgy?

Theurgy (θεουργία, *theourgia*), "work of the gods" or "divine work", is a term used by late ancient writers to denote spiritual practices that aim to develop the mind, deepen one's ethics, and purify and elevate the soul, awakening it to its divine nature.[6] The term first appeared in the *Chaldean Oracles*, a collection of verses from the late second century CE that were allegedly transmitted by the gods to Julian the Chaldean and his son, Julian the Theurgist.[7] The

5   For discussions of the Egyptian elements of Iamblichean theurgy, see Algis Uždavinys, *Philosophy and Theurgy in Late Antiquity* [2010] (Kettering, OH: Angelico Press/Sophia Perennis, 2014); Dennis Clark, "Iamblichus's Egyptian Neoplatonic Theology in *De Mysteriis*", *The International Journal of the Platonic Tradition* 2 (2008); and Gregory Shaw, *Theurgy and the Soul*, 21–23. Iamblichus also claims that other ancient Near Eastern cultures practiced theurgy—namely the Chaldeans and Assyrians, though he mentions these cultures less frequently than the Egyptians.
6   As Crystal Addey points out, theurgy is difficult to define. I am adapting parts of her definition here, which she has gleaned from Neoplatonic sources. See Addey, *Divination and Theurgy in Neoplatonism* (Burlington, VT: Ashgate Publishing, 2014), 24–25.
7   See Ruth Majercik, *The Chaldean Oracles: Text, Translation, and Commentary* (Leiden: Brill, 1989), 1–3. The two Julians also wrote works on theurgic rituals, daimons, and the planetary zones—none of which have survived. The *Chaldean Oracles* only survive in fragments, and most of these are gathered from citations found in Neoplatonic works. For further information on Chaldean theurgy, see also Hans Lewy, *Chaldean Oracles and Theurgy* (Paris: Augustinian Studies, 1978), and Sarah Iles Johnston, *Hekate Soteria: A Study of Hekate's Roles in the Chaldean Oracles and Related*

Oracles became immensely popular with Neoplatonists. As Ruth Majercik observes, "the Oracles were regarded by the later Neoplatonists—from Porphyry to Damascius—as authoritative revelatory literature equal in importance only to Plato's *Timæus*".[8] Porphyry was the first to write a commentary on the *Oracles* and evaluate the efficacy of theurgic rites, and his student, Iamblichus, expanded the scope of theurgy beyond the *Oracles* and developed it into a full-fledged philosophy of ritual.[9] Although scholars typically use the word "theurgy", the vocabulary used by ancient writers is more diverse: terms like *hieratikē technē* (priestly art or method); *telestikē* (to consecrate, initiate); *theosophia* (divine knowledge); and *hiera hagisteia* (sacred rites, temple worship) are often used synonymously with theurgy.[10] These terms all imply a mindset appropriate to ritual performance and communion with the gods; for theurgists, this sacred orientation is understood not only as a proper approach to ritual, but also as a way of being.[11] Ilinca Tanaseanu-Döbler argues that Iamblichus's contribution to theurgy is in "developing a theoretical frame, a ritual *technē* and *epistēmē* that is not tied to different traditions but transcends them".[12] Zosimos, as we have seen, is attempting something similar with his universalizing approach to alchemy, finding common theological concepts in Egyptian, Jewish, and Greek cultures that can be used as an overarching framework for the sacred art (*hiera technē*) of alchemy.

Literature (Atlanta: Scholars Press, 1990).

8   MAJERCIK, *The Chaldean Oracles*, 2. She also notes that Franz CUMONT was the first to refer to the Oracles as the "Bible of the Neoplatonists".

9   For a comparison of Chaldean and Iamblichean theurgy, see JOHNSTON, *Hekate Soteria*, ch. 6. On Iamblichus as the "first philosopher of religion", see Andrew Smith, "Iamblichus, The First Philosopher of Religion?" *Habis* 31 (2000), 345-353.

10   See Algis UŽDAVINYS's discussion of these terms in *Philosophy and Theurgy in Late Antiquity*, 79–82. See also Ilanca TANASEANU-DÖBLER, *Theurgy in Late Antiquity* (Göttingen: Vandenhoeck & Ruprecht, 2013), 14–16, 97–98.

11   I agree with ADDEY, who describes theurgy as "a *way of life* or, strictly speaking, as a *way of being*, as well as a nexus of ritual practices" in *Theurgy and Divination*, 24.

12   TANASEANU-DÖBLER, 102.

As Gregory Shaw has argued, Iamblichean theurgy can also be seen as a demiurgical practice: the theurgist imitates the Demiurge, the divine mind who created an orderly universe out of chaos, by creating an orderly soul out of the chaos of its embodied existence.[13] Zosimean alchemy is also demiurgical. Iamblichus and Zosimos both adhere to Plato's teaching (also prominent in Hermetic thought) that the cosmogonic will of the Demiurge is made manifest in the physical universe, and fulfilled when human souls return to their divine source: the natural world and the divine powers that create and sustain the world provide the very model of order and stability that the soul must emulate in order to ascend.[14] The divine work of theurgy is to bring the soul into harmony with the divine cosmic order so that it may attain union with the Demiurge (*nous*) and fully experience the unity of all things.[15] But for Zosimos at least, this demiurgical approach has roots that extend farther back than Plato: its foundations lie in the Egyptian myth

13   See SHAW, *Theurgy and the Soul*, 15 and ch. 4.
14   See PLATO, *Timaeus* 42B–D, 90D. Iamblichus notes that the Demiurge "sent down souls for this purpose, that they should return to him again", in DM VIII.8; in DM V.20 he explains that the natural order of the cosmos provides a "mode of access" to divine principles on which theurgic rites should be based. Hermetic views of creation and salvation are deeply inspired by Plato's *Timaeus*, and the idea that humans should contemplate and emulate the natural order in order to know god is found throughout the philosophical *Hermetica*.
15   In *De Mysteriis*, Iamblichus held that there were two Demiurges: the cosmic creator, and the pre-essential Demiurge who is the "god of gods" and the "first principle of the intelligible realm" (DM VIII.2.262). The One is the highest principle, but it is entirely transcendent and ineffable, and therefore beyond the reach of the soul. See SHAW's discussion in *Theurgy and the Soul*, 113; John DILLON's outline of Iamblichean metaphysics in *Iamblichi Chalcidensis in Platonis dialogos commentariorum fragmenta*, ed. and trans. John M. DILLON (Leiden: Brill, 1973), 29–39; see also D. CLARK, "Iamblichus's Egyptian Neoplatonic Theology in *De Mysteriis*", 167–169. There is a similar notion of two Demiurges in Hermetic thought: the father god is called Mind, and the cosmic creator is called the second Mind. As explained in chapter 4, Zosimos understands the highest divine powers as a trinity consisting of the father god, who is the source of all, and his "sons", the Demiurge and the Holy Spirit, who are the Mind and the Will of the father god and are responsible for the creation of the universe.

of the sun god's nightly descent into the dark underworld, where he and other gods must defeat the threatening monsters of chaos; the sun-god and his retinue rise triumphantly each morning, having defeated chaos and re-established the divine cosmic order (*maat*). This myth of the sun god's nightly descent echoes the Egyptian cosmogonical myth, in which the creator god fashions an orderly world out of chaos and non-being. These mythic patterns are prominent themes in Zosimos's writings, as we have seen in previous chapters: death and resurrection, the victory of light over darkness, and being in harmony with *maat* (cosmic and social order).

Their sacred orientation to ritual, which involves tracing cosmic sympathies from the material plane to hypercosmic noetic realities, and their emphasis on purification and elevation of the soul, are areas that Zosimos and Iamblichus have the most in common, and the grounds on which Zosimean alchemy can be considered theurgical.

"Cosmic" knowledge versus theurgical knowledge

Zosimos and Iamblichus are careful to distinguish their philosophical approaches from those that are merely "cosmic" in orientation. Cosmic knowledge can signify many things, but these authors most often use this trope to indicate superficial, limited, or false understandings of divine reality. This language is not meant to degrade the cosmos, which they believe is essentially divine; rather, it reflects their notions of spiritual ascent, in which divine reality is topographically imagined as being beyond the realm of the fixed stars; below this cosmic boundary is the realm of Fate, which signifies the spiritual ignorance from which the soul must be liberated. Two specific forms of cosmic orientation will be examined here—magic and rationality—because the ways in which Zosimos and Iamblichus critique these epistemologies (to varying degrees) help to introduce their theurgical orientation, which emphasizes divine revelation and divine causation.

I will start by saying that Egyptians did not typically distinguish between magic, religion, and philosophy. Thoth/Hermes is both a god of knowledge and a god of magic, and in the literature of the Hermetic tradition in which Zosimos is immersed, and which Iamblichus portrays as his theurgical heritage, there are collections of philosophical texts as well as collections of rituals and spells, and works dealing with alchemy, astronomy, and medicine.[16] As Garth Fowden has notably argued, these philosophical and technical treatises should be seen as a single spiritual "way" of Hermes, a path that is intended to unveil the mysteries of the cosmos and the heavens.[17] The collection of ritual texts known as the Greek Magical Papyri (*Papyri Graecae Magicae*, or PGM), which are thought to have been written by Egyptian priests, have "spells" for attracting lovers or cursing enemies, as well as rituals for spiritual ascent, communion, and mystical union with the gods.[18] Magical texts like these may have even contributed to the mystical turn in Neoplatonism that began with Plotinus. As Zeke Mazur has pointed out, Plato's notion of spiritual ascent culminates in a vision of the gods, but Plotinus is the first Platonist to imagine this as a mystical union, in which the soul conjoins with the god.[19] Mazur demonstrates that Plotinus's views were influenced by Gnostic and Hermetic ideas of mystical union, as well as by Egyptian magic, particularly the types of spells one finds in the PGM.[20] Although magic, religion, and philosophy are often seen as a hierarchy, with magic on the bottom and more prone to being associated with illicit practices, in these late ancient Egyptian and Neoplatonic currents, the terms and concepts are often "mixed".[21]

16 See FOWDEN, *The Egyptian Hermes* (1993 ed.), 57–68.
17 This is the thesis of FOWDEN's book cited above; quotation is from p. xxiv.
18 On Egyptian priests as possible authors of texts in the PGM, see ADDEY, 37–38.
19 Zeke MAZUR, "Unio Mystica I", *Dionysius* 21 (Dec 2003), 29–30.
20 Ibid, 35–52.
21 Brian COPENHAVER's phrase in *Hermetica*, xxxix.

The philosopher Iamblichus adopting the persona of an Egyptian priest to write a work on theurgy is a good example of the blurring of philosophical and religious boundaries. As Heidi Marx-Wolf argues, Iamblichus and other second- and third-century Platonists were in dialogue across social boundaries, theorizing about mainstream religious practices, and expressing their philosophical positions in more popular ways.[22] This is a way of gaining social capital: by positioning himself as a philosopher-priest, Iamblichus could lay claim to greater metaphysical insight than other philosophers or priests, perhaps making him more sought-after as a teacher or freelance ritual expert.[23] Zosimos, as we have seen in previous chapters, does a great deal of social positioning himself. He, too, styles himself as one of the intellectual elites in order to show his superiority over other alchemists and priests, probably as a way of gaining professional prestige. Zosimos, as a Hermetic priest and scribe, would already be seen as a philosopher-priest in his tradition: "the-one-who-loves-knowledge", rendered as *philosophos* in Greek, is an Egyptian epithet for the initiates and priests of the House of Life, and Zosimos refers to himself and respected priests in his tradition as philosophers.[24] Each in their own ways, Zosimos and Iamblichus position themselves as learned Hermetic priests (real or fictional) who have greater insight than others. Despite the mixing of magic, religion, and philosophy in this period, neither of them would consider their approaches to be magical, and they are also critical of being overly intellectual or logical.

As Brian Copenhaver rightly notes, Zosimos takes the "stron-

---

22 Heidi MARX-WOLF, *Spiritual Taxonomies and Ritual Authority* (Philadelphia: University of Pennsylvania Press, 2016), 63–64.
23 Ibid, 107–110.
24 See my discussion of Zosimos as a priest and scribe in the House of Life in chapter 2. On this epithet in the House of Life, see JASNOW and ZAUZICH, *Conversations in the House of Life*, 30–31. Zosimos frequently uses the term "philosopher" when referring to great alchemical authors like Democritus or Hermes, as well as to refer to philosophers outside his tradition, like Plato and Aristotle. He also uses it as a term of intellectual respect. There are numerous instances of this in *Auth.Mem.* 1, for example.

gest stand against magic of any Hermetic author".²⁵ In late ancient Mediterranean culture, magic was often associated with attempts to coerce the gods and other cosmic powers. Zosimos echoes this view in *On Apparatus and Furnaces (Letter Omega)*:

> [T]he spiritual man, who knows himself, should not direct anything through the use of magic, not even if it is considered a good thing, nor must he use force upon Necessity [Fate], but rather let it work in accordance with its own nature and divine decree. He should devote himself exclusively to self-understanding, and when he has come to know God, he must hold fast to the trinity that cannot be named and allow Destiny to do what it wants with its own clay, that is, the body".²⁶

Here Zosimos uses his rivals' magical manipulation of divine powers as a foil for his superior "spiritual" efforts to understand oneself and one's divine nature, and to work in harmony with these powers. To "know thyself" is to know God, and with proper understanding and the right orientation towards the divine, one could transcend the cosmic realm of Fate and attain divine unity.

Iamblichus doesn't have much to say about magic in *De Mysteriis*. As Crystal Addey observes, Iamblichus never uses the term *mageia*, and there are only two instances where he uses the term *goēteia* (sorcery), which carries a more negative connotation, yet it is clear from these sparse references that Iamblichus believes that theurgy is superior to magic.²⁷ Iamblichus's problem with magicians (and with less sophisticated ritual experts, which he discusses more frequently) is that they work solely within the cosmic realm and attempt to manipulate and command the cosmic gods and powers, whereas theurgists try to understand how these

---

25   COPENHAVER, *Hermetica*, xxxix.
26   *Auth.Mem.* 1.7, adapted from H. JACKSON's translation.
27   ADDEY, 34–35.

powers are divinely generated.²⁸ For example, in a discussion of divination, Iamblichus explains that visions brought about by magic (*goēteia*) are only illusions. He warns that one should not compare "the clearest visions of the gods to the images produced artificially from magic, for these have neither the energy, nor the essence of things seen, nor truth, but present mere images, reaching only as far as appearance".²⁹ He likens these artificial images to hallucinations that one experiences during a fever or illness; these illusions are products of the (unhealthy) body and the human imagination, and are therefore limited to the cosmic realm, having nothing in common with divine visions.³⁰ According to this view, magicians falsely believe that they can control the gods; this is a form of hubris, because the gods are "completely superior to all others, so also their operations are not like those of any other beings".³¹ Both Zosimos and Iamblichus would agree that the human will should be directed properly, not by compelling the divine (or forcing Fate, in Zosimos's terms), but rather toward being a conduit for experiencing the divine acting within oneself, and within the world.

Zosimos and Iamblichus make similar distinctions between human and divine causality in their critiques of rationalism, which they deem as another type of "cosmic" knowledge. Zosimos writes of the inferiority of rationalism, or "mortal intelligence", in what appears to be an assessment of Aristotle:³²

---

28   On magicians, see Emma CLARKE, *Iamblichus' De Mysteriis: A Manifesto of the Miraculous*, 21–22. As MARX-WOLF rightly points out, scholars have often over-estimated Iamblichus's opposition to magic. Iamblichus frequently criticizes certain ritual approaches, but he doesn't usually call them magical. MARX-WOLF, 109–110.
29   DM III.25.160–161.
30   Ibid.
31   Ibid.
32   Zosimos doesn't mention Aristotle by name in this passage, but it is preceded by a note saying "Here are the types of Aristotle". The passage is about a brilliant philosopher of "visible things", who is less skilled at discerning spiritual truths. FOWDEN assumes that Zosimos is speaking about Aristotle, and I also think this is likely.

ALCHEMY, THEURGY, & THE DIVINE COSMOS 207

> He [Aristotle?] was not [united with] the Divine Mind, but was rather a mortal man, a mortal intelligence and a mortal body. He was the most brilliant of the non-luminous beings, in contrast to the incorporeal beings. He possessed the power of appropriation or resistance over the corporeal and non-luminous beings, other than the superior intelligences and the grand celestial bodies. But since he was mortal, he could not elevate himself as far as the celestial sphere; nor did he know how to render himself worthy. This is why his science and his deeds stayed in the lower region of this sphere.[33]

Despite his intellectual brilliance—or rather, because of it—this brilliant philosopher could not ascend beyond the cosmic realm. His mind was too logical, too focused on the physical world, which prevented him from uniting with the divine mind of the Demiurge, the fount of all wisdom. Zosimos tells Theosebeia that she should instead apply her mind to transcending the cosmic sphere by focusing it toward the divine presence in her soul. He writes:

> But you, Madam, elevate your thought beyond the inferior sphere, which is a part of the visible universe; envision your soul [...] made with the two intelligences, that is to say with the Son of God, the Word, joined with the Divine Mind, and full of the spirituality of the Trinity. Communicate this without jealousy to those who are worthy of it and who will ask it of you, so that even here you possess a great good: I mean the souls that you will save and direct towards the incorporeal and incorruptible nature.[34]

---

33   CMA, Syr. II.12.4. My translation, based on DUVAL's French.
34   Ibid. See also G. FOWDEN's discussion of this passage, which is a continuation of the one above, in *The Egyptian Hermes*, 126. I have amended DUVAL's French translation slightly. He has "holy spirit" where I have "divine mind". I think Zosimos is referring to the Hermetic trinity, not the Christian one (though he does see them as analogous—see CAAG III.49

208   CHAPTER FIVE

Zosimos agrees with Iamblichus that knowledge is not solely the result of human effort; divine revelation also plays a role.[35] He explains that this worldly philosopher received the inspiration for his ideas from superior cosmic beings; but since these are cosmic divinities, their knowledge of the noetic realm is limited. This is why he excelled as a philosopher of "visible things", but was not able to adequately distinguish the "invisible things, such as the intelligences or spiritual substances", which belong to the noetic realm beyond the cosmos. Zosimos continues, "[t]he angels who inspired his science did not know them, and consequently, they could not communicate that which they did not possess".[36] Noetic revelation, as opposed to "cosmic" revelation, is necessary in order to perceive the whole of reality.

and my discussion of this in chapter 4).

35 Iamblichus upholds Plato's view that all knowledge is either divinely revealed or recollected by the soul due to its divine origins (see Plato's *Meno* dialogue). Rationality works hand in hand with divine inspiration; the latter is the source of ideas, though due to the limitations of the human mind, not all knowledge is clearly perceived, and is often misunderstood or misinterpreted. In late antiquity, the notion that knowledge is divinely inspired was quite prevalent, and the cosmology of that era gave rise to several classes of divine beings, all of whom had different capacities for inspiring humans, for good or for ill; not all revelation occurred at the noetic, hypercosmic level. Iamblichus believes that the cosmic gods can inspire humans, but that daimons cannot (DM III.7.114). Zosimos thinks that both cosmic gods and daimons can reveal knowledge, but the quality of information differs. See, for example, his encounters with daimons, especially Agathodaimon, in *On Excellence* (*Auth.Mem.* XI.2) discussed in chapter three. For a discussion of how Iamblichus's views of revelation and the limitations of discursive thought are related to the Socratic-Platonic ideal of *aporia*, or perplexity—the state in which one realizes one's ignorance and the limitations of human thought—and how this instills a desire for the divine by creating a desire for further knowledge, see SHAW, "After Aporia: Thuergy in Later Platonism", esp. 58–59, 73–75.

36 CMA, Syr. II.12.4. As I discussed in chapter four, Zosimos makes similar statements regarding rival "corporeal" alchemists, who only know things of the body, and nothing of the soul. These alchemists invoke daimons to assist them with their alchemical procedures, and Zosimos believes that the daimons only have a limited understanding of nature. The celestial beings that inspire this philosopher are superior to daimons, but they are cosmic entities nonetheless.

Iamblichus's critique of rationalism can be seen in *De Mysteriis*, which is a response to questions raised by Porphyry, who (in Gregory Shaw's words) thought that theurgy was "merely a *technē* for the philosophically immature".[37] In this philosophical dialogue, Iamblichus paints Porphyry as a pedantic intellectualist who relies too heavily upon human reasoning when it comes to divine matters.[38] For instance, he reproaches Porphyry for his intellectual hubris in "conceding" that the gods exist.[39] Knowledge of the divine, Iamblichus argues, cannot be obtained through "conjecture, or opinion, or some form of syllogistic reasoning", because these mental activities belong to temporal or cosmic reality.[40] Iamblichus insists that divine knowledge (*noēsis, gnōsis*) has its source in eternity and is innate within us; it can only be revealed through direct contact with the divine, not by human reason (*logismos*) alone.[41] As Addey points out, Porphyry isn't quite the rationalist that Iamblichus makes him out to be, so this debate might be best understood as an educational device in the literary tradition of the Platonic dialogue, where false or inferior lines of reasoning are exposed by the philosophic "hero" through the question and answer process.[42] In this case the hero is not a Platonic philosopher, but an Egyptian priest named Abamon; this is reminiscent of Plato's *Symposium*, where Socrates evokes Diotima, a priestess of the mysteries, to

---

37   Gregory SHAW, "After Aporia: Theurgy in Later Platonism", in *Gnosticism and Later Platonism*, ed. J. D. TURNER and R. MAJERCIK (Atlanta: Society of Biblical Literature, 2001), 74.

38   On the polemics between Porphyry and Iamblichus in *De Mysteriis*, see CLARKE, *Manifesto of the Miraculous*, 4–12.

39   DM I.3.7.

40   DM I.3.9. As the translators of this edition note, Iamblichus is making similar divisions between opinion (cosmic realm) and truth (the intelligible realm) as Plato did in his image of the Divided Line in *Republic* VI (509D–513E).

41   Iamblichus notes that true knowledge of the divine is not really "knowledge" *per se*, but contact with divine presence. See DM I.3.8–10, and I.21.65–66. Andrew SMITH analyzes Iamblichus's terminology in "Iamblichus' Views on the Relationship of Philosophy to Religion", in *The Divine Iamblichus*, ed. BLUMENTHAL and CLARK; see especially 77, 79.

42   ADDEY, 127–143.

teach a group of learned men about the "ladder of love", starting with particular and physical examples of love and ascending to more universal and spiritual forms.[43]

Critiques of rational, discursive modes of knowledge are prevalent in Neoplatonic philosophy. Plotinus contrasts discursive thought, in which the mind is separate from its object, with intellectual (noetic) thought, in which the mind is identical with its object; the latter is superior because the mind directly apprehends the noetic Forms.[44] Iamblichus echoes this distinction in claiming that Porphyry thinks *about* the divine, but has not experienced divine union; if he had, then Porphyry would not be granting that the gods exist, as if divine reality were merely a theoretical proposition.[45] As Andrew Smith observes, the primary difference between Iamblichus, Plotinus, and Porphyry regarding noetic union is that Plotinus and Porphyry consider this to be a human capacity, attained by human effort, whereas Iamblichus believes that it can only be achieved with the help of the gods.[46] Smith explains Iamblichus's position: "Unaided, human thought always stands outside the object it contemplates or reaches out towards (ultimately god). It is only through the divine causality that the barrier can be broken down, the human be made divine and united with the divine. Uniting, even at the noetic level, is the work of theurgy".[47]

The principle of identity between subject and object, which

---

43 PLATO, *Symposium* 210A–212C.
44 See Sara RAPPE's discussion of Plotinus in "Self-knowledge and Subjectivity in the *Enneads*", in The Cambridge Companion to Plotinus, ed. Lloyd P. GERSON (Cambridge: Cambridge University Press, 1996): 254–259. Iamblichus also makes this point in DM I.3.8.
45 In *De Mysteriis*, Iamblichus frequently distinguishes between theurgy and theoretical speculation about the divine in order to drive his point home to Porphyry. For example, after Iamblichus gives a summary of Egyptian theology, he is quick to point out that for the priests this is "not [...] purely a matter of theorizing, but they recommend that we ascend through the practice of sacred theurgy to the regions that are higher, more universal and superior to fate, towards the god who is the creator" (DM VIII.4.267).
46 A. SMITH, *Porphyry's Place in the Neoplatonic Tradition* (The Hague: Martinus Nijhoff, 1974), 84–88.
47 Ibid, 88.

Iamblichus calls "gnostic" or "noetic" knowledge, can also be seen in Zosimos's work. In the passages cited above, Zosimos encourages Theosebeia to envision her soul conjoined with the Divine Mind, and critiques Aristotle for not being able to do this. The highest form of gnosis is union with the divine mind of the creator, or Demiurge, but identity also occurs at various levels. In Zosimos's allegory of the alchemical opus, *On Excellence*, one of the main characters is a self-sacrificing priest who identifies with the metals as they are being transformed. The metals are personified in this narrative (alluding to the statues they will become) and their identities, as well as that of the alchemist, continually slip into one another: the alchemist-priest changes into a man of copper, the copper man eventually transforms into man of gold, who then becomes the alchemist-priest, and so forth.[48] The point of this allegory is that all of these beings are divine images of the One, and that ultimately, all these beings *are* One. The slippage seems to represent moments of identification with the divine images—and transcending them—during the course of the work, until one reaches the point of union with the Divine Mind.[49]

The problem with magic and rationalism, then, is that they are human contrivances and do not adequately represent or "work" with divine reality. Magicians impiously attempt to command the gods and overestimate their human powers and capabilities. Rationalists, on the other hand, assign too much power to human thought as a means of knowing the divine. In both cases, human causality is given priority over divine causality. Theurgy, by contrast, emphasizes the experience of divine union in which the soul is utterly identified with the divine; this "knowledge" is revealed through divine grace. Noetic union also allows one to experience the cosmos as a spiritual and physical whole, whereas "cosmic" knowledge provides only a partial understanding of the universe.

---

48   *Auth.Mem.*XI.1, 5.
49   See my exegesis of this text in chapter three.

The "divine work" of theurgy is to become intimate with the divine power that is innate within the self and the world, but which also transcends it. Through this work, the soul can become purified and ascend toward the noetic realms. But the work of theurgy *begins* with the material world.

The divine hierarchy

Zosimos and Iamblichus, whose understandings of cosmogony and salvation are influenced—either directly or indirectly—by Egyptian ideas as well as Plato's *Timaeus*, believe that the cosmos was created as a divine image of the noetic realms, and that one can experience the divine by contemplating the natural order. Within the physical, visible cosmos, however, there lies a spiritual, invisible order that creates, sustains, and moves the visible order. These realms are thoroughly intertwined. This invisible order consists of an array of divine beings, ranging from the highest gods to the lowliest of daimons, all of which are creations and agents of the Demiurge; they comprise a hierarchical network of divine power extending from heaven to earth. These beings administer the laws of Fate or Necessity and thereby create the cosmic condition from which the soul must be liberated, but as agents of divine providence they can also help the soul to ascend. The task of the human soul is to overcome its attachments to Fate by perceiving the providential order in the cosmos and bringing the soul into accordance with this order.

Heidi Marx-Wolf argues that the philosophical enterprise of ordering divine beings into a hierarchy by creating "spiritual taxonomies", as she calls them, can be a political move, a strategy to "establish various kinds of authority, garner social capital, and wrest these from other contemporary cultural entrepreneurs and experts".[50] She demonstrates how third century Platonists

---

[50] Marx-Wolf, *Spiritual Taxonomies*, 2.

like Iamblichus used these taxonomies to position themselves as "high priests of the highest gods" over and above the more local, traditional priests, who then became associated with the worship of lesser gods and spirits.[51] Zosimos, as we have seen, is involved in similar rivalries and positions himself as philosopher-priest who has greater insight into spiritual matters than others. These social and political maneuverings should be kept in mind, but I also think that Zosimos and Iamblichus are incredibly sincere in their piety and search for wisdom, and that power plays are not their primary motive. My purpose in this section is to give an overview of the divine cosmic frameworks imagined by these authors, and the ways in which spiritual and material realities intersect. This context is necessary for understanding their theurgical approaches to ritual and alchemy, which intentionally link the material and spiritual worlds. I will lead with Iamblichus, whose classification includes divine beings that are familiar in several pantheons. Zosimos does not offer a systematic taxonomy of divine beings, though he does talk about them in a hierarchical way. His ideas resonate with taxonomies found in Hermetic philosophy, which I will use to fill in the gaps.

In Iamblichus's system, the highest beings are the invisible gods, who are of the noetic realm. They preside over the visible gods, which are the stars and planets of the cosmic realm. Iamblichus explains that the visible gods are images of the invisible gods, produced as a result of the invisible gods "thinking their own divine forms".[52] The visible gods are thus continuous with the noetic gods, yet they are also a different order of being.[53] As cosmic gods, they are responsible for administering the laws of Fate; they generate and sustain life on earth, and they also impart worldly qualities to the human soul, both virtues and vices. Yet, Iamblichus claims

---

51   MARX-WOLF, "High Priests of the Highest God: Third Century Platonists as Ritual Experts", *Journal of Early Christian Studies* 18.4 (2010), 482.
52   DM I.19.57.
53   DM I.19.58.

that the cosmic gods can also release the soul from the realm of generation because of their intimacy with noetic gods.[54]

This divine chain of command continues from the celestial gods in the outer regions of the cosmos to the divine beings whose domains are progressively closer to the earth. The visible gods preside over archangels, who in turn rule over legions of angels. Below these are daimons and various other spirits, which mediate between the human soul and the higher beings. Some of these entities encourage virtue and help the soul to ascend, while others pollute the soul with worldly concerns and wickedness. Iamblichus explains that daimons are the "generative and creative powers of the gods in the furthest extremity of their emanations".[55] The terrestrial daimons are closest to earth and they have important, though limited, creative functions. They oversee the physical manifestation and growth of the natural world, and they are responsible for binding souls to bodies. The daimons also exist within the human body and control very specific aspects of somatic life; one daimon might control the sex drive, another hunger, while others are charged with regulating the rhythms of the breath and the beating heart.[56] Iamblichus mentions additional beings below the daimons, including heroes, who "assign life-giving powers" and can inspire human souls to greatness, and two classes of cosmic archons that rule over the sublunary cosmos and material affairs.[57] However, the roles of heroes and archons are not as well-defined and at times appear contradictory. As Marx-Wolf notes, Iamblichus's inclusion of these beings in his taxonomy, and the difficulty in making them fit, are revealing of his efforts to subsume local deities into a universal scheme and translate this across social boundaries.[58]

---

54 See DM I.19 and VIII.8.271 on the relationship between the visible and invisible gods and their role in the liberation of the human soul.
55 DM II.1.67. See also SHAW on this point, *Theurgy and the Soul*, 40–43.
56 See SHAW, *Theurgy and the Soul*, 140.
57 On heroes, see DM II.1, 2 and DM II.6.114; on the two classes of cosmic archons, see DM II.3.
58 MARX-WOLF, 62–64.

Zosimos's understanding of the divine hierarchy is similar in some ways to Iamblichus's, though Zosimos does not refer to any divinities as "gods" other than the noetic trinity, which consists of the Divine Mind (the One, or the Father) and his two "sons", the Demiurge (who is also called Mind, or *nous*) and the Son of God (*logos*, God's will or word).[59] He calls the celestial bodies "intelligences" or "luminous beings" and views them as divine beings that govern the realm of Fate.[60] His ideas are in keeping with several texts in the philosophical *Hermetica*, where the visible cosmos is viewed as divine image of the creator, and the invisible and visible aspects are interconnected.[61] The luminous planets and stars are created in the image of the Demiurge, who is "life and light"; this is particularly true of the sun, which holds a central place in Hermetic thought and in ancient Egyptian theology.[62] Although Zosimos never refers to the sun as a god in his surviving writings, he does view the sun as a visible manifestation of divine light. For example, in *On Apparatus and Furnaces (Letter Omega)*, he meditates on the fact that the sun is in the middle of the seven planetary spheres, just as the divine fire of the creator is at the center of all things.[63] And in another text, *The Book of Sophe the Egyptian*, he talks about terrestrial and celestial aspects of the sun, which is akin to the visible and invisible gods in the *Hermetica* and in Iamblichus's system.[64]

Angels are nearly absent from Zosimos's works and from the *Hermetica*. The only time that Zosimos mentions angels is to say

---

59   *Auth.Mem.* 1.7, 12.
60   CMA, Syr. II.12.4.
61   For different perspectives on the cosmos as a god and as a divine image of the creator, see: CH III.2–3; V (all); X.10, 14; and XI.22. See also Garth FOWDEN's discussion of the divine cosmic order in *The Egyptian Hermes*, 77–78.
62   E.g., CH V.3; IX.13; XIII.16; XVI (all).
63   See *Auth.Mem.* 1.9.
64   CAAG III.42.1.

that they gave Adam his name.⁶⁵ Angels are mentioned briefly in the Hermetic *Asclepius* as a type of good soul, and the *Poimandres* contains a reference to angelic beings called "powers", which are liberated souls that reside in the fixed stars.⁶⁶ Daimons are more common, however. Hermetic texts often refer to the ambivalent nature of daimons. In the hierarchy of divine beings, daimons are subordinate to the stellar and planetary intelligences, and their creative function is to preside over human affairs and to cause changes and turbulence within the soul.⁶⁷ Daimons also reside within the human body; as one text describes, they are "laying in ambush in our muscle and marrow, in veins and arteries, in the brain itself, reaching to the very guts".⁶⁸ Zosimos rails against the daimons and sees them as greedy, jealous beings with limited understanding, who cause turbulence in the soul as well as in society.⁶⁹ But there is some indication that he also views them as useful and necessary. In his allegory *On Excellence*, he describes how Agathodaimon, the "good daimon", imparts a brilliant white color to the metals and assists Zosimos when he loses his way during the course of his procedure, which is both a chemical transformation and a spiritual ascent.⁷⁰ He also mentions a little razor-working man who fixes

---

65 In Zosimos's critique of Aristotle (in CMA, Syr. II.12.4), translators BERTHELOT and DUVAL, who tend to Christianize Zosimos's terminology, translate one phrase as "Les anges qui lui inspirèrent la science ne les connaissaient pas, et ne pouvaient par conséquent communiquer ce qu'ils ne possédaient pas". (The angels who inspired [Aristotle's] science...). However, since Zosimos claims that these divinities have limited knowledge of the noetic realm, they are probably not angels or liberated souls, but the celestial intelligences that he mentions elsewhere in this passage. In *Apparatus and Furnaces (Letter Omega)*, Zosimos says that angels gave Adam his name. As Howard JACKSON points out, he is probably referring to the late ancient Jewish belief that Hebrew is the language of the angels. See *Auth.Mem.* I.9, and JACKSON, *Zosimos of Panopolis: On the Letter Omega*, 48, n. 42.
66 See *Asclepius* 37 and CH I.26.
67 See, for example, CH XVI.10–18; CH IX.3; CH X.18; CH XII.
68 CH XVI.14.
69 See, for example, CAAG III.51.7–8.
70 *Auth.Mem.* XI.2.

the "spirits" of the metals to their bodies, and guards these spirits while the metallic bodies are being melted down and transformed by the fire.[71] This character identifies itself as a spirit (πνεῦμα, *pneuma*) rather than a daimon, but in the allegory he is associated, in part, with underworld daimons in Egyptian mortuary traditions who oversee the cauldrons of annihilation that prepare souls for new life.[72]

Human souls are the lowest in the cosmic chain of being. Iamblichus believes that the soul's ascent can only be accomplished with divine assistance, and therefore theurgical rites are designed to honor and provide access to all of the divine powers that are capable of elevating the soul. He recommends that theurgists make an "accurate study" of these entities and perform rituals "in a manner that is agreeable to them in all cases".[73] Iamblichus honors even the lowest daimons because they are part of the divine cosmic order, and because it honors the gods who preside over them.[74] But he denies that the daimons are able to provide any sort of spiritual inspiration.[75] He says that they "weigh down the body", "drag the soul down to the realm of nature", and detain the soul within the realm of Fate.[76] The natural earthbound functions of daimons are akin to a gravitational force; this movement runs counter to the goal of spiritual ascent, and so their influences on the soul must be neutralized. This is accomplished by purifying the soul of its passions, and by directing one's worship to the benevolent deities that will help the soul ascend. Zosimos does not display the same piety toward the daimons as Iamblichus; he tells Theosebeia to perform

---

71 *Auth.Mem.* x.3.
72 Ibid. The knife-wielding daimons are found in an Egyptian mortuary text called the *Book of Caves*. In Roman era versions of this text, the boiling of the souls in cauldrons is said to prepare them for the state of non-being, which is a prerequisite for new creation. See HORNUNG, *Idea into Image*, 100–101.
73 DM V.25.237.
74 Ibid.
75 Iamblichus claims that inspiration comes from the gods, not from daimons. See DM III.7.114.
76 DM II.6.82.

rituals that drive the daimons away, not the rituals that nourish and entice them.[77] But they are in agreement that daimonic influences can be neutralized or transcended by purifying the soul of its passions.[78]

Divinity, then, has material and immaterial aspects that are thoroughly intertwined. Both Zosimos and Iamblichus talk about the luminous planets as visible images of the highest noetic gods, and daimons as governing the motions of bodies, both human bodies and metallic ones. Divine beings function as natural forces, and the creative activities and energies of these divine entities constitute an invisible order that supports and governs the visible order. As we shall see, theurgic practices focus intently on this interface between the material and the spiritual, and aim to purify the soul and ascend to the noetic realms by consciously activating links between these visible and invisible realms.

Linking spirit and matter through theurgic rites

Theurgy encompasses the proper mindset for ritual practice as well as the ritual practice itself. Iamblichus talks about how common rituals, like divination and sacrifice, can be practiced in theurgical and non-theurgical ways. What makes a ritual theurgical is that it purifies and elevates the soul and facilitates union with the highest gods. Iamblichus insists that theurgic rites should begin with matter, or with the visible gods, and proceed toward the invisible realms.[79] Zosimos, too, emphasizes an anagogical movement from the material to the spiritual; this applies to the practice of alchemy as well to other spiritual exercises he describes. Both writers advocate the contemplation of material objects as divine signatures, or "receptacles" for divine energies, which reveal and

---

77   CAAG III.51.8.
78   Ibid.
79   See, for example, DM V.14.217.

activate the lines of cosmic sympathy that connect the material object to its noetic source. Zosimos and Iamblichus have similar ideas about cosmic sympathy, which is noteworthy, because cosmic sympathy is usually treated as a uniform theory, but late ancient theories were actually quite diverse. I argue here that their common source of understanding lies in Egyptian concepts of *heka*, the vital power that animates and unifies all parts of the cosmos.

As Gregory Shaw has observed, Iamblichus believes that the ritual use of matter is the *only* way for the embodied soul to attain salvation.[80] Iamblichus writes: "the theurgic art [...] links together stones, plants, animals, aromatic substances, and other such things that are sacred, perfect, and godlike, and then from all these composes an integrated and pure receptacle [for the gods]".[81] He goes on to explain that these objects enable the soul to commune with the gods:

> For there is no other way in which the terrestrial realm or the men who dwell here could enjoy participation in the existence that is the lot of the higher beings, if some such foundation not be laid down in advance [...] [S]uch material rouses up the gods to manifestation, summons them to reception, welcomes them when they appear, and ensures their perfect representation.[82]

Zosimos does not promote material "foundations" like Iamblichus, perhaps because alchemy necessarily begins with material objects; instead, Zosimos insists that alchemy needs to be practiced in a spiritual way. He says that the true philosophers of alchemy do not focus merely on things pertaining to bodies, but also on things pertaining to the soul, and argues that a spiritual approach to alchemy is necessary in order to understand nature properly; he attributes the mistakes and faulty recipes of his com-

---

80 SHAW, *Theurgy and the Soul*, 24. Emphasis his.
81 DM V.23.233.
82 DM V.23.234.

petitors to their lack of spiritual understanding.⁸³ He also maintains that the goal of noetic union surpasses all other aspects of alchemy, saying that one must practice alchemy in both a corporeal and spiritual manner until perfection is reached; it is then that the "true object of one's desire" will be found, which surpasses the corporeal arts.⁸⁴

Zosimos's views of spirit and matter are complicated, because sometimes he expresses positive views of the material world, marveling at its beauty, order, and goodness, while other times he depicts it as chaotic and undesirable, as a chain for the soul.⁸⁵ A mix of pro-cosmic and anti-cosmic sentiments are found within Platonism, Hermetism, and Jewish/Christian Gnostic texts as well. These can represent the stances of particular thinkers: for example, the Middle Platonist, Numenius, who views matter as evil, as opposed to the pro-cosmism of Plotinus, Iamblichus, and other Neoplatonists.⁸⁶ In some cases, as we see in the *Hermetica* and in certain Gnostic texts, these different stances on the cosmos can also represent different viewpoints held during stages of spiritual development or initiation, with anti-cosmic ideas spurring the soul to purify itself of its material stains, separate from the body, and undergo the spiritual ascent.⁸⁷ But rather than viewing the

---

83   See, for example, CMA, Syr. II.8.1., CAAG III.49.2–4 and CMA, Syr. II.6.
84   CMA, Syr. II.11.21.
85   For both positive and negative examples, see his allegory, *On Excellence* (*Auth.Mem.* X–XII). He describes the soul as being "enchained in the four elements" in CAAG III.41.1.
86   Numenius makes a sharp distinction between the divine intelligibles, which give order to the cosmos, and matter, which exists independently of God and is the source of evil and disorder. See John DILLON, *The Middle Platonists* [1977] (Ithaca: Cornell University Press, 1996), 373–374. As for Plotinus's pro-cosmism, see, for example, his treatise against the anti-cosmism of certain Gnostics in *Ennead* II.9.
87   As FOWDEN has argued, the pro-cosmic and anti-cosmic sentiments in the philosophical *Hermetica* might reflect successive stages of spiritual understanding, See FOWDEN, *op.cit.*, 97–104. Wouter HANEGRAAFF has persuasively demonstrated that some of the Hermetic philosophical texts reflect an initiatory sequence in "Altered States of Knowledge: The Attainment of Gnōsis in the *Hermetica*", *The International Journal of the Platonic Tradition*

soul's journey as linear one, moving from matter to spirit, I think it is more appropriate to see it as circuitous: the ascent to the divine source allows for a noetic experience of spiritual union and rebirth, but the enlightened soul must return to the body and to ordinary consciousness, and through this journey it will have gained a deeper understanding of matter, spirit, and how they coalesce in the divine cosmic order.[88]

Iamblichus's ritual items are selected based upon their affinity with the gods who created them; a sunflower, for example, would be an appropriate ritual object to use when worshiping the sun because it resembles the sun in color and its "face" also follows the sun as it traverses the sky. Zosimos's materials cannot be purely symbolic, because his work with metals and chemicals must accomplish technical goals; nevertheless, metals, precious gems, and their colors all have a spiritual meaning in Egyptian thought. For example, gold corresponds to the sun and solar deities, and is also known as the "flesh of the gods"; the "bones of the gods" are silver, which corresponds to the moon and lunar deities (particularly goddesses); and blackened statues are associated with the underworld and with underworld deities like Osiris and Anubis.[89] Zosimos

---

2 (2008). Both Fowden and Hanegraaff indicate that the anti-cosmic statements represent the higher stages of the journey, when the soul longs only for God and loses desire to be in the world. In Zosimos's work, I think the reverse is more often true: anti-cosmic statements are made at the earlier stages of the spiritual journey to inspire the separation of the soul from body, which is necessary for spiritual ascent. CH VI is an anti-cosmic text, and many texts include a mix of pro- and anti-cosmic sentiments, e.g., CH I, X. A Gnostic example of dual cosmic perspectives held at different stages of the soul's journey can be found in *On the Origin of the World* (NHC II.5).

88   I disagree that anti-cosmism is the more enlightened perspective, because Egyptians typically viewed their land as a heaven on earth and celebrated the divine re-creation of the world each day. The return to the divine source allows for a rebirth in the body and more enlightened perspectives of the natural world, which reveal that the divine is everywhere. See for example CH XIII.10-11.

89   Gay ROBINS, "Cult Statues in Ancient Egypt", in *Cult Image and Divine Representation in the Ancient Near East*, ed. N. WALLS (Boston: American Schools of Oriental Research, 2005), 6; on underworld gods, see AUFRÈRE,

calls the copper that he has colored gold a "terrestrial" sun, and connects it to the celestial sun, which, he explains, is in turn a divine image of the Demiurge.[90] These associations were part of Egyptian statue-making culture, as was the art of proper timing, which also relies on cosmic sympathy. Zosimos says that certain alchemical operations, particularly those that deal with gold, are best performed in the summertime, when the sun is at the peak of its power.[91] He also recommends that mercury should be extracted from cinnabar at the heliacal rising of Sirius.[92] The heliacal rising of the star Sirius marks the Egyptian New Year, which coincides with the annual flooding of the Nile.[93] Mercury, a fluid, silvery substance, is a divine signature of the river, and both mercury and the Nile have an affinity with the star Sirius.[94]

In addition to alchemical practices, Zosimos recommends spiritual exercises or meditations that trace a series of correspondences, beginning with the physical and mundane and progressing toward the sublime. As we have seen, one of these shows how electrum, the substance from which mirrors are made, reflects not only one's physical image, but also the divine image within the soul; his meditation ends with an image of the entire cosmos as a mirror of noetic reality.[95] These exercises reveal that divine signatures are not limited to natural or material objects. Zosimos shows how the four letters of Adam's name correspond to the four cardinal directions, to the four elements, and ultimately to the Son of God, the divine presence within nature.[96] Iamblichus also considers certain quasi-material phenomena to be divine signatures, in-

L'Univers minéral dans la pensée Égyptienne, vol. 2, 451.
90   CAAG III.41.1.
91   See CAAG III.15.2 and *Auth.Mem.* 1, *On Apparatus and Furnaces (Letter Omega)*.
92   See CMA Syr. II.9.15, 18.
93   See R. T. RUNDLE CLARK, *Myth and Symbol in Ancient Egypt* (London: Thames & Hudson, 1978), 188.
94   Sirius is associated with the Egyptian goddess Sothis, later identified with Isis. See RUNDLE CLARK, ibid.
95   CMA, Syr. II.12
96   CAAG III.49.9–13.

cluding numbers, letters, and sounds. For example, he claims that music inspires the soul and functions as a receptacle for the gods because it reflects the divine harmony of the spheres:

> [T]hose things such as sounds and tunes are properly consecrated to each of the gods, and kinship is properly assigned to them in accord with their proper orders and powers, the motions in the universe itself and the harmonious sounds rushing from its motions. It is, then, in the virtue of such connections of the tunes with the gods that their presence occurs (for nothing intervenes to stop them) so that whatever has a fortuitous likeness with them, immediately participates in them, and a total possession and filling with superior being and power takes place at once.[97]

Iamblichus also criticizes certain understandings of cosmic sympathy, and this has led some scholars to argue that he refuted the notion of sympathy, or that he only embraced it to a certain extent.[98] But given that there were many theories of cosmic sympathy in late antiquity, it appears that he was trying to differentiate his theurgical understanding of sympathy (which he often calls *philia*, or friendship of the gods) from the others. For example, he explains that it is "absurd" to attribute the efficacy of theurgical rites solely to the physical correspondences of the ritual materials:

---

97 DM III.9.119.
98 Emma CLARKE argues that Iamblichus rejected cosmic sympathy; see CLARKE, *A Manifesto of the Miraculous*, 48. SHAW argues against a distinction made by Andrew SMITH (in *Porphyry's Place in the Neoplatonic Tradition*, 90–99), that "higher" theurgy works with the noetic realm and "lower" theurgy works with cosmic sympathies. Shaw claims that Iamblichus rejected practices based solely on natural sympathies on the grounds that they are not theurgical. See SHAW, "Theurgy: Rituals of Unification", 7–9, 25. I think Iamblichus's point, however, is that the cause of sympathy should be attributed to the noetic realm, and not solely to the cosmos. Theurgical rites work with sympathies, but theurgical understandings of the noetic source of these sympathies differ from the mainstream.

as for instance when one assigns the number sixty to the crocodile as being proper to the sun; or to natural-reason principles, as exemplified by the powers and activities of certain animals, such as the dog, the baboon or the field-mouse, all of which have an affinity to the moon; or to the forms in matter, as in the case of sacred animals, where one looks at them from the point of view of their colors and all their bodily traits [...] or any other such feature of a natural phenomenon as a cause of the [ritual] efficacy.[99]

Iamblichus says that physical resemblances are *auxiliary* causes for ritual efficacy—they are "necessary consequences" of cosmic sympathy—but the primary cause is rather to be sought in the "friendship and affinity" that "binds together creators with their creations and generators with their offspring".[100] In other words, the divine powers that generate the world form the bonds of sympathy, and if a ritual works, it is because the gods have found favor with it, not because of the materials one uses (though these may indeed please the gods).

Iamblichus is, in part, trying to distance theurgy from more popular ritual applications of cosmic sympathy that are based on manipulating one aspect of nature in order to affect another. This is particularly prominent in the "magical" belief in action at a distance, whereby one uses certain objects, such as fingernail clippings, rose petals, or bat wings to activate natural lines of sympathy and antipathy in order to affect another person or attain a desired outcome, such as winning over a lover or securing a financial profit. To the casual observer, a theurgic rite, which makes use of various stones, plants, and animals, might appear similar to a so-called magical rite.[101] But the difference is in the theurgical

---

99   DM V.8.208.
100 DM V.8–9.209.
101 This is probably why scholars have classified late ancient theurgy as a magico-religious practice. E. R. DODDS, for example, says that theur-

mindset and the goal, which is to elevate the soul so that it may attain divine union.

Iamblichus's views of cosmic sympathy, which extend to the noetic realm, differ from those of other philosophers. Plotinus and Porphyry, for example, think of cosmic sympathy solely as a property of the cosmos or World Soul. Since the cosmos is a single living organism that unites all parts to itself, there is necessarily sympathy (and antipathy) between all of its parts.[102] Many Stoics also held this view.[103] Iamblichus agrees with this to a certain extent, but he thinks that this explanation reduces sympathy to physical necessity and natural causes; he argues instead that the cause of sympathy is divine and utterly transcends the cosmic realm.[104] Andrew Smith points out that Iamblichus's preferred term for cosmic sympathy—*philia*, or friendship of the gods—is often connected with *nous*, and that it refers to the connective powers of the noetic gods.[105] Iamblichus's notion, then, might be more aptly described as "supracosmic" sympathy.[106]

Zosimos also views sympathy in a supracosmic way.[107] As we have seen, Zosimos criticizes other alchemists for their limited understandings and uses of cosmic sympathy, which pertain solely to the cosmic realm; they invoke daimons to assist them in their work based on their favorable or unfavorable aspects, but these daimons are just cogs in the cosmic machine, and the knowledge they grant

---

     gy "used the procedures of vulgar magic primarily to a religious end". DODDS, *Greeks and the Irrational*, Appendix II, 291.
102 See PLOTINUS, *Enneads* IV.4.32.
103 On differences between Stoic and Plotinian notions of cosmic sympathy, see Gary GURTLER, "Sympathy: Stoic Materialism, and the Platonic Soul", in *Neoplatonism and Nature*, ed. M. WAGNER (Albany: SUNY Press, 2002).
104 DM V.7.207–208. Translators CLARKE, DILLON, and HERSHBELL note that Iamblichus's insistence that cosmic sympathy has a noetic cause and source does not reject the theories held by Plotinus, Porphyry, and Stoic philosophers (particularly Posidonius), but rather upstages them.
105 SMITH, *Porphyry's Place in the Neoplatonic Tradition*, 93–94. See also DM V.9.211.
106 The translators of *De Mysteriis* have suggested this. See CLARKE, et al., *De Mysteriis*, 239, n. 299.
107 See, for example, the exercises in CMA, Syr. II.12 and CAAG III.49.

is limited.[108] He argues time and time again that alchemists need to lift their sights to noetic reality. He believes that the physical and spiritual dimensions of nature are a unified whole, and that one can only fully perceive or experience this wholeness by uniting with the Divine Mind, whose presence is everywhere in nature, but which also transcends it. Zosimos's "natural" methods, then, appear to make use of the same type of *supracosmic* sympathy that Iamblichus describes.

Zosimos and Iamblichus are most likely getting their ideas from ancient Egyptian notions of cosmic sympathy, or *heka*. *Heka* is the creative force, often translated as "magic", that animates all of life, protects against chaos, and links sympathetic powers into a unified whole. Geraldine Pinch, in a description of Egyptian priests' use of divine signatures and *heka*, explains: "*Heka* was the force that turned these connections into a kind of power network. It was through *heka* that an image or name could be made to stand for the real thing, a part could stand for the whole, and symbolic actions could have effects in the real world".[109] In addition to being a spiritual force, *heka* was also viewed as one of the oldest and most powerful gods. In Egyptian myth, Heka is the first creation of the primeval creator-god and can be seen as the hypostasis of his creative power.[110] Zosimos, as an Egyptian priest, was undoubtedly familiar with these concepts of *heka*, and Iamblichus, who adopts the persona of an Egyptian priest, appears to be familiar with *heka* as well. In Book VIII of *De Mysteriis*, Iamblichus outlines a taxonomy of the hypostases of noetic reality, both in Neoplatonic terms and in Egyptian ones, which he describes as a hierarchy of Egyptian gods. The first among them (though not the first discussed) is Eikton, whom Iamblichus describes as "the indivisible One", and the "first act of magic" (πρῶτον μάγευμα, *prōton*

---

108 On Zosimos's criticisms of alchemists who invoke daimons, see especially CAAG III.49.2–4.
109 Geraldine PINCH, *Magic in Ancient Egypt* (Austin: University of Texas Press, 2006 ed.), 16.
110 Robert RITNER, *The Mechanics of Ancient Egyptian Magical Practice*, 17.

mageuma), who is prior to the leader of the celestial gods (Kmeph) and the "primal object of intellection [...] worshiped by means of silence alone".[111] Eikton is not known in the Egyptian pantheon, but scholars have identified this god as Heka, based on Egyptian descriptions of Heka as the first born and self-generated god, who existed prior to duality.[112]

Heka is a vital, natural force that also transcends nature, generating the universe and binding the spiritual and material worlds as a plenitude. This concept is a likely source for notions of "One is the All" (ἓν τὸ πᾶν, *hen to pan*) in the Greco-Egyptian alchemical corpus. In Zosimos's writings, this is found in the form of a philosophical slogan: "One is the All and through it is All and to it returns the All; and if it did not contain the All, the All is nothing".[113] The idea of the unity of nature is an important alchemical principle, and while this is usually traced to Greek philosophical theories of a primary unifying element of the cosmos, the Egyptian idea of *heka* is much older and more supracosmic in scope, and was probably more integral to Egyptian alchemical arts of statue-making.

God-making

We have looked at theurgy from several angles thus far. I have shown how Zosimos and Iamblichus position their approaches as being superior to both magic and rationalism because they involve revelation rather than human contrivance. I've introduced

---

[111] DM VIII.3. I'm using Dennis CLARK's translation for the phrase "first act of magic". The manuscript reads μάγευμα (*mageuma*) but as translators DILLON, HERSHBELL, and CLARKE note, the meaning of this word isn't clear, so they follow GALE's conjecture of μαίευμα (*maieuma*) and translate this as "first product". See DILLON, et al., *On the Mysteries*, 311, n. 409; and Dennis CLARK, "Iamblichus' Egyptian Neoplatonic Theology in *De Mysteriis*", *The International Journal of the Platonic Tradition* 2 (2008), 166, n. 3.

[112] D. CLARK, ibid., 173–176. See also UŽDAVINYS, *Philosophy and Theurgy*, 104–105.

[113] *Auth.Mem.*VI.

their cosmologies and taxonomies of the divine hierarchy, which demonstrate their belief in supracosmic sympathy, as well as their practice of tracing symbols, or divine signatures, from the material to the noetic realms. In these last sections we shall examine theurgical ideas of two types of god-making: the sacred art of making divine statues, and the practice of purifying of the soul so that it may ascend and unite with the highest gods. This emphasis on god-making offers yet another theurgical perspective on the relationship between the spiritual and material worlds, this time through the lens of divine images.

Divine Statues

One of Zosimos's roles as a priest is to oversee the manufacture of religious statues and other religious objects. As discussed in Chapter One, many Greco-Egyptian alchemical recipes are for coloring metals, which matches up with what we know of metal statuary that has survived from ancient Egypt: most statues are polychromatic and display highly-advanced techniques for coloring metals. In his text *On Copper*, Zosimos gives recipes for several tinctures used in coloring statues, imparting hues of purple, red, coral-pink, yellow, black, white, blue, gold, and silver to the metals.[114] He clearly takes pride in his work, claiming that the coloration is so vivid and the form so perfect that when people see the statues, they believe they are living beings.[115] "How moving it is to admire the invention of these arts", he proclaims, "how beautiful is the sight!".[116]

In Greek, a cult statue was often known as an *agalma*, a word which indicated not so much the statue itself, but a relationship that forms between the statue and the viewer: the god's beauty elicits an æsthetic response that inspires adoration and worship, uplifting

---

114   See CMA, Syr. II.6.9, 12, 23, 25, 28, 30, 33-35, 40, 43-49, 53-54, 57, 61-63.
115   CMA, Syr. II.6.31.
116   CMA, Syr. II.6.30.

the soul to the divine.¹¹⁷ This resonates with Zosimos's descriptions of people feeling moved and amazed by the statue's beauty. As Algis Uždavinys points out, Platonists also refer to the cosmos as an *agalma*, a Demiurgic creation; the sun, moon, and stars are also *algamata*, inspiring humans with wonder and reverence.¹¹⁸ The term *agalma* is uncommon in Hermetic texts, but concepts of making vital spiritual connections with divine images—both humanly and divinely created—are prevalent.

Statue-making is praised in the Hermetic *Asclepius* as the art of "god making", which is worth quoting at length in order to convey the theology of statues as divine images that Zosimos and Iamblichus were likely familiar with as real or aspiring Hermetic priests:

> Just as the master and father—or god, to use his most august name—is maker of the heavenly gods, so it is mankind who fashions the temple gods who are content to be near to humans. Not only is mankind glorified; he glorifies as well. He not only advances toward god; he also makes the gods strong [...].
>
> Mankind certainly deserves admiration, as the greatest of all beings. All plainly admit that the race of gods sprang from the cleanest part of nature and that their signs are like heads that stand for the whole being. But the figures of gods that humans form have been formed of both natures—from the divine, which is purer and more divine by far, and from the material of which they are built, whose nature falls short of the human—and

---

117 See Catherine M. KEESLING, "Greek Statue Terms Revisited: What does ἀνδριάς mean?", *Greek, Roman, and Byzantine Studies* 57 (2017): 837–838, 840–843.

118 Algis UŽDAVINYS, "Animation of Statues in Ancient Civilization and Neoplatonism", in *Late Antique Epistemology: Other Ways to Truth*, ed. P. VASSILOPOULOU and S. R. L. CLARK (London: Palgrave Macmillan, 2009), 120–123.

they represent not only the heads but all the limbs and the whole body. Always mindful of its nature and origin, humanity persists in imitating divinity, representing its gods in semblance of its own features, just as the father and master made his gods eternal to resemble him.[119]

The *Asclepius* suggests that statue making is an act of divine *mimesis*: just as the Demiurge creates the heavenly gods in its own divine image, so humans create the gods in their own image. In this way, the likeness of the divine creator god radiates throughout the divine cosmos, appearing in both immaterial and material forms. The divine images manufactured by humans are not merely symbols meant to inspire spiritual contemplation—although they could function this way—but were more commonly viewed as physical bodies that concentrated and channeled divine power. These statues, as the *Asclepius* goes on to tell us, are "ensouled and conscious, filled with spirit and doing great deeds; statues that foreknow the future and predict it by lots, by prophecy, by dreams, and by many other means; statues that make people ill and cure them, bringing them pain and pleasure as each deserves".[120]

As discussed earlier, the statues were brought to life by a ritual called the "Opening of the Mouth", which was performed in temple workshops known as the House of Gold, where the finishing touches were put on the statues.[121] This ritual was not only performed on statues, but also on mummies as a means of rendering the corpse serviceable to the soul in the afterlife so that it could travel to the heavens and return to the physical body for nou-

---

119   *Asclepius* 23, trans. Brian COPENHAVER.
120   *Asclepius* 24, trans. B. COPENHAVER.
121   Zosimos alludes to this ritual in his alchemical allegory, *On Excellence*, and he was likely one of the high-ranking artisan-priests that was responsible for performing this rite. I discuss these allusions to the Opening of the Mouth ritual in chapter three. On high-ranking priests performing this rite on statues in the House of Gold, see P. DERCHAIN, "L'Atelier des Orfevres à Dendara et les origins de l'Alchimie", 220. See also D. LORTON, "The Theology of Cult Statues in Ancient Egypt", 147–179; and Jan ASSMANN,

rishment when needed.¹²² These animating rituals therefore provide a vital link between matter and spirit and facilitate the human soul's ascent to the gods. Algis Uždavinys captures the essential purpose of these Egyptian rites:

> For the ancient Egyptians, the world as a whole was animated from the beginning; therefore any secondary 'animation' is tantamount to re-establishing or reactivating the otherwise hidden theurgic relationship between an image…and a certain spiritual will or power, between a corporeal vehicle […] and its archetypal principle, its *neter*. Everything here below is an image of its spiritual archetype and is involved in a rhythmic series of 'ontological rituals' performed on different levels of being, including the mundane temple rites and funerary ceremonies.¹²³

Statue animation—also known as the telestic art (τελεστική, *telestikē*)—was popular among Neoplatonic theurgists, as well, and these animated statues were thought to have an oracular power. Porphyry endorsed the telestic art, and it was also popular among Iamblichus's successors.¹²⁴ Iamblichus's views on the matter are more difficult to assess. On the one hand he acknowledges the consecration of statues is an important theurgical rite, stating that the objects chosen for building temples and consecrating statues

---

Death and Salvation in Ancient Egypt (Ithaca, NY: Cornell University Press, 2005), 310–329.

122 In mortuary contexts, this ritual was performed in the entrance to the tomb of the deceased. See Emily TEETER, *Religion and Ritual in Ancient Egypt*, 139–145.

123 Algis UŽDAVINYS, "Animation of Statues in Ancient Civilization and Neoplatonism", in *Late Antique Epistemology: Other Ways to Truth*, ed. P. VASSILOPOULOU and S. R. L. CLARK (London: Palgrave Macmillan, 2009), 128.

124 For overviews, see E. R. DODDS, "Appendix II: Theurgy", in *Greeks and the Irrational*, 291–295; and P. ATHANASSIADI, "Dreams, Theurgy, and Freelance Divination: The Testimony of Iamblichus", *Journal of Roman Studies*

should be in harmony with the gods, and that these "foundations" make it possible for humans to participate in divine reality.[125] But on the other hand, he reproaches "image makers" (εἰδωλοποιοί, *eidōlopoioi*) claiming they are not theurgists but "artificers" since they are concerned merely with imitations and not with divine reality itself.[126] Upon closer reading of his complaints, however, it appears that these images might not have anything to do with statues, but rather with "wonder-working" attempts (θαυματουργία, *thaumatourgia*) to make images of divine beings appear in clouds of incense smoke, and the like.[127] Iamblichus says that although the image makers claim that their art descends from the Demiurge, this is not the case, because these images come from humans and not from the gods: "[T]he skill of producing images is, indeed, far removed from the creative workmanship of things genuine", he insists.[128] The human-created image is ephemeral, more like a shadow or a phantom, and Iamblichus thinks it absurd to regard these images as gods, because it devalues both the human soul and the gods.[129] He asks poignantly, "Why does the image maker, who does these things, so undervalue himself?"[130]

There is some ambiguity around images in Zosimos's writings, as well. In *On Copper* he mentions making figurines of several popular gods—gods like Agathodaimon, the Nile, Fortune, and Mother Earth (*Terra Mater*), who had broad appeal throughout the Mediterranean—as well as other figurines commonly used in rituals such as snakes, animals, fruits, and ears (so that the gods may hear one's prayers), and concludes his list with: "the image of those things which lend themselves to the error and illusion of

---

83 (1993), 122–123.
125 DM V.23.
126 DM III.28-30.
127 See ADDEY's discussion of this in *Divination and Theurgy in Neoplatonism*, 252–255. Iamblichus discusses ephemeral images that appear in incense offerings in DM III.29.
128 DM III.28.
129 DM III.29.
130 Ibid.

duped individuals".[131] He goes on to say, "I scorn the disciples of Neilos who were admiring things unworthy of admiration; they were indeed ignorant, and we directed their attention to the saying 'know thyself'—the very saying that they did not admire".[132] Since this passage comes directly after the one where he expresses pride in his profession and admiration for the arts, his objections to the things that Neilos's disciples are admiring aren't clear.[133] He gives a clue, perhaps, later in the passage when he describes how people admired the vivid colors of the statue and believed they were the "colors of living nature", with only a small number of priests knowing that this was the handiwork of men, since this was spoken of only in secret.[134] There is a marginal note on this page, probably by a Christian or Muslim scribe, which refers to statues as "idols" and calls the artisan an "imposter";[135] therefore, the statement about these statues leading to error and illusion could be a scribal interpolation.[136] But if instead this is an accurate rendering of Zosimos's words, then this might indicate a similar problem pointed out by Iamblichus: that people confuse human creative power with divine power.

---

131 CMA Syr. 11.6.31.
132 Ibid.
133 In this same text, Zosimos talks about the beautiful colors they are able to achieve, and how moving it is to see the inventions of these arts. CMA Syr. 11.6.30.
134 Ibid.
135 As noted by Ruelle in CMA, Syr.11.6.30: « (A la marge.) Que tous les passants admirent l'idole et s'enorgueillissent de l'objet sculptè, comme le fit Pabapnidos, fils de Sitos, l'imposteur. » In the passage itself, Zosimos credits Pabapnidos with being the inventor of a particular blue color, which Zosimos greatly admires for its beauty.
136 Another reason to believe this might be a Christian or Muslim interpolation is a clause noting that the River Nile is the same as the River Gihon—one of the four rivers of Paradise mentioned in Genesis 2:13, though it is certainly within the realm of possibility that Zosimos would make this connection himself, given his attempts to harmonize Egyptian ideas with Jewish and Christian thought. See CMA Syr. 11.6.31.

Beginning in the classical period, Greek thinkers classified images as belonging to the realms of *eikōna* or *eidōla*; these concepts are useful for thinking about this ambivalence in our authors' discussions of divine images.[137] As Deborah Tarn Steiner explains, an *eikōn* is an image that shares an essential quality with its source: it is a "stepping stone pointing to the original that gives the viewer access to a hidden or absent reality".[138] Ideally, divine images are viewed and worshiped as *eikōna* that partake in and provide access to divine reality. By contrast, *eidōla* do not share this intrinsic quality; they are merely visual resemblances.[139] Iamblichus refers to the images of gods conjured in incense smoke as *eidōla*, not as *eikōna* or *agalma*. The *eidōla* he describes are soulless phantoms and shadows.[140] However, as Tarn Steiner points out, these theoretical categories are not quite as simple and clear-cut when it comes to "real world" scenarios, which reveal a great deal of vacillation between the realms.[141] This is evident in Zosimos's statement about certain statues leading to error and illusion; the statues he mentions are popular pan-Mediterranean gods, which were probably sold in the marketplace rather than installed in the temples; the images themselves might be *eikōna*, but the ways in which they were viewed or ritually employed might cross over into the realm of *eidōla*, or surface resemblances. Zosimos's complaint is that certain priests admired things in these statues that weren't worthy of reverence; they did not "know themselves". Iamblichus's image-makers mistake their human-created images with divine reality; they, too, lack self-understanding. This hearkens back to Zosimos's and Iamblichus's insistence upon having a

---

137 My discussion of *eikōna* and *eidōla* are informed by Deborah TARN STEINER's work in *Images in Mind: Statues in Archaic and Classical Greek Literature and Thought* (Princeton: Princeton University Press, 2001). She defines these concepts on page 5, and traces them in ancient discussions, including Plato's dialogues, throughout chapter 1.
138 Ibid, 5.
139 Ibid.
140 DM III.29.
141 TARN STEINER, 5.

correct view of the divine cosmic hierarchy and the proper place of the human within it. Divine images can be slippery; gods create humans, but humans can also create gods to a certain degree. In order to properly understand this human-divine relationship, one must come to "know thyself" through the practice of purifying the soul. Through this process, the material stains upon the soul are cleansed, and the soul gradually manifests its true nature as an *eikōn* of the divine.

Divinizing the Soul

The purification of the soul is in itself a god-making process. Iamblichus explains that god-making is the goal of theurgy:

> [T]he whole of theurgy has a double aspect. On the one hand, it is performed by humans, and as such observes our natural rank in the universe; but on the other, it controls divine symbols and by virtue of them is raised up to union with the higher powers, and directs itself harmoniously in accordance with their dispensation, which enables it quite properly to assume the mantle of the gods. It is in virtue of this distinction, then, that the art both naturally invokes the powers from the universe as superiors, inasmuch as the invoker is a human, and yet on the other hand gives them orders, since it invests itself, by virtue of the ineffable symbols, with the hieratic role of the gods.[142]

In regards to this statement by Iamblichus, Jan Assmann remarks that "[t]he basic principle of ancient Egyptian ritual practice could not be expressed more clearly", and goes on to explain that during ritual performances, Egyptian priests did not act as

---

142   DM IV.2. I have slightly amended the translation by CLARKE, et al. by translating ανθρωπος as "human" here, rather than "man".

humans, but as gods.¹⁴³ In order to prepare for these encounters with the divine, and even to enter the temple, priests underwent certain forms of physical purification, including ritual washings several times a day, shaving their heads, not eating certain foods, and wearing prescribed garments (particularly linen) so that they would not pollute the temple.¹⁴⁴ Different levels of purity were required in certain areas of the temple, and high priests were expected to uphold greater standards of purity than priests in the lower ranks.¹⁴⁵ Only certain high priests and kings were considered ritually pure enough to have contact with the temple's cult statue, which was housed in the inner sanctum.¹⁴⁶ Purity requirements for temple metallurgists are unknown, but we can surmise that they followed the same hierarchical rules, where higher ranking priests and scribes, like Zosimos, would be held to higher purity standards than lower-level artisans. Zosimos makes it clear that purity is important to alchemy; as he explains to his student, Theosebeia, "If you are impure, you won't work well, you won't understand".¹⁴⁷

For Zosimos, purification is a way to "know thyself". Purification rites such as ablutions and sacrifices can easily become empty rituals (like *eidōla*) if one fails to do the inner work of purifying the soul, of activating and bringing forth the divine image and purpose within. This involves having an acute awareness of one's thoughts, passions, and sensory experiences, and the ability to detect and transcend one's material "stains". Zosimos recommends meditation for this purpose. "Rest your body, calm your passions, resist desire, pleasure, anger, grief, and the twelve portions of death [i.e., the influences of the zodiac]", he tells his colleague, Theosebeia: "By righting yourself in this way, you will summon the divine to you, and it will come, that which is everywhere and nowhere".¹⁴⁸

143   ASSMANN, *Death and Salvation in Ancient Egypt*, 246.
144   See, for example, SAUNERON, *The Priests of Ancient Egypt*, 35–42; and TEETER, *Religion and Ritual in Ancient Egypt*, 32–34.
145   TEETER, 32.
146   ROBINS, "Cult Statues in Ancient Egypt", 7.
147   CMA, Syr. II.II.21.
148   CAAG III.51.8.

ALCHEMY, THEURGY, & THE DIVINE COSMOS 237

Zosimos's instructions allude to the astrological belief—very popular in Greco-Roman philosophy and religion—that the planets impart both virtues and vices to the soul as it makes its descent through the cosmos to be born on earth. When the soul ascends, it must relinquish these planetary "gifts" by transcending personal desires and attachments in order to merge with the divine. This journey of ascent through the planetary spheres (and beyond) is described in detail in the Hermetic *Poimandres*, where it is tantamount to the god-making process:

> First, in releasing the material body you give the body itself over to alteration, and the form that you used to have vanishes. To the demon you give over your temperament, now inactive. The body's senses rise up and flow back to their particular sources, becoming separate parts and mingling again with the energies. And feeling and longing go on toward irrational nature. The human being rushes up through the cosmic framework, at the first zone surrendering the energy of increase and decrease; at the second evil machination...; at the third the illusion of longing...; at the fourth the ruler's arrogance...; at the fifth unholy presumption and daring recklessness...; at the sixth the evil impulses that come from wealth...; at the seventh zone the deceit that lies in ambush. And then, stripped of the effects of the cosmic framework, the human enters the region of the ogdoad; he has his own proper power, and along with the blessed he hymns the father....[H]e also hears certain powers that exist beyond the ogdoadic region and hymn god with sweet voice. They rise up to the father in order and surrender themselves to the powers, and, having become powers, they enter into god. This is the final good for those who have received knowledge: to be made god.[149]

---

[149] CH I.24–26. Translation, COPENHAVER.

Iamblichus has similar ideas about the soul's ascent, and he believes that the soul travels to and from the heavens in a sort of ethereal body or envelope called the soul-vehicle (ὄχημα-πνεῦμα, *ochēma-pneuma*). As an intermediary between the physical body and the immaterial soul, the soul-vehicle is considered an integral part of the human being, thought to be the organ of sense perception and the seat of the imagination.[150] The soul-vehicle acquires material impurities from the cosmic gods and powers as it descends to earth to be born, manifesting ultimately as a material body; the theurgist must purify the vehicle of these impurities so that it can make its journey of ascent through the cosmos to the realm of the heavenly gods.[151] The soul can be helped or hindered by spiritual beings along the way, and so it is guarded by its personal daimon until it unites with its ruling god in the celestial realm.[152] In the higher stages of ascent, the soul-vehicle is illuminated by a process called *phōtagōgia*, or "evoking the light". According to Iamblichus, this:

> illuminates with divine light the ethereal and luminous vehicle of the soul, from which divine visions take possession of our imaginative power, moved by the will of the gods. For the entire life of the soul and all the powers in it move subject to the gods, in whatever way its leaders decree.[153]

Gregory Shaw claims that "in the critical moment of *phōtagōgia*, the theurgist no longer seeks the god, he becomes the god".[154]

---

150   J. FINAMORE, *Iamblichus and the Theory of the Vehicle of the Soul* (Chico: Scholars Press, 1985), 1-2; see also E. R. DODDS, trans. and ed., *Proclus: The Elements of Theology* (Oxford: Oxford University Press, 2004 [1963]), 316.
151   FINAMORE, 50–53
152   DM IX.6.
153   DM III.14. Blending here SHAW's translation (see note below) with CLARKE, DILLON, and HERSHBELL's.
154   SHAW, "Theurgy and the Platonist's Luminous Body", in *Practicing Gnosis: Ritual, Magic, Theurgy, and Liturgy in Nag Hammadi, Manichaean, and Other Ancient Literature, Essays in Honor of Birger A. Pearson*, A. DECONICK, G. SHAW, and J. TURNER, eds. (Leiden: Brill, 2013), 550.

I don't see evidence of this as the culminating rite of theurgy in the same way that Shaw does, because Iamblichus describes *phōtagōgia* as a rite of divination which can be used for many purposes, and the light can manifest in many ways, all according to the will of the gods.[155] However, Shaw is right in that the divinized soul is filled with light. Iamblichus mentions the illumination of the soul (also called *ellampsis*) at several points in the *De Mysteriis*. As with *phōtagōgia*, the illumination is always performed by the gods in response to the theurgist creating a pure receptacle for that light, that is to say, the purified soul. Iamblichus writes:

> in the case of the purified soul, the impression manifested is fiery, the fire being undefiled and unmixed; its interior light and form appear pure and stable, and follow after the leader [god] elevating it while rejoicing in his good will, and itself displays its proper order in its works.[156]

Once the soul has united with its leader god, the purified soul-vehicle (containing the irrational parts of the soul) is given over to the leader god's care, leaving the rational soul—the only part of the soul created by the Demiurge, for the purpose of revealing the Ineffable—to continue the ascent to the noetic realm to unite with the Demiurge.[157] Iamblichus describes this unified or divinized soul as "a formless fire manifesting itself around the entire cosmos as a whole, indivisible, and formless soul of the All".[158]

The concept of "spirit" as an ethereal envelope is also found in some of the *Hermetica*. For example, a text called *The Key* says that soul is the garment of mind, and spirit is the garment of the

---

155   DM III.14.
156   DM II.7.
157   On the ruling god and the rational soul transcending its vehicle, see FIN-AMORE, 148–150. On the Neoplatonic understanding of reason, see Jean TROUILLARD, cited by SHAW, in "Theurgy and the Platonist's Luminous Body", 540.
158   DM II.7.

soul. Spirit is united to the physical body through the bloodstream, where it "governs" and "moves" the human being. The purified mind eventually strips its spirit and soul garments and puts on a "fiery tunic" in which it ascends to the noetic realms.[159] In Iamblichus's theory of the soul's ascent, the purified soul-vehicle is left behind in the celestial realm so that the rational soul can ascend to the noetic realm. This Hermetic text indicates a similar process, where mind sheds the soul and rises to the noetic realms in its garment of fire. The thoughts of the Demiurge are also described as having a fiery body, and this divine fire is the instrument with which he creates divine works.[160] Other Hermetic texts describe the process of inner illumination as a means of becoming god. In *Poimandres*, for example, the initiate sees "an endless vision in which everything became light—clear and joyful—and in seeing the vision, I came to love it".[161] After the light is identified as the mind of god, the initiate is told that this divine light is identical with his own mind: "that in you which sees and hears is the word of the lord, but your mind is god the father; they are not divided from one another, for their union is life".[162]

Zosimos shares these traditions of soul purification and illumination. As we have seen in his *On the Letter Omega*, he refers to shedding one's "Adam"—that is, one's material and worldly self, or ordinary consciousness—to reveal the inner "man of light" (Phōs), the divine image within.[163] In this text, Zosimos explains the concept of the illuminated soul to Theosebeia in Christian theological terms as well as Greek, and his purpose is to show how aspects of these traditions are shared by Hebrews, Greeks, and Egyptians. He does not elaborate on the Egyptian concepts, however; he seems more interested in translating these ideas into the theological language of other cultures. But it is worth looking

---

159   CH X.13–18.
160   CH X.18.
161   CH I.4.
162   CH I.6. See also HANEGRAAFF's discussion of light in this text in "Altered States of Knowledge: The Attainment of Gnōsis in the *Hermetica*", 139–140.
163   *Auth.Mem.* 1.10.

ALCHEMY, THEURGY, & THE DIVINE COSMOS 241

at Egyptian ideas of the soul, because they are relevant and help contextualize the theurgical aspects of alchemy.

According to ancient Egyptian theology, the soul has three manifestations. First is the *ka*, which is linked to a person's vitality, character, and social status, and is also associated with the tomb; Erik Hornung relates that the *ka* "represents a bridge between the physical world and the realm of the spirit".[164] Next is the *ba*, or the soul of the individual, which is distinct from the *ka* as social self. The *ba* can move freely between the physical and spiritual worlds and acquire spiritual wisdom, but it is dependent on the physical body and must return to it for nourishment.[165] There is also the *akh*, which is the part of the soul that has been transfigured after death. The *akh* accompanies the gods and can intercede on behalf of the living, or cause harm if not appeased.[166] While the *akh* is sometimes described in wrathful terms, it was also understood as a perfected and deified soul; mortuary texts like the popular *Book of the Dead* refer to this type of transfiguration, where the gods dress the deceased in "pure clothes" and deify its entire body.[167] Deities also have *kau* and *bau* (plural of *ka* and *ba*). The *ka* of a deity is its cult statue, and a deity's *ba* is its divine essence; the *ba* of a god is what irradiates the statue with divine presence.[168] Although the *ba* of a god is not dependent on its statue in the same way that human *bau* are dependent on the physical body, the god's *ba* is encouraged to reside in its statue through daily cult offerings, including the washing, dressing, and feeding of the statue.[169] The term *ba* implies one thing emerging from another, which is consistent with

---

164 See ASSMANN, *Death and Salvation in Ancient Egypt*, 96–102; and HORNUNG, *Idea into Image*, 175.
165 ASSMANN, ibid, 14, 90–96; HORNUNG, ibid, 179–181.
166 TEETER, *Religion and Ritual in Ancient Egypt*, 148–152.
167 TEETER, ibid; RIGGS, *Beautiful Burial in Roman Egypt*, 28; and HORNUNG, *The Ancient Egyptian Books of the Afterlife*, 21. TEETER, on page 149, discusses a cult known as *akh iker n Re* ("able spirit of Re") that thrived in the Thebaid region (Zosimos's area) and honored the *akh* as perfected spirit.
168 TEETER, 44–45.
169 Ibid, 44–51.

the idea of the *ba* as a divine image that radiates throughout the cosmos on different levels of existence.[170] The *bau* of the gods can be present in people, animals, and forces of nature. For example, *heka*, the creative, vital force that animates the universe, is considered a *ba* of the solar creator god, Re.[171] The hawk is a *ba* of Horus; the baboon and ibis are *bau* of Thoth.[172] In other words, *bau* are divine signatures of the deity; they are *eikōna* that partake in the divine essence.

Zosimos, as we saw in chapter three, relies heavily on Egyptian mortuary texts and traditions in his allegory of the alchemical arts. He uses images of violence and death to convey the "violence" done to the metals as they are being smelted, but also to illustrate the importance of separating soul from body so that it may be transfigured and perfected. In Egyptian thought, death involves dismemberment and separation of the *ba* and *ka*, but mortuary cult is replete with rituals for preserving the body so that the soul can be nourished with offerings; the same is true for divine statues in that the physical receptacles for the gods enable them to receive offerings and praise. The links between the physical and the spiritual realms are therefore very important, imagined as a concatenation of divine images that, when properly aligned and realized, reveal the divinity in matter and make humans into gods.

God-making is the quintessential sacrament of the sacred arts of alchemy and theurgy. It involves knowing one's self and one's place in the divine cosmic order, so that one does not confuse human effort with divine revelation. This relationship between god and human changes as one progresses on the path of spiritual ascent. The process of purifying the soul is like a distillation of the self, whereby more subtle and spiritual forms of the person emerge. This transformation enables the soul to become illuminated with the fiery divine light, or *heka*, that pervades and unites all things, and to fully experience unity with the godhead.

170   HORNUNG, *Idea into Image*, 183.
171   RITNER, *The Mechanics of Ancient Egyptian Magical Practice*, 24.
172   MORENZ, *Egyptian Religion*, 157.

The enlightened soul will continue to nourish and be nourished by this light.

Conclusion

In conclusion, there are different approaches to theurgy, just as there are different approaches to alchemy, and care needs to be taken when comparing or conflating these arts. But in the case of Iamblichean theurgy and Zosimean alchemy, there is a strong alignment between the two. Iamblichus points to Egyptian religion as the wellspring for his views of theurgy, and comparing his writings with Zosimos, an Egyptian priest, allows for a closer look at how Egyptian religion and Neoplatonism were feeding each other in the latter third century, and how Zosimos's approach to alchemy fits in with Neoplatonic philosophical currents that were enormously influential in his day.

Iamblichean theurgy is about fostering a certain mindset—an approach to ritual, to philosophy, to life—that aims to unite matter and spirit and prepare the soul for union with the divine. Zosimos has a remarkably similar approach. They both believe that the soul's journey to the divine source begins with the material world. The soul must become aligned with the natural order and experience the revelations of the hierarchy of divine cosmic beings during the course of its ascent. Experiencing the divine cosmos and harmonizing with its perfect order enables the soul to transcend its limited "cosmic" perspectives and attain union with divine mind of the Demiurge. Thus the soul becomes divinized, comprehending the divine totality of heaven and earth, realizing the divine image of the One within the All. Given these shared approaches and aims, Zosimos's approach to alchemy can be considered theurgical, at least according to Iamblichus's framing of theurgy. These similarities also lend credence to Iamblichus's claim that his approach to theurgy is rooted, in part, in the Egyptian hieratic arts.

Coda

My aim in writing a cultural biography of Zosimos of Panopolis has been to examine his religious thought and the Egyptian contexts in which he lived and worked, which reveal some clues about the origins of western alchemy. The earliest alchemical texts come from Roman Egypt and were written in Greek. Although these texts incorporate some Greek natural philosophy, this is not their dominant feature, and I opened this book by challenging two prevailing scholarly narratives about the origins of alchemy: (1) the assumption that alchemists were primarily concerned with the transmutation of base metals into gold, and (2) the claim that alchemy originated in the Greco-Roman period when Egyptian metallurgists began using theories from Greek natural philosophy to explain their crafts. Looking closely at the earliest recipes in the Greco-Egyptian alchemical corpus, it is evident that many of them are instructions for coloring metals a variety of hues, such as blue, red, coral, yellow, black, and silver, as well as gold. These recipes align with specimens of ancient Egyptian metal statuary, particularly religious statuary crafted in temple workshops, which display highly advanced polychromatic techniques. Indeed, polychromy was a signature feature of Egyptian metalwork for at least a thousand years before Zosimos's time, from the Third Intermediate Period through the Roman period. Egyptian metalwork was prized throughout the Mediterranean, including their blackened silver, and a durable alloy they produced known as Corinthian bronze, which could be colored gold or silver. This evidence provides a more nuanced understanding of the Greco-Egyptian alchemical recipes, which are not just about gold-making. Zosimos indicates that he and his colleagues were responsible for making statues of the gods, vessels, and other goods for the temples. Religious ideas and rituals are interwoven into the work of these artisan-priests, and this book uncovers some of these Egyptian traditions. The idea that alchemy originated with Greek philosophy deserves to be questioned, because it is steeped in biases stemming from the European Enlightenment that bifurcate science and religion, privileging rational science and philosophy over religious teachings and mystical insights. This narrative has been used to argue that alchemy is a type of proto-chemistry, built on the rational foundations of Greek science. This Eurocentric view implies that Egyptian priests had no theories about their ancient technologies until Greek science came along, and I hope this book has demonstrated that this is not the case.

Another purpose of this cultural biography has been to flesh out what the alchemical profession might have been like in Panopolis and the Thebaid region around the time that Zosimos was active. Although alchemy originated in ancient Egyptian temple traditions, Zosimos is writing in the late-third to early-fourth century (ca. 270–325 CE), and traditions undergo changes over time. Zosimos identifies himself as a priest of Hermes, and evidence from his writings indicates that he worked as a scribe in a House of Life, which were centers of learning and knowledge production, usually affiliated with the main temple in town. As a scribal priest and high-ranking craftsman, Zosimos was responsible for preserving and translating ancient Egyptian metallurgical recipes, and for supervising temple artisans. But Zosimos was also an advisor to metallurgists outside of the temple tradition, particularly his Christian colleague, Theosebeia, who was most likely a member of a trade guild. Trade guilds were organized along familial and community ties, and they were often commissioned to do work for the temples, so there was some overlap between temple and trade guild economies. Trade guilds in Egypt began to flourish under Roman rule, and it is significant that the earliest alchemical texts also date from this period. This new economic arrangement challenged temple traditions of craft secrecy, thus paving the way for the alchemical recipes to be circulated more widely.

Roman Egyptian society was multicultural, and Panopolis had been a center of Greek culture and learning under Ptolemaic rule. Zosimos's writings reflect a Hellenized mode of expression that was common amongst educated Egyptians, but he was also making a more conscious attempt to blend cultures. He was reading Greek philosophy, Jewish pseudepigraphal works, and gnostic Christian texts and trying to harmonize these teachings with alchemical theories, both religious and technical, in order to provide a universal theory of alchemy. Universalizing efforts are also found among Neoplatonists like Iamblichus, who draws upon Egyptian, Greek, and Chaldean teachings to present theurgy as a universal philosophy of religion that transcends cultural boundaries.

Zosimos uses Jewish and Christian thought to illustrate the difference between his "natural" (*physika*) methods of alchemical practice and the "unnatural" (*aphysika*) methods of his rivals. Natural methods involved preparing substances in accordance with celestial, seasonal, and diurnal cycles, which was in keeping with ancient Egyptian craft traditions. His rivals used a newer method in which they appealed to the daimons of the zodiac to assist them in their work. Zosimos gives several reasons why this method is inadequate, but the thrust of his argument is that the daimons preside over very precise locations of the cosmos and therefore have only a partial understanding of nature; one should rather appeal to the divine creator who can reveal knowledge of heaven and earth as a totality. Some of the Jewish texts that Zosimos references contain instructions for this kind of "unnatural" demonology, and Zosimos's hermeneutical skill is impressive for the way he twists these texts and plays them off others to show how even though they contain some "errors", they essentially support his natural methods, which work in harmony with the natural rhythms and cosmic order established by the creator god.

Zosimos and his contemporaries shared a basic cosmological framework—the Ptolemaic view that the earth is surrounded by concentric planetary spheres, which are bounded by the realm of the fixed stars—but there was disagreement about the invisible powers that move and govern the cosmos. This is particularly evident in the theories of cosmic sympathy circulating in that era, all of which postulated that there are hidden spiritual forces linking all parts of nature, but these forces were imagined in different ways. This lack of uniformity was problematic for universalists like Zosimos and Iamblichus, because the divine cosmic order is the epitome of consistency and universality, a reflection of the divine mind and divine providence (or *maat*, in Egyptian terms). Iamblichus formulated a taxonomy of divine beings so that people could properly understand this order and work effectively with spiritual forces, and Zosimos had a similar hierarchical order of divine beings in mind, each with its own capacity for divine revelation. One of the spiritual exercises they had in common was to contemplate or ritually link a series of divine images, beginning with material objects and progressing to more universal, spiritual realities. This theurgical practice helps to elevate and purify the soul, and once the soul has been purified, it can experience union with the divine mind of the creator, who reveals the truth of the divine cosmic order.

Although most of Zosimos's religious writings focus on harmonizing ideas from different cultures, there are some distinctly Egyptian elements in his work that aid in understanding the alchemical tradition he inherited. His allegory of the alchemical opus, *On Excellence*, contains several allusions to Egyptian statue-making and mortuary traditions. For example, there are references to the Opening of the Mouth ritual, which is performed on new statues to invoke the presence of the deity in the world, as well as on new mummies to enable the soul to travel to and from the spirit world, where it will ideally become perfected. Zosimos emphasizes these religious ideas in one form or another throughout his work. Although Egyptian metallurgists made extensive use of polychromatic techniques, gold was prized as the most precious metal. It was known as the "flesh of the gods", and was considered a divine image of the creator, the sun god Re. Since gold is impervious to tarnish or rust, it was an emblem of purity and perfection and was used in religious contexts to convey supreme holiness. Zosimos's allegory links the alchemical process of coloring a metal gold to the spiritual process of purifying the soul, and this idea, rooted in ancient theologies of metals, has left an indelible impression on western alchemy.

Zosimos, living at the turn of the fourth century, was on the cusp of tremendous social and religious change. By the end of that century, the empire had been Christianized and ideological battles between Christians and pagans had resulted in rampant iconoclasm and the official closing of Egyptian temples. The alchemical arts persisted, of course; divorced from temple traditions, they were adapted to new contexts. Zosimos's efforts to articulate a universal theory of alchemy that would appeal to all religions and cultures, especially Christianity, proved to be a wise move at that point in history. His texts survived and helped ensure that future generations of metallurgists would persevere in the art of becoming gold.

Bibliography

ABT, Theodor, ed. *The Book of Pictures Mushaf as-suwar by Zosimos of Panopolis.* Corpus Alchemicum Arabicum Series, ed. T. ABT and W. MADELUNG. Zurich: Living Human Heritage Publications, 2007.

ADDEY, Crystal. *Divination and Theurgy in Neoplatonism: Oracles of the Gods.* Ashgate Studies in Philosophy and Theology in Late Antiquity Series, ed. M. EDWARDS and L. AYERS. Burlington: Ashgate Publishing, 2014.

ALSTON, Richard. "Trade and the City in Roman Egypt", in *Trade, Traders, and the Ancient City*, ed. Helen PARKINS and Christopher John SMITH. London: Routledge, 1998.

———. *The City in Roman and Byzantine Egypt.* London: Routledge, 2002.

ALSTON, Richard, and Robert D. ALSTON. "Urbanism and the Urban Community in Roman Egypt", *Journal of Egyptian Archaeology* 83 (1997): 199–216.

ANTON, John P. "Theourgia—Demiourgia: A Controversial Issue in Hellenistic Thought and Religion", in *Neoplatonism and Gnosticism*, ed. R. T. WALLIS and J. BREGMAN. Albany: State University of New York Press, 1992.

ARISTOTLE. *Metaphysics.* Translated by W. D. ROSS, in *The Complete Works of Aristotle*, vol. 2, ed. J. BARNES. Bollingen Series LXXI: 2. Princeton: Princeton University Press, 1995.

ARLANDSON, James Malcolm. *Women, Class, and Society in Early Christianity: Models from Luke–Acts.* Peabody, MA: Hendrickson Publishers, 1997.

ARMSTRONG, A. H., ed. *Classical Mediterranean Spirituality.* World Spirituality: AnEncyclopedic History of the Religious Quest, vol. 15.

New York: Crossroad, 1986.

ARNAOUTOGLOU, Ilias N. "*Collegia* in the Province of Egypt in the First Century AD", *Ancient Society* 35 (2005): 197–216.

ASSMANN, Jan. *The Mind of Egypt: History and Meaning in the Time of the Pharaohs.*Translated by A. JENKINS. New York: Metropolitan Books, 1996.

———. *Moses the Egyptian: The Memory of Egypt in Western Monotheism.* Cambridge: Harvard University Press, 1998.

———. *Death and Salvation in Ancient Egypt.* Translated by D. LORTON. Ithaca, NY: Cornell University Press, 2005.

———, and D. FRANKFURTER, "Egypt", in *Ancient Religions*, ed. Sarah Isles JOHNSTON. Cambridge: Belknap Press, 2007.

ATHANASSIADI, Polymnia. "Dreams, Theurgy, and Freelance Divination: The Testimony of Iamblichus", *The Journal of Roman Studies* 83 (1993): 115–130.

———. "The Chaldean Oracles: Theology and Theurgy", in *Pagan Monotheism in Late Antiquity*, ed. P. ATHANASSIADI and M. FREDE. Oxford: Clarendon Press, 1999.

AUFRÈRE, Sydney. *L'Univers Minéral Dans La Pensée Égyptienne*. 2 vols. Cairo: Institut Français d'Archéologie Orientale, 1991.

AUGUSTINE OF HIPPO. *The City of God*. Translated by Marcus DODS. Vol. 1. Edinburgh: T. & T. Clark, 1881.

AURELIUS, Marcus. *Meditations*. Translated by Maxwell Staniforth. London: Penguin, 1964.

BAGNALL, Roger S. *Egypt in Late Antiquity*. Princeton: Princeton University Press, 1993.

———., et al. *The Encyclopedia of Ancient History*. West Sussex, UK: Wiley-Blackwell, 2013.

BAINES, John. *Visual and Written Culture in Ancient Egypt*. Oxford: Oxford University Press, 2007.

BALL, Philip. *Bright Earth: Art and the Invention of Color*. New York: Farrar, Straus and Giroux, 2002.

BARCLAY, John M. G. *Jews in the Mediterranean Diaspora: From Alexander to Trajan*. 1996. Berkeley: University of California Press, 1999.

BARNES, J., ed. *The Complete Works of Aristotle: The Revised Oxford Translation*. 2 vols. Bollingen Series LXXI: 2. Princeton: Princeton University Press, 1995.

BARTON, Tamsyn. *Ancient Astrology*. London: Routledge, 1994.

BERETTA, Marco. *The Alchemy of Glass: Counterfeit, Imitation, and Transmutation in Ancient Glassmaking*. Sagamore Beach, MA: Science History Publications USA, 2009.

BERTHELOT, Marcellin. *Les origines de l'alchimie*. Paris: G. Steinheil, 1885.

———. and Ch.-Ém. RUELLE. *Collection des Anciens Alchimistes Grecs*. 3 vols. 1888. Osnabrück: Otto Zeller, 1967.

———. and R. DUVAL. *La Chimie au Moyen Age*. 3 vols. 1893. Osnabrück: Otto Zeller, 1967.

BETZ, Hans Dieter. *The Greek Magical Papyri in Translation*, 2nd ed. Chicago: University of Chicago Press, 1992.

BIDEZ, Joseph, and Franz CUMONT. *Les Mages Hellénisés*, 2 vols. Ancient Religion and Mythology Series, ed. W. R. CONNOR. 1938. New York: Arno Press, 1975.

BLACK, Matthew, trans. and ed. *The Book of Enoch or 1 Enoch*. Studia in Veteris Testamenti Pseudepigrapha vol. 7, ed. A. M. DENIS and M. DE JONGE. Leiden: Brill, 1985.

BLUMENTHAL, Henry J. and E. Gillian CLARK, eds. *The Divine Iamblichus: Philosopher and Man of Gods*. London: Bristol Classics Press, 1993.

BOAK, A. E. R. "The Organization of Gilds in Greco-Roman Egypt", *Transactions and Proceedings of the American Philological Association*, 68 (1937): 212–220.

BORKOWSKI, Zbigniew. *Une description topographique des immeubles à Panopolis*. Warsaw: Panstwowe Wydawnictwo Naukowe, 1975.

BOROWSKI, Oded. *Daily Life in Biblical Times*. Atlanta: Society of Biblical Literature, 2003.

BOWERSOCK, G. W. *Hellenism in Late Antiquity*. Jerome Lectures, no. 18. Ann Arbor: University of Michigan Press, 1990.

BRAIN, Peter. *Galen on Bloodletting*. Cambridge: Cambridge University Press, 1986.

BRAKKE, David, and Andrew CRISLIP. *Selected Discourses of Shenoute the Great: Community, Theology, and Social Conflict in Late Antique Egypt.* Cambridge: Cambridge University Press, 2015.

BREMMER, Jan, and Jan VEENSTRA, eds. *The Metamorphosis of Magic from Late Antiquity to the Modern Period.* Groningen Studies in Cultural Change, ed. M. GOSMAN. Leuven: Peeters, 2002.

BROWNE, C. A. "Rhetorical and Religious Aspects of Greek Alchemy, Including a Commentary and Translation of the Poem of the Philosopher Archelaos Upon the Sacred Art: Part I", *Ambix* 2 (Dec. 1946): 129–137.

———. "Rhetorical and Religious Aspects of Greek Alchemy: Part II", *Ambix* 3 (May 1948): 15–25.

BROWN, Peter. *The Making of Late Antiquity.* Carl Newell Jackson Lectures. Cambridge, MA: Harvard University Press, 1978.

BURFORD, Alison. *Craftsmen in Greek and Roman Society.* Aspects of Greek and Roman Life, ed. H. H. SCULLARD. Ithaca: Cornell University Press, 1971.

BURKHALTER, Fabienne. "La production des objets en metal (or, argent, bronze) en Égypte hellénistique et romaine à travers les sources papyrologiques", in *Commerce et artisanat dans l'Alexandrie hellénistique et romaine : Actes du colloque d'Athènes 11–12 décembre 1988*, ed. Jean-Yves EMPEREUR. Athènes: École française d'Athènes, 1998.

BURNHAM, Daniel. "Explorations of the Alchemical Idiom of the Pyramid Texts", *Discussions in Egyptology* 60 (2004): 11–20.

CALEY, Earl Radcliffe, trans., and William. B. JENSEN, ed. *The Leyden and Stockholm Papyri: Greco-Egyptian Chemical Documents from the 4th Century AD.* Oesper Collections in the History of Chemistry. Cincinnati: University of Cincinnati, 2008.

CERBELAUD, Dominique. "Le nom d'Adam et les points cardinaux : recherches sur un theme patristique", *Vigiliæ Christianæ* 38.3 (1984): 285–301.

CHARLESWORTH, J. H., ed. *The Old Testament Pseudepigrapha,* vol. 1. New York: Doubleday, 1983.

CHARRON, Régine. "The Apocryphon of John (NHC II, 1) and the Græco-Egyptian Alchemical Literature", *Vigiliæ Christianæ* 59.4

(2005): 438–456.

CHEAK, Aaron. "The Perfect Black: Egypt and Alchemy", in *Alchemical Traditions: From Antiquity to the Avant-Garde*, ed. A. CHEAK. 2013. Rev. ed. Auckland: Rubedo Press, forthcoming.

_____, ed. *Alchemical Traditions: From Antiquity to the Avant-Garde*. 2013. Rev, ed. Auckland: Rubedo Press, forthcoming.

CLAGETT, Marshall. *Ancient Egyptian Science*. 3 vols. Philadelphia: American Philosophical Society, 1989–1999.

CLARK, Dennis C. "Iamblichus' Egyptian Neoplatonic Theology in De Mysteriis", *The International Journal of the Platonic Tradition*, no. 2 (2008): 164–205.

CLARKE, Emma C. *Iamblichus' De Mysteriis: A Manifesto of the Miraculous*. New Critical Thinking in Theology and Biblical Studies Series, no. 1152. Aldershot: Ashgate Publishing, 2001.

COPENHAVER, Brian P., trans. and ed. *Hermetica*. Cambridge: Cambridge University Press, 1992.

CORNFORD, F. M. *From Religion to Philosophy: A Study in the Origins of Western Speculation*. 1912. Princeton: Princeton University Press, 1991.

CROSLAND, Maurice P. *Historical Studies in the Language of Chemistry*. 1962. New York: Dover, 1978.

DALY, Robert J. "The Power of Sacrifice in Ancient Judaism and Christianity", *Journal of Ritual Studies* 4.2 (1990): 181–198.

DAUMAS, Francois. "L'alchimie a-t-elle une origine égyptienne?", in *Römisch Byzantinische Ägypten. Akten des internationalen Symposions 26–30 September 1978 in Trier* (Mainz am Rhein: P. von Zabern, 1983), 109–118.

DAVID, A. Rosalie. "Mummification", in *Ancient Egyptian Materials and Technology*, ed. P. T. NICHOLSON and I. SHAW. Cambridge: Cambridge University Press, 2000.

DAVIS, Tenney L. "The Problem of the Origins of Alchemy", *The Scientific Monthly* 43.6 (Dec. 1936): 551–558.

DECONICK, April D., Gregory SHAW, and John D. TURNER, eds. *Practicing Gnosis: Ritual, Magic, Theurgy, and Liturgy in Nag Hammadi, Manichæan, and Other Ancient Literature*. Essays in Honor of Birger

Pearson. Leiden: Brill, 2013.

DeConick, April D. "Gnostic Spirituality at the Crossroads of Christianity: Transgressing Boundaries and Creating Orthodoxy", in *Beyond the Gnostic Gospels: Studies Building on the Work of Elaine Pagels*, ed. E. Iricinschi, L. Jenott, N. Denzey Lewis, and P. Townsend. Studies and Texts in Antiquity and Christianity, 82. Tübingen: Mohr Siebeck, 2013.

Delange, Élisabeth. "The Complexity of Alloys: New Discoveries About Certain 'Bronzes' in the Louvre", in *Gifts for the Gods: Images from Egyptian Temples*, ed. M. Hill with D. Schorsch, technical ed. Catalog of exhibition held at the Metropolitan Museum of Art, New York, Oct. 16, 2007–Feb.18, 2008. New Haven: Yale University Press, 2007.

Derchain, Philippe. "L'Atelier des Orfevres à Dendara et les origins de l'Alchimie", *Chronique d'Egypte* LXV (1990): 219–242.

Dick, Michael B., ed. *Born in Heaven, Made on Earth: The Creation of the Cult Image in the Ancient Near East*. Winona Lake, IN: Eisenbrauns, 1999.

Dickie, Matthew. *Magic and Magicians in the Greco-Roman World*. London: Routledge, 2001.

Dillon, John M., ed. and trans. *Iamblichi Chalcidensis in Platonis dialogos commentariorum fragmenta*. Leiden: Brill, 1973.

———. *The Middle Platonists 80 BC to AD 220*. 1977. Ithaca: Cornell University Press, 1996.

Dodds, E. R. *The Greeks and the Irrational*. Berkeley: University of California Press, 1951.

———, trans. and ed. *Proclus: The Elements of Theology*. 1963. Oxford: Oxford University Press, 2004.

Dufault, Olivier. "Transmutation Theory in the Greek Alchemical Corpus", *Ambix* 62.3 (2015): 215–244.

Duling, D. C., trans. *Testament of Solomon*, in *The Old Testament Pseudepigrapha*, vol. 1, ed. J. H. Charlesworth. New York: Doubleday, 1983.

Dunand, Françoise, and Christiane Zivie-Coche. *Gods and Men in Egypt: 3000 BCE to 395 CE*. Translated by David Lorton. Ithaca:

Cornell University Press, 2004.

DUPRÉ, Sven, ed. *Laboratories of Art: Alchemy and Art Technology from Antiquity to the Eighteenth Century*. Archimedes 37. Switzerland: Springer International, 2014.

DUQUESNE, Terence. "Egypt's Image in the European Enlightenment", *Seshat 3* (1999): 32–51.

EATON-KRAUSS, Marianne. "Artists and Artisans", in *The Oxford Encyclopedia of Ancient Egypt*, ed. Donald B. REDFORD. Online ed. Oxford: Oxford University Press, 2005.

EGBERTS, A., B.P. Muchs, and J. Van Der Vliet, eds. *Perspectives on Panopolis: An Egyptian Town from Alexander the Great to the Arab Conquest. Acts from an International Symposium Held in Leiden on 16, 17 and 18 December 1998*. Leiden: Brill, 2002.

EL-DALY, Okasha. *Egyptology: The Missing Millennium: Ancient Egypt in Medieval Arabic Writings*. London: UCL Press, 2005.

ELIADE, Mircea. *The Forge and the Crucible: The Origins and Structures of Alchemy*. Translated by Stephen Corbin. 2nd ed. Chicago: Chicago University Press, 1978.

ELIAS, Jonathan. "Akhmim", in *Encyclopedia of Ancient History*, ed. R. BAGNALL, et al. West Sussex, UK: Wiley-Blackwell, 2013.

EMPEREUR, Jean-Yves, ed. *Commerce et artisanat dans l'Alexandrie hellénistique et romaine: Actes du colloque d'Athènes 11-12 décembre 1988*. Athènes: École française d'Athènes, 1998.

FAIVRE, Antoine. "Hermetism", in *Hidden Truths: Magic, Alchemy, Religion, and the Occult*, ed. Lawrence E. SULLIVAN. Religion, History, and Culture: Selections from The Encyclopedia of Religion, ed. Mircea ELIADE. New York: Macmillan, 1987.

⸺⸺⸺. *Access to Western Esotericism*. Albany: SUNY Press, 1994.

FELDMAN, Louis H. *Jew and Gentile in the Ancient World*. Princeton: Princeton University Press, 1993.

FERRARIO, Gabriele. "The Jews and Alchemy: Notes for a Problematic Approach", in *Chymia. Science and Nature in Medieval and Early Modern Europe*, ed. M. LÓPEZ PÉREZ, D. KAHN, and M. R. BUENO. Newcastle upon Tyne: Cambridge Scholars Publishing, 2010.

FESTUGIÈRE, A.-J. *La Révélation D'Hermès Trismégiste*, 4 Vols. 2nd ed.

Paris: Gabalda, 1950.

———. *Hermétisme et Mystique Païenne*. Paris: Aubier-Montaigne, 1967.

FINAMORE, John F. *Iamblichus and the Theory of the Vehicle of the Soul*. American Classical Studies 14. Chico, CA: Scholars Press, 1985.

FINNESTAD, Ragnhild Bjerre. "The Meaning and Purpose of Opening the Mouth in Mortuary Contexts", *Numen* 25.2 (1978), 118–134.

———. "Temples of the Ptolemaic and Roman Periods: Ancient Traditions in New Contexts", in *Temples of Ancient Egypt*, ed. Byron SHAFER. Ithaca: Cornell University Press, 1997.

FORBES, R. J. *Studies in Ancient Technology*, vol. 1. Leiden: Brill, 1955.

FOUCAULT, Michel. *The Order of Things: An Archaeology of the Human Sciences*. New York: Vintage Books, 1994.

FOWDEN, Garth. "The Pagan Holy Man in Late Antique Society", *The Journal of Hellenic Studies* 182 (1982): 33–59.

———. *The Egyptian Hermes: A Historical Approach to the Late Pagan Mind*. Cambridge: Cambridge University Press, 1986.

FRANKFORT, Henri, Mrs. H. A. FRANKFORT, et al. *Before Philosophy: The Intellectual Adventure of Ancient Man*. 1946. Reprint, New York: Penguin Books, 1974.

FRANKFURTER, David. *Religion in Roman Egypt: Assimilation and Resistance*. Princeton: Princeton University Press, 1998.

———. "Histories: Egypt, Later Period", in *Religions of the Ancient World: A Guide*, ed. Sarah Iles JOHNSTON. Cambridge: Harvard University Press, 2004.

———. "Religious Practice and Piety", in *The Oxford Handbook of Roman Egypt*, ed. C. RIGGS. Oxford: Oxford University Press, 2012.

FRASER, Kyle. "Zosimos of Panopolis and the Book of Enoch: Alchemy as Forbidden Knowledge", *Aries* 4.2 (2004): 125–147.

———. "Baptized in Gnôsis: The Spiritual Alchemy of Zosimos of Panopolis", *Dionysius* 25 (2007): 33–54.

GAGER, John G. *Moses in Greco-Roman Paganism*. Society of Biblical Literature Monograph Series 16. Nashville: Abingdon Press, 1972.

GALEN. *Three Treatises on the Nature of Science*. Translated by Richard

Walzer and Michael Frede. Indianapolis: Hackett Publishing Co., 1985.

GARDINER, Alan H. "The House of Life", *The Journal of Egyptian Archæology* 24.2 (1938), 157–179.

GEENS, Karolien. "Panopolis, A Nome Capital in Egypt in the Roman and Byzantine Period (ca. AD 200-600)". PHD diss., Katholieke Universiteit Leuven, 2007.

———. "Hellenism as a Vehicle for Local Traditions in Third Century Egypt: The Evidence from Panopolis", in *Faces of Hellenism: Studies in the History of the Eastern Mediterranean, 4th Century B.C. to 5th Century A.D.*, ed. Peter NUFFELEN. Leuven: Peeters, 2009.

GERSH, Stephen and Charles KANNENGIESSER, eds. *Platonism in Late Antiquity*. Christianity and Judaism in Antiquity, vol. 8, ed. C. KANNENGIESSER. Notre Dame, IN: University of Notre Dame Press, 1992.

GERSON, Lloyd P., ed. *The Cambridge Companion to Plotinus*. Cambridge: Cambridge University Press, 1996.

GESSLER-LÖHR, Beatrix. "Mummies and Mummification", in *The Oxford Handbook of Roman Egypt*, ed. Christina RIGGS. Oxford: Oxford University Press, 2012.

GEUS, Klaus and Mark J. GELLER, eds. *Esoteric Knowledge in Antiquity*. TOPOI—Dahlem Seminar for the History of Ancient Sciences, vol. II. Berlin: Max Planck Institute for the History of Science, Preprint 454, 2014.

GILLY, C. and C. van HEERTUM, eds. *Magia, Alchimia, Scienzia dal '400 al '700: L'influsso di Ermete Trismegisto / Magic, Alchemy and Science, 15th-18th Centuries: The Influence of Hermes Trismegistus*, vol. I. Florence: Centro Di, 2002.

GIUMLIA-MAIR, Alessandra and P. T. CRADDOCK. *Corinthium æs: das schwarze Gold der Alchimisten*. Mainz am Rhein: P. von Zabern, 1993.

GIUMLIA-MAIR, Alessandra. "Zosimos the Alchemist, Manuscript 629, Cambridge, Metallurgical Interpretation", in *I bronzi antichi: Produzione e tecnologia, Atti del XV Congresso Internazionale sui Bronzi Antichi, Università di Udine, 22–26 Maggio, 2001*, ed. A. GIUMLIA-MAIR. Montagnac: Éditions Monique Mergoil, 2002.

_____, ed. *I bronzi antichi: Produzione e tecnologia, Atti del* xv *Congresso Internazionale sui Bronzi Antichi, Università di Udine, 22–26 Maggio, 2001.* Montagnac: Éditions Monique Mergoil, 2002.

GRANT, Robert M. *Miracle and Natural Law in Græco-Roman and Early Christian Thought.* Amsterdam: North Holland, 1952.

GRIMES, Shannon. *Zosimus of Panopolis: Alchemy, Nature, and Religion in Late Antiquity.* PHD dissertation, Syracuse University, 2006.

_____. "Natural Methods: Examining the Biases of Ancient Alchemists and Those Who Study Them", in *Esotericism, Religion, and Nature*, ed. A. VERSLUIS, C. FANGER, L. IRWIN, and M. PHILLIPS. Minneapolis: North American Academic Press, 2010.

GURTLER, Gary M. "Sympathy: Stoic Materialism and the Platonic Soul", in *Neoplatonism and Nature: Studies in Plotinus' Enneads*, ed. M. F. WAGNER. Albany: SUNY Press, 2002.

HAAS, Christopher. *Alexandria in Late Antiquity: Topography and Social Conflict.* Baltimore: The John Hopkins University Press, 1997.

HADOT, Pierre. *Philosophy as a Way of Life.* Translated by M. Chase. Malden, MA: Blackwell Publishing, 1995.

_____. *What is Ancient Philosophy?* Translated by M. Chase. Cambridge: Belknap Press of Harvard University Press, 2002.

HALLEUX, Robert. *Les Textes Alchimique.* Typologie des Sources du Moyen Âge Occidental, ed. L. Genicot, Fasc. 32. Turnhout, Belgium: Brepols, 1979.

_____. *Papyrus de Leyde, Papyrus de Stockholm Recettes.* Les Alchimistes Grecs, Tome I. Paris: Les Belles Lettres, 1981.

HALLUM, Benjamin. *Zosimus Arabus: The Reception of Zosimos of Panopolis in the Arabic/Islamic World.* PHD dissertation, Warburg Institute, 2008.

_____. "The Tome of Images: An Arabic Compilation of Texts by Zosimos of Panopolis and a Source of the Turba Philosophorum", *Ambix* 56.1 (2009): 76–88.

HAMILTON, E. and H. CAIRNS, eds. *The Collected Dialogues of Plato.* Bollingen Series LXXI. Princeton: Princeton University Press, 1961.

HAMMER-JENSEN, Ingeborg. *Die älteste Alchemie. Det Kongelige Danske*

Videnskabernes Selskab. Historiskfilologiske Meddelelser IV, 2. Copenhagen: Host & Son, 1921.

HANEGRAAFF, Wouter. "Altered States of Knowledge: The Attainment of Gnōsis in the *Hermetica*". *The International Journal of the Platonic Tradition* 2 (2008), 128–63.

HARKER, Andrew. "The Jews in Roman Egypt: Trials and Rebellions", in *The Oxford Handbook of Roman Egypt*, ed. C. RIGGS. Oxford: Oxford University Press, 2012.

HARLAND, Philip. *Associations, Synagogues, and Congregations: Claiming a Place in Ancient Mediterranean Society*. Minneapolis: Augsburg Fortress Press, 2003.

HARRISON, Peter. *The Territories of Science and Religion*. Chicago: University of Chicago Press, 2015.

HEALY, John F. *Mining and Metallurgy in the Greek and Roman World*. Aspects of Greek and Roman Life, ed. H. H. Scullard. London: Thames & Hudson, 1978.

HERODOTUS. *The Histories*. Translated by R. Waterfield. Oxford: Oxford University Press, 1998.

HERSHBELL, Jackson P. "Democritus and the Beginnings of Greek Alchemy", *Ambix* 34.1 (1987): 5–20.

HILL, Marsha, ed., with Deborah SCHORSCH, technical ed. *Gifts for the Gods: Images from Egyptian Temples*. Catalog of exhibition held at Metropolitan Museum of Art, New York, Oct. 16 2007–Feb. 18 2008. New Haven: Yale University Press, 2007.

HILL, Marsha. "Heights of Artistry: The Third Intermediate Period (ca. 1070-664 B.C.)", in M. HILL, ed., with D. SCHORSCH, technical ed. *Gifts for the Gods: Images from Egyptian Temples*. Catalog of exhibition held at Metropolitan Museum of Art, New York, Oct. 16 2007–Feb. 18 2008. New Haven: Yale University Press, 2007.

———. "Lives of the Statuary", in M. Hill, ed., with D. Schorsch, technical ed. *Gifts for the Gods: Images from Egyptian Temples*. Catalog of exhibition held at Metropolitan Museum of Art, New York, Oct. 16 2007–Feb. 18 2008. New Haven: Yale University Press, 2007.

HIMMELFARB, Martha. *Ascent to Heaven in Jewish and Christian Apocalypses*. New York: Oxford University Press, 1993.

HOLMYARD, E. J. *Alchemy*. 1957. Reprint, New York: Dover, 1990.

HOPKINS, Arthur John. "Earliest Alchemy", *The Scientific Monthly* 6.6 (1918): 530–537.

———. "A Modern Theory of Alchemy", *Isis* 7.1 (1925): 58–76.

———. *Alchemy: Child of Greek Philosophy*. 1933. Reprint, New York: AMS Press, 1967.

———. "A Defence of Egyptian Alchemy", *Isis* 28.2 (1938): 424–431.

———. "A Study of the Kerotakis Process as Given by Zosimus and Later Alchemical Writers", *Isis* 29.2 (1938): 326–354.

HORNUNG, Erik. *Conceptions of God in Ancient Egypt: The One and the Many*. Translated by J. Baines. Ithaca, NY: Cornell University Press, 1982.

———. *Idea into Image: Essays on Ancient Egyptian Thought*. Translated by E. Bredeck. New York: Timken Publishers, 1992.

———. *The Secret Lore of Egypt: Its Impact on the West*. Translated by D. Lorton. Ithaca, NY: Cornell University Press, 2001.

HUNTER, Erica C. D. "Beautiful Black Bronzes: Zosimos's treatises in Cam. Mm.6.29", in *I bronzi antichi: Produzione e tecnologia, Atti del XV Congresso Internazionale sui Bronzi Antichi, Università di Udine, 22-26 Maggio, 2001*, ed. Alessandra GIUMLIA-MAIR (Montagnac: Éditions Monique Mergoil, 2002), 655–660.

IAMBLICHUS. *Iamblichus Chalcidensis in Platonis dialogos commentariorum fragmenta*. Translated and edited by J. DILLON. Philosopha Antiqua Series, vol. XXIII. Leiden: Brill, 1973.

———. *On the Pythagorean Life*. Translated by Gillian Clark. Translated Texts for Historians, vol. 8. Liverpool: Liverpool University Press, 1989.

———. *De Mysteriis*. Translated by E. Clarke, J. Dillon, and J. Hershbell. Writings from the Greco-Roman World Series, no. 4. Atlanta: Society of Biblical Literature, 2003.

IDEL, Moshe. "The Origin of Alchemy According to Zosimos and a Hebrew Parallel", in *Kabbalah and Alchemy: An Essay on Common Archetypes by Arturo Schwarz*. Northvale, NJ: Jason Aronson, 2000.

IRBY-MASSIE, Georgia, and Paul T. KEYSER. *Greek Science of the Hellenistic Era: A Sourcebook*. London: Routledge, 2002.

ISAAC, E., trans. *I Enoch*, in *The Old Testament Pseudepigrapha*, vol. 1, ed. J. H. Charlesworth. New York: Doubleday, 1983.

JACKSON, Howard, ed. and trans. *Zosimos of Panopolis on the Letter Omega*. Society of Biblical Literature Graeco-Roman Religions Series, No. 5. Missoula: Scholars Press, 1978.

JACOBSON, David. "Corinthian Bronze and the Gold of the Alchemists", *Gold Bulletin* 33.2 (2000): 60–66.

JANES, Dominic. *God and Gold in Late Antiquity*. Cambridge: Cambridge University Press, 1998.

JANOWITZ, Naomi. *Magic in the Roman World: Pagans, Jews, and Christians*. Religion in the First Christian Centuries, ed. D. Sawyer and J. Sawyer. New York: Routledge, 2001.

———. *Icons of Power: Ritual Practices in Late Antiquity*. Magic in History Series. University Park, PA: Pennsylvania State University Press, 2002.

JASNOW, Richard and Karl-Theodor ZAUZICH. *Conversations in the House of Life: A New Translation of the Ancient Egyptian Book of Thoth*. Wiesbaden: Harrassowitz Verlag, 2014.

JOHNSTON, Sarah Iles. *Hekate Soteira: A Study of Hekate's Roles in the Chaldean Oracles and Related Literature*. American Classical Studies 21. Atlanta: Scholars Press, 1990.

———. "Rising to the Occasion: Theurgic Ascent in its Cultural Milieu", in *Envisioning Magic: A Princeton Seminar and Symposium*, ed. P. SCHÄFER and H. KIPPENBERG. Studies in the History of Religions (Numen Book Series) vol. LXXV. Leiden: Brill, 1997.

———, ed. *Religions of the Ancient World: A Guide*. Cambridge: Harvard University Press, 2004.

———, ed. *Ancient Religions*. Cambridge: Belknap Press, 2007.

JONAS, Hans. *Gnostic Religion: The Message of the Alien God and the Beginnings of Christianity*. 2nd ed. Boston: Beacon Press, 1963.

JORDAN, David, Hugo MONTGOMERY, and Einar THOMASSEN, eds. *The World of Ancient Magic. Papers from the Norwegian Institute at Athens 4*. Bergen: Norwegian Institute at Athens, 1999.

JUNG, C. G. *Alchemical Studies*. Translated by. R. F. C. Hull. 2nd ed. Bollingen Series XX. Princeton: Princeton University Press, 1967.

―――. *Mysterium Coniunctionis*, trans. R. F. C. Hull. 2nd ed. Princeton: Princeton University Press, 1970.

KAHN, Didier and Sylvain MATTON, eds. *Alchimie: art histoire, et mythes, Actes du 1er colloque international de la Société d'Étude d l'Histoire de l'Alchimie (Paris, Collège de France, 14-16 mars 1991)*. Textes et Travaux de Chrysopoeia 1. Paris: S.É.H.A., 1995.

KARPENKO, Vladimir. "The Chemistry and Metallurgy of Transmutation", *Ambix* 39.2 (1992): 47–62.

―――. "Not All That Glitters is Gold: Gold Imitations in History", *Ambix* 54.2 (2007): 156–175.

KEESLING, Catherine M. "Greek Statue Terms Revisited: What does ἀνδριάς mean?" *Greek, Roman, and Byzantine Studies* 57 (2017): 837–861.

KEYSER, P. T. "Alchemy in the Ancient World: From Science to Magic", Illinois Classical Studies 15 (1990): 353–378.

KLEMM, D., R. KLEMM, and A. MURR, "Gold of the Pharaohs: 6000 Years of Gold Mining in Egypt and Nubia", *African Earth Sciences* 33 (2001), 643–659.

KING, Karen. *What is Gnosticism?* Cambridge, MA: Belknap Press of Harvard University Press, 2003.

KINGSLEY, Peter. *Ancient Philosophy, Mystery, and Magic: Empedocles and Pythagorean Tradition*. Oxford: Clarendon Press, 1995.

KUHLMANN, K. *Materialien zur Archäologie und Geschichte des Raumes von Achmim*. Mainz am Rhein: Philipp von Zabern, 1983.

LELLI, Fabrizio. "Hermes Among the Jews: *Hermetica* as Hebraica from Antiquity to the Renaissance", in *Magic, Ritual, and Witchcraft* 2.2 (2007): 111–135.

LESKO, Leonard. "Ancient Egyptian Cosmogonies and Cosmology", in Byron SHAFER, ed., *Religion in Ancient Egypt*. Ithaca: Cornell University, 1991.

LETROUIT, Jean. "Hermetism and Alchemy: Contribution to the Study of Marcianus Græcus 299 (=M)", in *Magia, Alchimia, Scienzia dal '400 al '700: L'influsso di Ermete Trismegisto/Magic, Alchemy and Science, 15th-18th Centuries: The Influence of Hermes Trismegistus*, vol. I, ed. C. GILLY and C. van HEERTUM. Florence: Centro Di, 2002.

LEWY, Hans. *Chaldaean Oracles and Theurgy: Mysticism, Magic and Platonism in the Later Roman Empire*. 1956. 3rd ed., edited by Michel Tardieu. Paris: Institut d'Études Augustiniennes, 2011.

LIDDELL and SCOTT. *A Greek-English Lexicon*. Revised by Sir H. S. JONES and R. MCKENZIE. Oxford: Clarendon Press, 1940.

LINDEN, Stanton J., ed. *The Alchemy Reader: From Hermes Trismegistus to Isaac Newton*. Cambridge: Cambridge University Press, 2003.

LINDSAY, Jack. *The Origins of Alchemy in Græco-Roman Egypt*. London: Frederick Muller, 1970.

LLOYD, G. E. R. *Magic, Reason, and Experience: Studies in the Origins and Development of Greek Science*. 1979. Reprint, Indianapolis: Hackett, 1999.

LONG, A. A. *Hellenistic Philosophy: Stoics, Epicureans, Sceptics*. 1974. 2nd ed. Berkeley: University of California Press, 1986.

LONG, Pamela O. *Openness, Secrecy, Authorship: Technical Arts and the Culture of Knowledge from Antiquity to the Renaissance*. Baltimore: John Hopkins University Press, 2001.

LÓPEZ PÉREZ, M., D. KAHN, and M. R. BUENO, eds. *Chymia. Science and Nature in Medieval and Early Modern Europe*. Newcastle upon Tyne: Cambridge Scholars Publishing, 2010.

LORTON, David. "The Theology of Cult Statues in Ancient Egypt", in *Born in Heaven, Made on Earth: The Creation of the Cult Image in the Ancient Near East*, ed. Michael B. DICK. Winona Lake, IN: Eisenbrauns, 1999.

LUCAS, Alfred. *Ancient Egyptian Materials and Industries*. 1926. 4th ed. London: Edward Arnold Publishers, 1962.

LUCK, Georg. "Theurgy and Forms of Worship in Neoplatonism", in *Religion, Science, and Magic*, ed. J. NEUSNER, E. FRERICHS, and P. V. M. FLESHER. New York: Oxford University Press, 1989.

MAJERCIK, Ruth, trans. and ed. *The Chaldean Oracles: Text, Translation, and Commentary*. Studies in Greek and Roman Religion, vol. 5. Leiden: Brill, 1989.

MARTELLI, Matteo. "Greek Alchemists at Work: 'Alchemical Laboratory' in the Greco Roman Egypt", *Nuncius* 26 (2011): 271–311.

———. *The Four Books of Pseudo-Democritus*. Sources of Alchemy and

Chemistry: Sir Robert Mond Studies in the History of Early Chemistry. Leeds: Maney Publishing; *Ambix* 60, supplement 1 (2013).

———. "The Alchemical Art of Dyeing: The Fourfold Division of Alchemy and the Enochian Tradition", in *Laboratories of Art: Alchemy and Art Technology from Antiquity to the Eighteenth Century*, ed. S. DUPRÉ. Archimedes 37. Switzerland: Springer International, 2014.

MARTELLI, Matteo and Maddelena RUMOR. "Near Eastern Origins of Græco-Egyptian Alchemy", in *Esoteric Knowledge in Antiquity*, K. GEUS and M. GELLER, eds. TOPOI—Dahlem Seminar for the History of Ancient Sciences vol. 11. Berlin: Max Planck Institute for the History of Science, Preprint 454, 2014.

MARTINÓN-TORRES, Marcos. "Some Recent Developments in the Historiography of Alchemy", *Ambix* 58.3 (2011): 215–237.

MARX-WOLF, Heidi. "High Priests of the Highest God: Third Century Platonists as Ritual Experts", *Journal of Early Christian Studies* 18.4 (2010): 481–513.

———. *Spiritual Taxonomies and Ritual Authority: Platonists, Priests, and Gnostics in the Third Century* C.E. Divinations: Rereading Late Ancient Religions Series, ed. D. Boyarin, et al. Philadelphia: University of Pennsylvania Press, 2016.

MAZUR, Zeke. "Unio Mystica 1", *Dionysius* 21 (2003): 23–52.

MENN, Stephen. *Plato on God as Nous*. Journal of the History of Philosophy Monograph Series, ed. R. A. Watson and C. M. Young. Carbondale: Southern Illinois University Press, 1995.

MERKUR, Daniel. "The Study of Spiritual Alchemy: Mysticism, Gold-Making, and Esoteric Hermeneutics", *Ambix* 37.1 (1990): 35–45.

MERTENS, Michèle. "Project for a New Edition of Zosimus of Panopolis", in *Alchemy Revisited: Proceedings of the International Conference on the History of Alchemy at the University of Groningen, 17-19 April 1989*, ed. Z. R. W. M. von MARTELS. Collection de Travaux de L'Academie Internationale d'Histoire des Sciences, Tome 33. Leiden: Brill, 1990.

———. "Alchemy, Hermetism and Gnosticism at Panopolis c. 300 A.D.: The Evidence of Zosimus", in *Perspectives on Panopolis: An Egyptian Town from Alexander the Great to the Arab Conquest. Acts from an International Symposium Held in Leiden on 16, 17, and 18 December*

1998, ed. A. EGBERTS, B. P. MUCHS, and J. VAN DER VLIET. Leiden: Brill, 2002.

———, trans. and ed. *Zosime de Panopolis: Mémoires authentiques*. Les alchimistes grecs, vol. IV, part 1. 2nd ed. Paris: Les Belles Lettres, 2002.

MILLER, Patricia Cox. "In Praise of Nonsense", in *Classical Mediterranean Spirituality*, ed. A. H. ARMSTRONG. World Spirituality: An Encyclopedic History of the Religious Quest, vol. 15. New York: Crossroad, 1986.

MINAS-NERPEL, Martina. "Egyptian Temples", in *The Oxford Handbook of Roman Egypt*, ed. C. RIGGS. Oxford: Oxford University Press, 2012.

MIRECKI, Paul. "Manichaean Allusions to Ritual and Magic: Spells for Invisibility in the Coptic Kephalia", in *The Light and the Darkness: Studies in Manichaeism and its World*, P. MIRECKI and J. BEDUHN, eds. Leiden: Brill, 2001.

MIRECKI, Paul and Jason BEDUHN, eds. *The Light and the Darkness: Studies in Manichaeism and its World*. Leiden: Brill, 2001.

MORENZ, Siegfried. *Egyptian Religion*. Translated by A. Keep. Ithaca: Cornell University Press, 1973.

MOSHER, Jr., Malcolm. "The Book of the Dead Tradition at Akhmim During the Late Period", in *Perspectives on Panopolis: An Egyptian Town from Alexander the Great to the Arab Conquest. Acts from an International Symposium Held in Leiden on 16, 17, and 18 December 1998*, ed. A. EGBERTS, B. P. MUCHS, and J. VAN DER VLIET. Leiden: Brill, 2002.

MOYER, Ian. *Egypt and the Limits of Hellenism*. Cambridge: Cambridge University Press, 2011.

MULTHAUF, Robert. *The Origins of Chemistry*. London: Oldbourne, 1966.

NEEDHAM, Joseph. *Science and Civilisation in China*, vol. 5, part II. Cambridge: Cambridge University Press, 1974.

NEUSNER, J., E. FRERICHS, and P. V. M. FLESHER, eds. *Religion, Science, and Magic*. New York: Oxford University Press, 1989.

NEWMAN, William R. and Lawrence M. PRINCIPE. "Alchemy vs. Chemistry: The Etymological Origins of a Historiographical Mistake", *Early Science and Medicine* 3 (1998): 32–65.

NEWMAN, William and Anthony GRAFTON, eds. *Secrets of Nature: Astrology and Alchemy in Early Modern Europe*. Cambridge, MA: The MIT Press, 2001.

NEWMAN, William R. "Brian Vickers on Alchemy and the Occult: A Response", *Perspectives on Science* 17.4 (2009): 482–506.

NICHOLSON, Paul T. and Ian SHAW, eds. *Ancient Egyptian Materials and Technology*. Cambridge: Cambridge University Press, 2000.

NUFFELEN, Peter, ed. *Faces of Hellenism: Studies in the History of the Eastern Mediterranean, 4th Century B.C. to 5th Century A.D.* Leuven: Peeters, 2009.

OGDEN, Jack. *Ancient Jewellery*. Berkeley: University of California Press, 1992.

————. "Metals", in *Ancient Egyptian Materials and Technology*, Paul T. NICHOLSON and Ian SHAW, eds. Cambridge: Cambridge University Press, 2000.

ORSI, Robert A. *Between Heaven and Earth: The Religious Worlds People Make and the Scholars Who Study Them*. Princeton: Princeton University Press, 2005.

————. *History and Presence*. Cambridge, MA: The Belknap Press of Harvard University Press, 2016.

PAPTHANASSIOU, Maria. "Stephanus of Alexandria: Pharmaceutical Notions and Cosmology in His Alchemical Work", *Ambix* 37.3 (1990): 121–133.

PARKINS, Helen, and Christopher John SMITH, eds. *Trade, Traders, and the Ancient City*. London: Routledge, 1998.

PARTINGTON, J. R. *A History of Chemistry*, vol. 1, part 1. London: MacMillan, 1970.

PATAI, Raphael. **The Jewish Alchemists**. Princeton: Princeton University Press, 1994.

PEARSON, Birger. "Jewish Elements in Corpus Hermeticum I (Poimandres)", in *Studies in Gnosticism and Hellenistic Religions*, ed. R. VAN DEN BROEK and M. J. VERMASEREN. Leiden: Brill, 1981.

PESTE, Jonathan. *The Poimandres Group in Corpus Hermeticum: Myth, Mysticism and Gnosis in Late Antiquity*. PHD dissertation, University of Göteborg, 2002.

PHOTIUS, *Bibliotecha*. Translated by J. H. Freese. London: SPCK, 1920.

PINCH, Geraldine. *Egyptian Mythology: A Guide to the Gods, Goddesses, and Traditions of Ancient Egypt*. Oxford: Oxford University Press, 2002.

———. *Magic in Ancient Egypt*. Rev. ed. Austin: University of Texas Press, 2006.

PLATO. *Timaeus*. Translated by F. M. Cornford. Indianapolis: Bobbs-Merrill, 1959.

———. *Apology*. Translated by Hugh Tredennick, in *The Collected Dialogues of Plato*, ed. E. HAMILTON and H. CAIRNS. Bollingen Series LXXI. Princeton: Princeton University Press, 1961.

———. *Phaedrus*. Translated by R. Hackforth, in *The Collected Dialogues of Plato*, ed. E. HAMILTON and H. CAIRNS. Bollingen Series LXXI. Princeton: Princeton University Press, 1961.

PLINY THE ELDER. *Natural History*. Loeb Classical Library. Cambridge, MA: Harvard University Press, 1962.

PLOTINUS. *Enneads*. Translated by A. H. Armstrong. Loeb Classical Library. Cambridge, MA: Harvard University Press, 1966.

PLUTARCH. *De Iside et Osiride*. Translated and edited by John Gwyn Griffiths. Cambridge: University of Wales Press, 1970.

PORPHYRY. *On Abstinence from Killing Animals*. Translated by Gillian Clark. Ithaca: Cornell University Press, 2000.

PRINCIPE, Lawrence M. and William R. Newman. "Some Problems with the Historiography of Alchemy", in *Secrets of Nature: Astrology and Alchemy in Early Modern Europe*, ed. W. NEWMAN and A. GRAFTON. Cambridge, MA: The MIT Press, 2001.

PRINCIPE, Lawrence M. *The Secrets of Alchemy*. Chicago: University of Chicago Press, 2013.

QUACK, Joachim Friedrich. "Religious Personnel: Egypt", in *Religions of the Ancient World: A Guide*, ed. Sarah Iles JOHNSTON. Cambridge: Harvard University Press, 2004.

QUIRKE, Stephen G. J. "Administrative Texts", in *Oxford Encyclopedia of Ancient Egypt*, online ed. Oxford: Oxford University Press, 2005.

RAPPE, Sara. "Self-knowledge and Subjectivity in the Enneads", in *The*

Cambridge Companion to Plotinus, ed. Lloyd P. Gerson. Cambridge: Cambridge University Press, 1996.

REDFORD, Donald B., ed. *The Oxford Encyclopedia of Ancient Egypt*. Online ed. Oxford: Oxford University Press, 2005.

RIGGS, Christina. *The Beautiful Burial in Roman Egypt: Art, Identity, and Funerary Religion*. Oxford: Oxford University Press, 2005.

————, ed. *The Oxford Handbook of Roman Egypt*. Oxford: Oxford University Press, 2012.

RITNER, Robert Kreich. *The Mechanics of Ancient Egyptian Magical Practice*. Studies in Ancient Oriental Civilization no. 54. Chicago: Oriental Institute of the University of Chicago, 1993.

ROBINS, Gay. "Cult Statues in Ancient Egypt", in *Cult Image and Divine Representation in the Ancient Near East*, ed. N. WALLS. American Schools of Oriental Research Book Series, no. 10. Boston: American Schools of Oriental Research, 2005.

ROBINSON, James M., gen. ed. *The Nag Hammadi Library*. Rev. ed. San Francisco: HarperCollins, 1990.

RUDOLPH, Kurt. *Gnosis: The Nature and History of Gnosticism*. San Francisco: HarperSanFrancisco, 1987.

RUNDLE CLARK, R. T. *Myth and Symbol in Ancient Egypt*. London: Thames & Hudson, 1959.

SAFFREY, Henri Dominique. « Mort et transformation de la matière: à propos d'un locus desperatus des Mémoires Authentiques de Zosime de Panoplis (x 6.130) », in *L'Alchimie et ses racines philosophiques: La tradition grecque et la tradition arabe*, ed. Cristina VIANO. Paris: Vrin, 2005.

SAMBURSKY, S. *The Physical World of the Greeks*. Translated by M. Dagut. Princeton: Princeton University Press, 1956.

————. *The Physical World of Late Antiquity*. Translated by M. Dagut. Princeton: Princeton University Press, 1962.

SAUNERON, Serge. *The Priests of Ancient Egypt*. Translated by D. Lorton. 1957. Rev. ed., Ithaca: Cornell University Press, 2000.

SCHÄFER, P. and H. KIPPENBERG, eds. *Envisioning Magic: A Princeton Seminar and Symposium*. Studies in the History of Religions (Numen Book Series) vol. LXXV. Leiden: Brill, 1997.

SCHEEL, Bernd. *Egyptian Metalworking and Tools*. Shire Egyptology. Aylesbury: Shire Publications, 1989.

SCHORSCH, Deborah. "The Manufacture of Metal Statuary: 'Seeing the Workshops of the Temple'", in M. HILL, ed., with D. SCHORSCH, technical ed. *Gifts for the Gods: Images from Egyptian Temples. Catalog of exhibition held at Metropolitan Museum of Art, New York, Oct. 16 2007–Feb. 18 2008*. New Haven: Yale University Press, 2007.

SCHRENK, Lawrence P., ed. *Aristotle in Late Antiquity*. Studies in the Philosophy and the History of Philosophy, vol. 27, ed. J. P. DOUGHERTY. Washington, DC: The Catholic University of America Press, 1994.

SHAFER, Byron E., ed. *Religion in Ancient Egypt: Gods, Myths, and Personal Practice*. Ithaca: Cornell University Press, 1991.

———. "Temples, Priests, and Rituals: An Overview", in B. SHAFER, ed., *Temples of Ancient Egypt*. Ithaca: Cornell University Press, 1997.

———, ed. *Temples of Ancient Egypt*. Ithaca: Cornell University Press, 1997.

SHAW, Gregory. "Theurgy: Rituals of Unification in the Neoplatonism of Iamblichus". *Traditio* 41 (1985): 1–28.

———. *Theurgy and the Soul: The Neoplatonism of Iamblichus*. University Park, PA: Pennsylvania State University Press, 1995.

———. "After Aporia: Theurgy in Later Platonism", in *Gnosticism and Later Platonism: Themes, Figures, and Texts*, ed. J. D. TURNER and R. MAJERCIK. Society of Biblical Literature Symposium Series 12, ed. C. R. Matthews. Atlanta: Society of Biblical Literature, 2001.

———. "Theurgy and the Platonist's Luminous Body", in *Practicing Gnosis: Ritual, Magic, Theurgy and Liturgy in Nag Hammadi, Manichaean, and Other Ancient Literature. Essays in Honor of Birger Pearson*. A. DeConick, G. Shaw, and J. Turner, eds. Leiden: Brill, 2013.

SHEPPARD, H. J. "The Ouroboros and the Unity of Matter in Alchemy: A Study in Origins", *Ambix* 10.2 (1962): 83–96.

SIORVANES, Lucas. *Proclus: Neo-Platonic Philosophy and Science*. New Haven: Yale University Press, 1996.

SMITH, Andrew. *Porphyry's Place in the Neoplatonic Tradition: A Study in Post-Plotinian Neoplatonism*. The Hague: Martinus Nijhoff, 1974.

_____. "Iamblichus' Views on the Relationship of Philosophy to Religion in De Mysteriis", in *The Divine Iamblichus: Philosopher and Man of Gods*, ed. H. J. BLUMENTHAL and E. G. CLARK. London: Bristol Classics Press, 1993.

_____. "Iamblichus, The First Philosopher of Religion?" *Habis* 31 (2000), 345–353.

SMITH, Jonathan Z. "Trading Places", in *Ancient Magic and Ritual Power*, ed. M. MARVIN and P. MIRECKI. 1995. Reprint, Boston: Brill, 2001.

SMITH, Mark. "Aspects of the Preservation and Transmission of Indigenous Religious Traditions in Akhmim and its Environs During the Graeco-Roman Period", in *Perspectives on Panopolis: An Egyptian Town from Alexander the Great to the Arab Conquest. Acts from an International Symposium Held in Leiden on 16, 17, and 18 December 1998*, ed. A. EGBERTS, et al. Leiden: Brill, 2002.

_____. *Traversing Eternity: Texts for the Afterlife from Ptolemaic and Roman Egypt*. Oxford: Oxford University Press, 2009.

STILLMAN, John Maxson. *The Story of Alchemy and Early Chemistry*. 1924. Reprint, New York: Dover, 1960.

STOLZENBERG, Daniel. "Unpropitious Tinctures: Alchemy, Astrology, and Gnosis According to Zosimos of Panopolis", *Archives internationales d'histoire des sciences* 49.142 (1999): 3–31.

STROUMSA, Guy. *The End of Sacrifice: Religious Transformations in Late Antiquity*. Translated by Susan Emanuel. Chicago: Chicago University Press, 2009.

SULLIVAN, Lawrence E., ed. *Hidden Truths: Magic, Alchemy, and the Occult. Religion, History, and Culture Selections from The Encyclopedia of Religion*, ed. Mircea Eliade. New York: Macmillan, 1987.

TAMBIAH, Stanley. *Magic, Science, Religion, and the Scope of Rationality*. Lewis Henry Morgan Lectures, 1984. Cambridge: Cambridge University Press, 1990.

TANASEANU-DÖBLER, Ilinca. *Theurgy in Late Antiquity: The Invention of a Ritual Tradition*. Göttingen: Vandenhoeck & Ruprecht, 2013.

TARN STEINER, Deborah. *Images in Mind: Statues in Archaic and Classical Greek Literature and Thought*. Princeton: Princeton University Press, 2001.

TAYLOR, F. Sherwood. "A Survey of Greek Alchemy", *The Journal of*

Hellenic Studies 50, part 1 (1930): 109–139.

———. "The Origins of Greek Alchemy", *Ambix* 1 (1937–38): 30–47.

———. "Translation of 'The Visions of Zosimos'", *Ambix* 1 (1937–38): 88–92.

———. "The Alchemical Works of Stephanos of Alexandria: Part One", *Ambix* 1 (1937–38): 116–139.

———. "The Alchemical Works of Stephanos of Alexandria: Part Two", *Ambix* 2.1 (1938): 38–49.

———. *The Alchemists*. 1952. Reprint, St. Albans: Paladin, 1976.

TEETER, Emily. *Religion and Ritual in Ancient Egypt*. New York: Cambridge University Press, 2011.

THOMAS, Thelma K. *Late Antique Egyptian Funerary Sculpture: Images for this World and the Next*. Princeton: Princeton University Press, 1999.

TORJIANO, Pablo. *Solomon, the Esoteric King: From King to Magus, Development of a Tradition*. Supplements to the Journal for the Study of Judaism, vol. 73, ed. John J. Collins. Leiden: Brill, 2002.

TRAUNECKER, Claude. «Le Château de l'Or de Thoutmosis III et les magasins nord du temple d'Amon». *Cahiers de Recherches de l'Institut de Papyrologie et d'Égyptologie de Lille* 11 (1989): 89–111.

TURNER, John D. and Ruth MAJERCIK, eds. *Gnosticism and Later Platonism: Themes, Figures, and Texts*. Society of Biblical Literature Symposium Series 12, ed. C. R. Matthews. Atlanta: Society of Biblical Literature, 2001.

UŽDAVINYS, Algis. "Animation of Statues in Ancient Civilizations and Neoplatonism", in *Late Antique Epistemology: Other Ways to Truth*, ed. Panayiota VASSILOPOULOU and Stephen R. L. CLARK. London: Palgrave Macmillan, 2009.

———. *Philosophy & Theurgy in Late Antiquity* [2010]. Kettering, OH: Angelico Press/Sophia Perennis, 2014.

VAN DEN BROEK, R. and M. J. VERMASEREN, eds. *Studies in Gnosticism and Hellenistic Religions*. Leiden: Brill, 1981.

VAN DEN BROEK, Roelof. *Studies in Gnosticism and Alexandrian Christianity*. Leiden: Brill, 1996.

VAN DEN BROEK, Roelof, and Wouter J. HANEGRAAF, eds. *Gnosis and Hermeticism from Late Antiquity to Modern Times*. Albany: SUNY

Van Minnen, Peter. "Urban Craftsmen in Roman Egypt", in *Münstersche Beiträge zur Antiken Handelsgeschichte* VI. Ostfildern: Scripta Mercaturae Verlag, 1987.

———. "Did Ancient Women Learn a Trade Outside the Home? A Note on SBXVIII 13305", *Zeitschrift für Papyrologie und Epigraphik* 123 (1998), 201–203.

———. "The Letter (and Other Papers) of Ammon: Panopolis in the Fourth Century AD", in *Perspectives on Panopolis: An Egyptian Town from Alexander the Great to the Arab Conquest. Acts from an International Symposium Held in Leiden on 16, 17, and 18 December 1998*, ed. A. Egberts, et al. Leiden: Brill, 2002.

Vassilopoulou, Panayiota and Stephen R. L. Clark, eds. *Late Antique Epistemology: Other Ways to Truth*. London: Palgrave Macmillan, 2009.

Venticinque, Philip F. "Family Affairs: Guild Regulations and Family Relationships in Roman Egypt", *Greek, Roman, and Byzantine Studies* 10 (2010), 273–294.

———. *Honor Among Thieves: Craftsmen, Merchants, and Associations in Roman and Late Roman Egypt*. New Texts from Ancient Cultures Series. Ann Arbor: University of Michigan Press, 2016.

Verner, Miroslav. *Temple of the World: Sanctuaries, Cults, and Mysteries of Ancient Egypt*. Cairo: The American University in Cairo Press, 2013.

Versluis, Arthur, C. Fanger, L. Irwin, and M. Phillips, eds. *Esotericism, Religion, and Nature*. Minneapolis: North American Academic Press, 2010.

Viano, Cristina. « Olympiodore l'alchimiste et les présocratiques: une doxographie de l'unité », in *Alchimie: art histoire, et mythes, Actes du 1er colloque international de la Société d'Étude d l'Histoire de l'Alchimie (Paris, Collège de France, 14–16 mars 1991)*, ed. Didier Kahn and Sylvain Matton. Textes et Travaux de Chrysopoeia 1. Paris: S.É.H.A., 1995.

———. « Aristote et l'alchimie grecque: La transmutation et le modèle aristotélicien entre théorie et pratique », *Revue d'histoire des sciences* 49, no. 2–3 (1996): 189–213.

———. « Les alchimistes gréco-alexandrins et le Timée de Platon », in *L'alchimie et ses racines philosophiques. La tradition grecque et la tradition arabe*, ed. Cristina VIANO. Paris: Vrin, 2005.

_____, ed. *L'alchimie et ses racines philosophiques. La tradition grecque et la tradition arabe*. Paris: Vrin, 2005.

_____. « Mixis and Diagnôsis: Aristotle and the 'Chemistry' of the Sublunary World », *Ambix* 62.3 (2015): 203–214.

VICKERS, Brian. "The Discrepancy Between res and verba in Greek Alchemy", in *Alchemy Revisited: Proceedings of the International Conference on the History of Alchemy at the University of Groningen 17–19 April 1989*, ed. Z. R. W. M. von MARTELS. Collection de Travaux de L'Academie Internationale d'Histoire des Sciences, Tome 33. Leiden: Brill, 1990.

_____. "The 'New Historiography' and the Limits of Alchemy", *Annals of Science* 65 (2008): 127–156.

VON MARTELS, Z. R. W. M., ed. *Alchemy Revisited: Proceedings of the International Conference on the History of Alchemy at the University of Groningen, 17–19 April 1989*. Collection de Travaux de L'Academie Internationale d'Histoire des Sciences, Tome 33. Leiden: Brill, 1990.

WAGNER, Michael F., ed. *Neoplatonism and Nature: Studies in Plotinus' Enneads*. Studies in Neoplatonism, 8. Albany: SUNY Press, 2002.

WALKER, Christopher and Michael B. DICK, "The Induction of the Cult Image in Ancient Mesopotamia: The Mesopotamian *mīs pî* Ritual", in *Born in Heaven, Made on Earth: The Creation of the Cult Image in the Ancient Near East*, ed. M. B. DICK. Winona Lake, IN: Eisenbrauns, 1998.

WALLIS, Richard T. *Neoplatonism*. 2nd ed. Indianapolis: Hackett, 1995.

WALLIS, Richard T. and Jay BREGMAN, eds. *Neoplatonism and Gnosticism*. Albany: State University of New York Press, 1992.

WALLS, Neal H., ed. *Cult Image and Divine Representation in the Ancient Near East*. American Schools of Oriental Research Book Series, no. 10. Boston: American Schools of Oriental Research, 2005.

WILLIAMS, Michael A. *Rethinking "Gnosticism": An Argument for Dismantling a Dubious Category*. Princeton: Princeton University Press, 1996.

WILLIS, William and Klaus MARESCH, eds. *The Archive of Ammon Scholasticus of Panopolis, vol. 1, The Legacy of Harpocration*. Weisbaden: Springer Fachmedien, 1997.

Index

Abamon 199, 209
Abraham 159
Abt, Theodor 15, 106, 251
Adam 124–25, 184–85, 187–88, 191, 215–16, 222, 240, 254 (see also: anthropos, primal human)
Addey, Crystal 199, 200, 203, 205, 209, 232, 251
Agalma (cult statue) 228–29, 234 (see also: statues, divine)
Agathodaimon (Agathos Daimon) 35, 91, 109, 147–49, 165, 208, 216, 232
  Hellenized Egyptian god Shai 81
  Goldsmith in Panopolis 91
Air 24, 33, 61–62, 125 (see also: elements, four)
Akh (soul concept) 241
Alchemical debates 26, 63–64, 107–09, 155 ff, 172, 194 ff
Alchemical instruction 34–35, 48, 49, 64, 69, 83, 102, 117–18, 144, 166, 169, 172, 183, 237, 245, 247
Alchemical manuscripts:
  Arabic 15, 28, 103–06, 108, 109,
  Greek 27–28, 29–30, 133, 110, 176
  Gnostic (see Nag Hammadi) 16
  Latin 28
  Syriac 28, 29–30, 38
Alchemical processes
  Distillation 31–32, 51, 95–96, 109, 132, 133, 160–61, 162–63, 177, 193, 242
  Cementation 160–61, 177
  Diplōsis 157, 159, 161
  Kērotakis 48, 132, 135, 147, 160–161
  Natural and unnatural methods 26, 62, 65, 100, 107, 108, 112, 155 ff, 156, 163, 165–67, 169, 172, 178, 180, 181, 191, 194, 226, 247, 260
Alchemy, theory vs. practice 46
Alchemy, traditional definitions of 29 ff, 44–52, 53–56
Alexander the Great 122
Alexandria 50, 76, 156
Allegory 26, 29, 87, 117, 126, 127–151, 160, 169, 211, 216–17, 242, 248, 249
Amalgamation 148–49, 157
Ammon (high priest), manuscripts of 80, 81, 274, 275
Amulets 35, 122, 190,
Angels 149, 168–73, 173–80, 186, 208, 214, 215–16
Anthropos (primal human) 156, 181–92, (see also: Adam, Phōs)
  as Son of God (Hermetic tradition) 183, 185–89, 191, 207, 215, 222,
Anti-cosmic 152–53, 220–21
Anti-Semitism, Egyptian 193
Anubis 38, 221,
Apilis, son of Gagios 160, 164, 172
Apatheia 119, 129–30 (see also: meditation)
Apophis 143–44
Aporia 208–09
Arab traditions of alchemy 20, 27–28, 47, 77–78, 103–06, 108–09, 155,
Archangels 214 (see also: Angels)

278   INDEX

Archon 168, 181, 185, 188, 214
Argyropoeia (silver making) 19
Aristotle 51, 53–56, 132, 204, 206–07, 211, 216, 251, 253, 271, 275,
Arsenic 31, 45, 51, 136
Artisan-priests (temple artisans) 18, 25, 33–35, 41, 42, 46, 53, 70–72, 75, 84, 89–94, 97–98, 103, 112–13, 130, 138, 153, 157, 194, 230, 233, 236, 246
  initiation of 94, 98, 99, 192
  ranks of 71–72, 94, 236
  and craft secrets 95–98, 157, 163
Ascent, spiritual 26, 117, 119, 123, 124, 126, 130, 140, 142, 148–50, 165, 170, 178, 202–03, 216–17, 220–21, 231, 237–42, 261, 263,
Asclepius (God) 80 (Hermetic text) 216, 229–30
Asōmata (incorporeals, metallic "spirits") 52,
Assaying tests (cupellation) 42
Assmann, Jan 73, 75, 85, 138–139, 144, 158, 194, 230–31, 235–36, 241, 252
Astrology 22, 54, 58, 64, 78, 82, 108, 164, 165–67, 168, 178–79, 182, 194, 253, 268, 272 (see also: sun; moon; planetary spheres; jupiter; saturn; tinctures, opportune; zodiac)
Aufrère, Sydney 18, 33, 69, 86–87, 90, 221–22, 252
Aurelius, Marcus 120, 252
Aurifaction vs. aurifiction 44–45

Ba (soul concept) 137, 241–42
Barber (razor-working man) 139–40
Barclay, John 163, 252
Becoming gold (divinizing matter) 24, 66, 249
Berthelot, Marcellin 27–28, 46, 59, 127, 132, 134, 139, 148, 157, 162, 164, 176, 216, 253
Black earth (alchemy as) 20
Black bronzes 38, 40–41, 43, 48, 221, 228, 245, 262 (see also: Corinthian bronze)

Blackening 48, 50, 66, 135–36, 140, 228, 245 (see also: color)
Blasphemy 118–19, 188
Blood 134, 136, 139, 147, 184, 240, 253
Bloodletting 139
Bolus of Mendes 58–59
  author of *On Sympathies and Antipathies* 58
  as "the Democritean" 59
Book of Enoch 156, 164, 173–80, 193, 253, 258, 263, 266
Bronze, bronzing, bronzesmiths 36, 41, 45, 89–90, 93–94, 171, 254 (see also: Corinthian bronze, black bronzes)

Caligula (smelting orpiment to produce gold) 41
Castor oil 35
Cauldron
  of annihilation (Egyptian texts) 136–37, 217 mixing bowl (Platonic and Hermetic texts) 141–42, 145 (see also: *phialē*)
Causality, human vs. divine 206–212
Celestial bodies
  planets 58, 73, 75, 122–125, 130, 142, 149–150, 166, 167–69, 171–72, 178, 185–86, 188, 199, 213, 215–16, 218, 237, 248 stars 62, 87, 120, 140, 142, 144, 173–74, 202, 213, 215–16, 222, 229, 248
  sun 62, 65–66, 70, 75, 84, 87, 103–04, 122, 125, 138, 143–44, 149–50, 162–63, 166, 173–74, 185, 202, 215, 221–22, 224, 229, 249
  moon 62, 75, 87, 103–04, 106, 138, 147–48, 173–74, 185, 221, 224, 229, as intelligences/luminous beings 215–16, 218
Cementation methods 160–61, 177
Chaldean Oracles 199–200, 252, 263, 265
Chaos 62, 65, 70, 131, 143–44, 201–02, 226 (see also isfet)

Chema 174–75, 180
Chēmia (chymia, chēmeia) 19–20, 96, 175
Chemistry, and alchemy 19–22, 55, 174, 246 (see also science and alchemy)
Christianity 16, 18, 19, 26, 30, 34, 66, 76, 81, 82, 110–11, 113, 128, 155–95, 197, 207, 216, 220, 233, 240, 246–47, 249, 251, 260, 261, 263
  and Gnosticism, 16, 66, 164, 181–183, 185, 187–89, 220–21, 247, 256, 263, 273
  and Judaism 16, 19, 26, 30, 66, 110–11, 113, 116, 128, 155–95, 197, 220, 233, 255, 259, 261, 263,
  in Panopolis 110–11, 182, 192
  populations in Egypt 110–11
Chrysopoeia (gold making) 19, 21, 44–45, 246
Cinnabar 45, 149–50, 166, 222
Cleopatra (pseudo) 32–33, 51, 61–62, 133, 143
Color
  color fabrication, and origins of alchemy 31–33, 179–80
  color transmutation, four stages 48–49, 135
    blackening (*melanōsis*) 48, 50, 66, 135–36, 140, 228, 245, 228
    whitening (*leukōsis*) 35, 48, 50, 62, 107, 121, 134, 135–36, 138, 146–48, 150, 216, 228
    yellowing (*xanthōsis*) 41, 42, 45, 47–48, 50, 134, 135–36, 146, 150, 161–62, 228, 245
    reddening (*iōsis*) 45, 48–49, 61, 135–136, 146, 150, 184, 228, 245
  coloring metals 25, 34–36, 38, 41, 42, 44–45, 47, 50–52, 60, 63, 66, 116, 117, 132, 135, 139, 140, 148, 150, 159, 162, 165, 166, 221, 222, 228, 233, 246, 249
Contemplation (natural, spiritual) 116, 117, 122, 128–30, 152, 178–79, 218–19, 230 (see also: spiritual exercises)
Corinthian bronze 49–50, 245, 262, 263
Cosmic gods 166, 205–06, 208, 213–14, 238
Cosmic knowledge 202–12
  and magic 205–06, 211, 224–25, 226–27
  and rationality 206–12
Cosmic order, visible and invisible 210
Cosmic sympathy and antipathy
  magical theories of 58–59
  different theories of 221–24
Counterfeiting (aurifiction) 44–45
Craft secrecy (see also: secrecy) 25, 94–99, 157, 163, 247
  in the priesthood 94–95, 98
  Zosimos's views of 96–99
  and distillation vs. furnaces 95–96
  oaths of secrecy for trade associations 95, 97, 98
  and royalty 95–97, 99
  and Jewish metallurgists 96–97, 163
  as corrupting influence 97–98, 99–101
  and jealousy 96, 98, 99
  and divine revelation 99–101
  and daimons (demons) 99–100
Cultural biography 19, 245–46

Daimons 63–65, 99–101, 130, 149, 165–173, 175, 178–83, 189–91, 194, 197, 199, 208, 212, 214–18, 225–26, 238, 247
  cosmic role of 149, 166–69, 178, 191, 212, 214–16, 225–26, 247
  according to Iamblichus 212, 214, 217–18, 238
  in Hermetic thought 180, 215–16
  and unnatural methods 65, 99–101, 165, 167, 169, 172, 178–83, 189, 191

280   INDEX

and meditation 101, 119, 149, 217–218
Daumas, Francois 18, 161, 255
De Mysteriis 199–201, 205, 209–10, 226–27, 239, 255, 262, 272
Death and resurrection 32, 65, 67, 87, 106, 127, 132, 144, 151–52, 188, 202, 241–42, 252
Delange, Elisabeth 36, 41, 256
Demiurge 141–42, 145–46, 185–86, 188, 201, 207, 211–12, 215, 222, 230, 232, 239–40, 243
Demotic script, papyri 73, 78, 80
Dendera, Temple of 77, 83, 85, 86
Depletion gilding 50–51
Derchain, Philippe 18, 83–84, 192, 230, 256
Dialogue of Cleopatra and the Philosophers 32, 51, 61
Diaspora 156, 163, 252
Diotima 126, 209
Diplōsis 157, 159, 161
Discursive thought (see: cosmic knowledge and rationality)
Dismemberment 134, 136, 144, 151–52, 242
Distillation (see: alchemical processes)
Divine hierarchy 116, 212–18, 226–28, 235, 243
Divine mind 16, 122–24, 141, 146, 151, 173, 194, 201, 207, 211, 215, 226, 243, 248
Divine revelation 16, 26, 94, 135, 140, 150, 178–79, 203, 208, 228, 242–43, 248
   noetic vs. cosmic 208
   of alchemical methods 179–80
Divinization 199
   of the soul 26, 239, 243
Dualism 152, 187, 221, 227
Duat 87, 131 (see also: underworld)
Dufault, Olivier 50–53, 55–56, 256
Duval, Rubens 28, 30, 216, 253
Dyeing 15, 31, 41, 56, 60, 91, 92, 94, 102, 113, 180, 266

Earth 20, 24, 33, 35, 51, 53, 61, 70, 86, 87, 120, 125, 139, 140, 141, 142, 145, 152, 162, 173, 174, 183, 184, 212, 213, 214, 217, 221, 232, 237, 238, 243, 247, 248, 252, 256, 268 (see also: elements, four)
Egypt, romanticization of 17, 69
Egyptian Book of the Dead 63, 78, 144, 241, 267
Egyptian mortuary traditions 26, 71, 127, 131, 135, 138, 151, 217, 231, 241, 242, 248, 258
Egyptian thought
   associative nature of 56–57
   punning, word play 57, 106
   cultural synthesis 57
Ekstrophē (transformation) 50–51
Electrum 37, 39–40, 44–45, 86, 122–24, 171–72, 222 (see also: *On Electrum*)
Elements, four 24, 32–33, 61, 125, 132, 145, 220, 222
Eliade, Mircea 15, 22, 53, 257
Embalming 71, 134–40
Enlightenment
   European 18, 21, 246, 257
   spiritual 66, 118, 188, 221, 243
Ephoroi 167
Epimetheus 181, 184, 188
Epistemology 200, 202
Esarhaddon, King of Assyria 115
Esoteric, esotericism 21–22, 69, 164, 198, 257, 259, 266, 274
Etymology of alchemy 19–20
Exercise of death 151, 197

Faivre, Antoine 22, 198, 257
Fallen angels 174–80
Fate, ideas of 26, 64–65, 80–81, 179, 182–92, 197, 202–06, 210, 212–13, 215, 217
Female metallurgists/alchemists 15, 48, 101, 102–03, 107 (see also: Maria the Jewess, Theosebeia, Paphnuteia)

INDEX

Final Account 27, 95, 99,–101, 107–08, 119, 142, 149, 163, 167
Finnestad, Ragnhild Bjerre 34, 71–72, 74, 138, 258
Fire 33, 42, 44, 125, 134, 137, 140, 146, 149, 151–152, 162, 184, 215, 217, 239–40 (see also: elements, four)
Fortune 35, 64, 81, 148, 183
  popular Roman goddess 35, 232
Fowden, Garth 57, 198, 203, 220–21 258
Fraser, Kyle 13, 64, 164, 166, 174, 175, 182, 198, 258
Funerary offerings 35

Geens, Karolien 20, 77–80, 85, 87, 90, 110–11, 182, 192, 259
Gellius, Aulus 60
Gemstones 85–86
  artificial 44
Gilding (see: gold)
Gnosticism, gnostic 24, 66, 119, 164, 181–183, 185, 187–89, 197, 198, 203, 211 220–21, 247, 256, 263, 264, 266, 270, 273, 275
God-making 26, 66, 84–85, 112, 116–17, 151, 227–243 (see also statues, divine)
  as divine mimesis 230
  as goal of theurgy 235–36
  and origins of alchemy 17–18, 84
  and purification of the soul 151, 228, 235–243
  and statue animation (telestic art) 231
  and fire or light (*phōtagōgia*) 66, 238–39
Gold 20, 29, 35, 37, 38, 39, 40–52, 85–87, 89, 96, 108, 117, 121–22, 135–36, 140, 146, 149–50, 152, 159, 162, 166, 171, 176, 211, 221–22, 228, 245–46, 248–49
  definitions, ancient vs. modern 41–42
  as flesh of the gods 66
  as spiritual realization 66, 122,

135–36, 149–50, 152, 211, 249
  value of 86–87
  symbolism in Egyptian ritual 66, 87, 122–22
  and sun, sun god 87, 122, 149, 162, 166, 221–22
  and Osiris 87
  touchstone test 42
  Gold-making (see: *chrysopoeia*)
Goldsmiths 25, 84–86, 89–94, 102, 112
  as wealthiest metallurgists 90
  as overseers of artisans 25, 89, 93
  as contractors with the temple 89
Grapes 135, 138
Greco-Egyptian alchemical corpus 15, 27–28, 33–35, 41, 47, 51–52, 55, 66, 73–74, 113, 127, 227, 245, 253, 256
Greek education 57, 80–81, 83
Greek influences 29, 83
Greek Magical Papyri 155, 203, 253
Greek philosophy 17, 21, 25, 30, 47–49, 53–55, 67, 165, 246–47, 262 (see also: natural philosophy, Greek)
Greeks 53–54, 77, 79, 80, 97, 155, 193–94, 240, 256, 270

Hades 32, 130 (see also: underworld)
Hadot, Pierre 116–17, 119–20, 151, 260
Hallum, Benjamin (Bink) 15, 28, 48, 103, 106, 108–09, 260
Harrison, Peter 54, 261
Hathor (as underworld goddess of metals) 85–86
Hebrew metallurgy and alchemy 111, 156–67
Hebrews 155, 161–62, 193, 240
Heka 57–60, 65, 219, 226–27, 242,
  and Eikton 226–227
  and supracosmic sympathy 225–26, 228
  definition of 57–58, 226
  as god 57, 226–27
Hermes 64, 74, 80, 109, 148, 155, 158, 173, 176–77, 203–04, 246, 258, 264

282　　　　　　　　　INDEX

(see also: Thoth)
Hermes Trismegistus 148, 259
Hermetic tradition, literature 74, 83,
　　125, 129, 141–42, 144, 148, 155–56,
　　173, 176, 180–81, 183–88, 191, 194,
　　197, 199, 201, 203–05, 207, 213,
　　215–16, 229, 237, 239–40, 255, 273
Hermetica 215, 216, 220, 229, 237, 239,
　　255, 261, 264, 268,
Hermetic priests 27, 199, 204, 229,
Herodotus 20, 79, 161, 261
Heroes 214
Hiera technē (sacred art) 19, 67, 117,
　　119, 200
Hieratic script 73, 112
Hieroglyphs 38, 51, 71–5, 112
　　as a form of cryptography 73
Historiography of alchemy 19–24,
　　266, 267, 269, 275
Hopkins, Arthur (theory of color
　　transmutation) 47–49, 52, 78, 132,
　　135–36, 262
Hornung, Erik 13, 36, 51, 56, 63, 132,
　　136–37, 152, 217, 241–42, 262
Hōrologoi (astronomer priests) 74,
　　166,–67
Hōroskopoi (astronomer priests) 74,
　　167
House of Gold 18, 83–84, 94, 230–31
　　as goldsmiths' workshop 84
　　and mouthopening/statue making rituals 84, 230–31
　　selective admission to 84, 94–95
　　Thoth and Seshat as presiding deities of 84
House of Life 70–79, 106–07,
　　152, 153, 204, 246, 259, 263
　　Artisans and craftsmen under 70–73
　　scribes, scribal priests 74–75
　　Zosimos as scribal priest 74, 152, 246
　　Zosimos as master craftsman 75
　　types of scribal priests 71–72
　　astronomer priests (see also: *hōroskopoi*)

Hygromanteia of Solomon 172

Iamblichus 26, 145, 194, 197–235,
　　337–40, 243, 247–48, 252, 253, 255,
　　258, 262, 271–72
Illumination 239–40
　　phōtagōgia 238–239
　　ellampsis 239
Image, divine 36, 71, 146, 183, 191,
　　211–12, 215, 222, 228–30, 234–36, 240,
　　242–43, 248–49
Imagination 107, 149, 206, 238
Inlays 36–38, 40
Iōs, iōsis 48–49, 51
Isfet (chaos) 65
Isis 81, 87, 106, 144, 176, 180, 222
Isis to Horus 176, 178, 180

Jacobson, David 49–50, 263
Janowitz, Naomi 23, 110, 263
Jesus 128, 181, 186–88
Jewish alchemy 111, 156–67
Jewish pseudepigrapha 26, 157,
　　163–164, 168, 171, 174, 247, 253, 254,
　　256, 263
Jewish/Judaic 16, 19, 26, 30, 49, 66, 83,
　　97, 110–11, 113, 128, , 155–94, 197,
　　200, 216, 220, 233, 247, 261, 268
Jung, C.G. 22, 103, 127, 139, 164, 263–64
Jupiter (Zeus) 122, 184

Ka (spirit concept) 58, 137, 241–42
Kērotakis 48, 132, 135–36, 147, 160–61,
　　262
Km/kmt (black earth) 20 (see also:
　　etymology of alchemy)
"Know thyself" (Delphic maxim) 107,
　　115, 123–24, 205, 233, 235–36
Kronos (Saturn) 124

Lead 41–42, 48, 107, 135,
　　147, 148, 150
Leiden and Stockholm papyri 31,
　　92, 254
Letrouit, Jean 23, 166, 264

Light 32, 65, 66, 123, 125, 137, 142–43, 150, 152–53, 184, 186–89, 191–92, 197, 202, 215, 238–40, 242–43, 267 (see also: illumination; man of light)
Like begets like 177, 180
Lindsay, Jack 18, 20, 60, 90, 101, 110, 166, 176–177, 265
Logos 185–86, 215
Lustration (metallic sheen) 35, 38

Maat (concept, goddess) 62–63, 65, 67, 70, 112, 116, 138, 180, 191, 202, 248
Macrocosm and microcosm 70, 121, 141
Magic 21–23, 32, 54, 59, 65, 74, 144, 168, 175, 190, 198, 202–06, 211, 225–27, 254, 255, 256, 257, 259, 263, 264, 265, 267, 269, 270, 271, 272 (see also: *heka*)
Magnesia 148
Man of flesh 184, 187–88, 191, 197 (see also: Adam)
Man of light 66, 125, 184, 187–89, 191–92, 197 (see also: Phōs)
Manichæans 190
Maria the Jewess 48, 72–73, 109–11, 157–61, 193
Martelli, Matteo 20, 46, 59, 69, 91–92, 265–66
Marx-Wolf, Heidi 204, 206, 212–14, 266
Master craftsmen 46–47, 75, 88, 92, 93, 98–99, 106, 113, 159–160
Materia medica 58–60
Materiality 126, 130, 151–53, 162
 ambiguity of (corrupting or divine) 126, 152–153, 187
Mazur, Zeke 203, 266
Meditation 16, 100, 119, 124, 130, 146–47, 222
 and *apatheia* 119, 129–30
 as intellectual or philosophical sacrifice 128, 129–30, 151, 218, 272 (see also: purification of the soul)
Mercury (substance, principle) 31, 45, 51, 103, 121, 136, 143, 148, 166, 190, 222
Mertens, Michele 15, 27, 63, 65, 72, 76, 132, 134, 138, 142, 148, 150, 160, 161, 185, 188, 166–67
Mesoupanisma 149–50
Metal, casting of 35, 89, 93, 147
Metallic bodies and spirits 32, 51–52, 131, 132, 139–40, 142, 160, 162–63, 217, 218, 230
Metallurgy/metallurgists 18, 23, 25, 31–33, 35, 42, 45–47, 49, 51–53, 56, 66, 73, 75, 83, 86, 89–90, 94–95, 98, 111–113, 155–67, 171–74, 179–82, 192–94, 236, 245–46, 248–49, 259, 261, 264
Metals, symbols of 73
Metaphysics 16, 24, 63, 83, 116, 141, 197, 201, 204, 251
Mimic Daimon 188–91
Min, Egyptian god 20, 76–87, 90–91, 112
 ithyphallic 77, 86
 god of mines and quarries 85
 patron deity of goldsmiths 86, 90
 patron deity of Panopolis 85
 patron deity of Coptos and the "goldsmiths of Min" 85, 90
Mirror 122–24, 150, 222 (see also: electrum)
Monotheism and polytheism 30, 111, 158, 167, 252
Moon 62, 75, 87, 103–06, 138, 147–48, 173–74, 185, 221, 224, 229
Mortuary cult 26, 71, 242 (see also: Egyptian mortuary traditions)
Moses/Mosaic 157–59, 168, 252, 258
Music 223
Mysticism 15, 20, 22, 54, 61, 120, 124, 203, 246, 265, 266, 268

Nag Hammadi 16, 164, 181, 238, 255, 270, 271
Natural and unnatural methods 26, 62, 65, 100, 107, 108, 112, 155 ff, 156, 163, 165–67, 169, 172, 178, 180, 181,

191, 194, 226, 247, 260
Natural rhythms 62, 120, 131, 141, 214, 231, 247
Natural philosophy, Greek 17, 23, 25, 29, 31, 53–55, 66, 245
Needham, Joseph 42–46, 267
Neilos (priest and rival of Zosimos) 25, 103, 107–09, 111, 233
Neoplatonism 24, 26, 139, 141, 194, 197, 199–203, 210, 220, 223–232, 239, 243, 247, 251, 255, 260, 265, 271, 273, 275
New Year ceremonies, Egyptian 84, 86, 222
Newman, William 19, 21–23, 267–69
Nicanor gate, Jewish Temple 49–50 (see also: Corinthian bronze)
Nikotheos 124, 189
Nile River 20, 35, 72, 75, 85, 166, 222, 232–33
Nine letters 170, 189–91
Noetic realms 119, 124, 126, 130, 140, 144, 145, 197, 202, 208, 210–28, 239–40 (see also: divine mind)
Nous 139, 141, 185, 201, 215, 225, 266

Occult 21–23, 58, 175, 257, 268, 272
Ogdoad (realm of fixed stars) 142, 144, 237
Olympiodorus 159, 176–77
On Apparatus and Furnaces (Letter Omega) 56, 63–64, 74, 78, 80, 107–08, 118, 124–25, 156, 165, 181–82, 185, 188, 190, 193, 205, 215–16, 222, 240, 263
On Electrum 35, 122, 150, 160, 170, 187, 190
One nature (formula) 24, 130, 132, 143–46, 151, 177 (see also: ouroboros)
On Excellence 26, 66, 74, 87, 91, 106, 117, 126, 127–53, 160, 166, 169, 192, 198, 208, 211, 216, 220, 230, 248
On Iron 118–19
On Lime 121

On Mercury 117, 190
On the Divine Water 121
On the Work of Copper 34, 36, 38, 50
On Tin 173, 177
Ontology, Egyptian 65–66
Opening of the Mouth ritual 84, 130–31, 137–38, 192, 230, 248, 258
Orpiment 41–44
Osiris 84, 87, 106, 144, 152, 221
and Isis 87, 106, 144
Ostanes 32, 69, 148, 158
Ouroboros 32, 143–44, 148, 271

P. Berl.Bork 76, 90–93, 110–13, 192
Panopolis 15, 20, 25, 69–111, 182, 192, 246–47
names 20, 77
and astronomy 78
and *Book of the Dead* tradition 78
and Hellenism 79–81
and mining, metallurgy, goldsmithing 85-86, 90–91, 112
and weaving 85
Pantheism 152
Phialē (alchemical vessel/altar) 132–34, 141, 145–46, 149 (see also: cauldron)
Philia (friendship) as cosmic sympathy 223–25
Philosopher-priests 204, 213
Phōs 66, 125, 184–85, 240,
Phōtes 187–88
Phrygian 34
Physika kai Mystika (ps.-Democritus) 31, 45, 60, 69
Physiologoi 53 (see also: natural philosophy)
Planetary spheres 122, 123, 130, 149, 207, 215, 223, 237, 248
Plato, Platonism 55–56, 106, 118–20, 126, 132, 141, 145, 180, 197, 200–01, 203–04, 208–10, 213, 220, 225, 229, 234, 256, 259, 260, 265, 266, 269, 271, 273, 274 (see also: Neoplatonism)

Phædrus 119–20, 269
Symposium 126, 209–10
Timæus 132, 141, 145, 200–01, 212, 269
Pliny the Elder 38, 41–42, 54, 59, 60, 269
Plotinus 124, 128, 203, 210, 220, 225, 259, 260, 269
Poimandres 142, 147, 183, 185, 216, 237, 240, 268
Polychromy (metallic statuary) 25, 35–41, 47, 52, 66–67, 136–37, 228, 245, 248
coloring metals, statues 25, 35–36, 41, 60, 66, 116, 228, 245
Porphyry 124, 128–30, 194, 200, 209–10, 223, 225, 231, 269, 271
Powers (liberated souls) 216
Pre-socratic philosophers 53–56
Priests, Egyptian 33, 35, 69–70–75, 78, 80, 82–84, 88, 91, 95, 97–101, 103, 111–14, 166–67, 192, 194, 203, , 204, 209–10, 226, 228, 233, 235–36, 243, 246, 266, 270, 271
purity requirements for 236
various types and ranks of 71–76
part-time employment of 88, 112–13
(see also: artisan priests, Hermetic priests, House of Life, sacrificing priest)
Principe, Lawrence 20–22, 29–30, 103, 267, 269
Pro-cosmic 220
Prometheus 181–87
Prophet (high-ranking Egyptian priest) 46, 73–76, 80, 96, 176
Providence 65, 80, 141, 192, 194, 197, 212, 248
Pseudo-science, alchemy as 20–21
Ptolemaic Egypt 36–37, 57, 71–72, 77, 79, 85, 92–93, 96–97, 156, 247–48, 258, 272
Ptolemais 79
Ptolemy I Soter 79

Purification of the soul 15, 116–20, 127, 130, 165, 202, 235–36, 240
and ascent 119–20, 130, 165
and soul vehicle 139, 238–40, 258
(see also: meditation, illumination, god-making)
Pythagoras 54, 128–30, 262, 264

Razor-working man 134–40, 146–49, 216
Re (solar deity) 57–58, 87, 137–38, 144, 163, 241–42, 249
Reason 21, 26, 54, 108, 140–141, 209, 224, 239, 265
Reciprocity 140–41
Religion
and magic 203–04, 247
and science 54, 56–57, 100, 155, 246
and universal theory of alchemy 247, 249
Religious studies and alchemy 22–24, 30–31
Revelation 16, 26, 94, 140, 150, 178–79, 181, 203, 208, 228, 242–43, 248
Ritual 23, 26, 33, 70, 82–83, 86, 89, 112, 128, 130, 138, 164, 182, 200, 202–06, 213, 218–24, 230, 235–36, 243, 263
sacrificial 26, 128
(see also: opening of the mouth)
Roman Egypt, scholarship on 17–19
Ruelle, Charles-Emile 27, 127, 162, 164, 176, 233, 253

Sacred art, alchemy as 19, 26, 32–33, 67, 72, 99, 117, 119, 141, 153, 194, 200, 228, 254 (see also: *hiera technē*)
as corporeal and spiritual 117, 141, 153, 194–95
Sacrifice 26, 99–100, 127–135, 138, 141–46, 149–52, 167–69, 211, 218, 236, 255, 272
alchemical imagery of 127–51
spiritual versus animal sacrifice 128–30 (see also: meditation)

sacrificing priest 132, 135–142, 149, 211
Saffrey, H. D. 27, 193
Saturn (Kronos) 124
Science, alchemy and 20–23, 31–32, 54–58, 61, 72, 77, 98, 100, 132, 155, 162–63, 175, 179, 194, 198, 207–08, 246, 255, 257, 258, 258, 259, 261–62, 264–68, 271–72, 274–75
Scoring 38
Scribes (see: priests, Egyptian)
Scribes, Christian and Muslim 30
Separation of spirit from matter 131–32, 152, 221, 242
(see also: exercise of death)
Serpent 143–44, 148
(see also: ouroboros)
Seven (days, heavens, spheres, zones, planets, doors, steps, bottles, jars, punishments) 62, 90, 123, 124, 142, 146, 170–72, 186, 215, 237
Shaw, Gregory 86, 124, 137, 145, 199, 201, 208–09, 214, 219, 223, 238–39, 255, 268, 271
Signatures, divine 122–125, 130, 137, 151, 163, 165, 191, 218, 222, 226, 228, 242 (see also: sympathies, *synthēmata*)
Silver 19, 20, 35, 37–41, 44–45, 48–51, 85–86, 94, 96, 121–22, 135–37, 138, 140, 148, 150, 159, 166, 171, 176, 221–22, 228, 245
man of, 135
Silversmiths 89–90, 94, 110
Sirius 166, 168, 222
Smith, Andrew 200, 209, 210, 223, 225, 271–72
Socrates 126, 208–09
Solomon 156, 164, 167–73, 190, 193, 256, 273
Sōmata (metallic "bodies") 51–52, 132, 217 (see also: *asōmata*)
Son of God 183, 185–89, 191, 207, 215, 222
Soul vehicle (*ochēma pneuma*) 139, 238–40, 258

Spirit and matter, relationship between 24, 197, 220
Spiritual approach to alchemy 22, 219
(see also: reason; Enlightenment, European)
Spiritual exercises 115–53, 178, 218, 222, 248,
Spiritual taxonomies 212–14, 226, 248, 266
Statues, divine 26, 33, 66–67, 81, 84, 112, 136–37, 151, 153, 162, 192, 228–35, 242
agalma (cult statue) 228–29, 234
Hermetic views of 229–30
as animated, ensouled 36, 192, 230–31
telestic art 200, 231,
eidōla vs. *eikōna* 234–236
and purity requirements 151, 236
relation of *ka* and *ba* to 241–42
types mentioned by Zosimos 34–36
Stephanus (7th century) 148, 268, 273
Steps (seven and fifteen in *On Excellence*) 142–43, 146, 150
Stoicism 55, 65, 120, 125, 225, 260, 265
Stroumsa, Guy 128, 129, 272
Sublimation 51, 106, 160
Sulfur 31, 51, 61, 103, 134–36
Sulfur water 136 (see also: water, divine)
Sun
and gold 87, 122, 149, 162, 221–22
visible and invisible 215
Synthemata (divine signatures) 122, 124–25, 165
as ladder of ascent 124, 126, 210
Sympathy 26, 53, 57–58, 60–61, 122, 163, 165, 167, 173, 183, 184, 191, 202, 219, 222–26, 228, 248, 260
On Sympathies and Antipathies 58
Supracosmic 225–28
Synagogues 110, 156, 261
Syncretism 25–27, 57, 155, 194
Synthesis, cultural and literary 57, 67, 83, 114

Talmud 156–57
Tanaseanu-Döbler, Ilinca 200, 272
Tattooing (statues) 38
Taylor, Frank Sherwood (F.S.) 21, 32, 42, 44, 48, 62, 73, 127, 131–35, 138–42, 145, 148–50, 157, 160–61, 166, 272–73
Technical recipes, alchemical 25, 31, 34–35, 38, 44–47, 49–50, 60, 66, 73, 76, 78, 92, 94, 97–99, 112–13, 117–18, 121, 157–59, 219, 228, 245–47
Temple artisans 18, 25, 34,–35, 46, 97, 157, 194, 246
Temples, Egyptian
  as cosmos in miniature 76, 112,
  as texts 83
  in Zosimus's *On excellence* 129, 142–45, 152
  of Min 20, 76–91
Temple grammar 83–84, 86
Temple traditions 17–18, 67, 193, 246–47, 249
Terracotta figurines 35
Testament of Solomon 156, 168–71, 174, 193, 256 (see also: Solomon)
Theodosius 33
Theophilus 160, 164
Theosebeia 15, 25, 28
  and Christianity 192–93, 240, 246
  and Zosimos 75, 97–111, 119, 122, 136, 142, 149, 156, 159–60, 167, 169, 172–75, 177, 180–83, 191, 194, 207, 211, 217, 236, 240
  as *soror mystica* 103, 106
  with Zosimos, as sun and moon, in the *Tome of Images* 103–06
The True Book of Sophe the Egyptian 27, 161, 192, 215
Theurgy 197–243
  Definitions 199–202
  Synonyms 200
  as demiurgical practice 201–02
  and divine hierarchy 212–18
  as linking material and spiritual worlds 128–27
  theurgical and non-theurgical approaches to ritual 218–27

Thoth 73–74, 78, 84, 106–07, 138, 148, 184, 203, 242, 263
  and Hermes 74, 148, 203
  as patron deity of the House of Life 74
Tinctures 44–45, 48, 51–52, 228
  opportune or timely (*kairikai katabaphai*) 62–64, 74, 95, 97, 99–100, 163–69, 177, 181–82, 198, 272
Tome of Images (Mushaf as-Suwar) 15, 103–06, 109, 260
Trade associations (guilds) 25, 69–114,
  function of 88–89
  membership 88, 94–95, 110, 113
  in Roman period 88, 113
  and trade networks 88
  religious dimensions of 88, 110, 113, 156, 164
  relationship to temple 92–93, 113, 246
  of goldsmiths 89–91, 110
  of silversmiths 89–90, 93–94, 110
  of bronzesmiths 93–94
Translation 25, 30, 47, 73, 74, 76, 78, 82, 112, 116, 127, 139, 226, 240, 246
Transmutation 25, 29, 32, 41–53, 55, 61, 66, 135, 174, 180, 245, 253, 256, 264, 274
Trinity, Hermetic 185–88, 201, 205, 207, 215

Underworld 51, 65, 87
  Egyptian (Amduat, Duat) 87, 131, 136, 137, 143
  death and resurrection (torture of metals, bodies) 87, 130, 136–37, 217
  Hades 32, 130
  Osiris 87, 144, 152–53, 221,
  and blackening stage in alchemy 51–52, 66
  journey through the underworld 65–66, 143, 201–02, 217
Union, divine/noetic 151–53, 201, 203, 205, 210–11, 218, 220–21, 225, 235, 240, 242–43, 248

Unity of nature 24, 32, 33, 60, 135, 143–45, 201, 227,
Universalism 26, 34, 57, 82–83, 121, 126, 155, 173, 181, 194–95, 200, 210, 214, 247–49
　as mark of Egyptian thought 34, 57, 82–83, 155–56
Unnatural methods (see: natural and unnatural methods)
Uždavinys, Algis 199–200, 227, 229–31, 273

Van Minnen, Peter 80–81, 88–89, 93, 102–03, 274
Viano, Cristina 55, 159, 193, 270, 274–75
Violence
　imagery of 127–28, 130–32, 144, 147
　done to metals 130, 242
　and the opening of the mouth ritual 130, 138
　and the embodied soul 136, 140, 242

Water 24, 32–33, 121, 125, 131, 6–62, 70, 99–100, 134–36, 138, 140, 142–44, 160, 170 (see also: four elements)
　divine 62, 121, 131, 134, 136, 138 (see also: sulfur water)
　primordial 70, 144
Wonder-working (thaumaturgy) 232
Workshops 88–94
　annexed to temples 92, 113, 230, 245
　in the necropolis 92–93
　owned by state or high ranking officials 93
　(see also: trade associations)

Zodiac 100, 123, 125, 150, 168, 236, 247
　in Temple of Min 77–80
　in Panopolis 80–81
　(see also: astrology; jupiter; moon; planetary spheres; tinctures, opportune or timely; saturn; sun)

Zosimos of Panopolis
　epithets 15
　as last of his kind 33
　Works:
　Final Account 27, 95, 99,–101, 107–08, 119, 142, 149, 163, 167
　On Apparatus and Furnaces (Letter Omega) 56, 63–64, 74, 78, 80, 107–08, 118, 124–25, 156, 165, 181–82, 185, 188, 190, 193, 205, 215–16, 222, 240, 263
　On Electrum 35, 122, 150, 160, 170, 187, 190
　On Excellence 26, 66, 74, 87, 91, 106, 117, 126, 127–53, 160, 166, 169, 192, 198, 208, 211, 216, 220, 230, 248
　On Iron 118–19
　On Lime 121
　On Mercury 117, 190
　On the Divine Water 121
　On the Work of Copper (Letter Waw) 34, 36, 38, 50
　On Tin 173, 177
　The True Book of Sophe the Egyptian 27, 161, 192, 215

ABOUT THE AUTHOR

DR. SHANNON GRIMES (PHD, SYRACUSE UNIVERSITY) is a scholar of religion and philosophy in the Græco-Roman era, with a particular emphasis on Gnostic, Hermetic, and Platonic traditions—the so-called roots of western esotericism. Her publications have focused on alchemy and cultural astronomy in the Roman period, while her research and teaching explore religious views of nature and the cosmos, a passion that stems from her own wonderment of the natural world.

Since 2006, Professor Grimes has taught at Meredith College, a women's university in Raleigh, North Carolina, where she is currently head of the Department of Religious and Ethical Studies. She teaches courses in world religions, early Christianity, philosophy, and environmental ethics, and has had the pleasure of leading several study abroad programs in Iceland and Italy.

www.ingramcontent.com/pod-product-compliance
Lightning Source LLC
Chambersburg PA
CBHW062025290426
44108CB00025B/2788